Dick West

Cover illustration by Dick West, art director,
found on an undated Christmas card to this author
from Loretta, Frank, Sara Sue and Willard,
sent while they were at Bacone Indian College in Oklahoma.
The message inside is a fitting statement for this biography:

It's all here in Dick West's Original.
The star–the cross–the steeple form a setting for
Creative fellowship with these fine Indian people.
You are here too, in our prayers and plans.
This enterprise is yours, and His who gave his Son
And that high and holy commission to tell the ages
The King Has Come!
We Thompsons share the prayer of Tiny Tim–
God bless you every one!

JUSTICE, PEACE AND GOD

A Minister's Personal Odyssey

Barbara Mills

HERITAGE BOOKS
2006

HERITAGE BOOKS
AN IMPRINT OF HERITAGE BOOKS, INC.

Books, CDs, and more—Worldwide

For our listing of thousands of titles see our website
at
www.HeritageBooks.com

Published 2006 by
HERITAGE BOOKS, INC.
Publishing Division
65 East Main Street
Westminster, Maryland 21157-5026

Other books by the author:

"Got My Mind Set on Freedom" Maryland's Story of Black and White Activism, 1663-2000

Providence: 1630-1800—Women Are Part of Its History

International Standard Book Number: 0-7884-4097-7

A special thanks
to Scott, Frank's son,
and to the many relatives, friends
and parishioners
who shared with me their memories,
and sent photos and other memorabilia
to be used in Frank's biography.

CONTENTS

ILLUSTRATIONS

(Most are from Frank's albums, scrapbooks and files. With very few exceptions, the others were sent to the author for use in this biography.)

ILLUSTRATIONS (continued)

Author's Note

I'd just finished *"Got My Mind Set on Freedom," Maryland's Story of Black & White Activism, 1663-2000*, and discussions were beginning about a "preemptive war" with Iraq. My thoughts turned to the Rev. Francis Willard Thompson who'd passed on to me his pacifism; his belief that war was not the way to settle disputes between nations, his belief that we might win wars but seemed incapable of winning a lasting peace—and who'd also passed on his abiding concern for the underdog, be he poor or of another race or culture. It seemed an appropriate time to tell his story.

† † †

I'd never heard of a mentor back in the 40s when Frank was my minister and I was in high school. I'm still not sure what one is. But if it is someone who is there for you, who influences your thinking and the direction your life will take, then he was my mentor. His powerful sermons, delivered in a deep resonant voice, connected the Bible's teachings to current-day happenings of significance. He deglamorized the war raging world-wide, and gave another perspective to the propaganda that surrounded us in films, newscasts and elsewhere. He invited Mennonites who were against all war to speak at our Sunday services—and a Japanese-American college student who told us of her family's experiences; suddenly uprooted from homes and jobs in California and thrust into one of our now-infamous war-time concentration camps.

But perhaps most important of all was the personal interest Rev. Thompson took in me. As I look back, I wonder why. Why did he pick me to go to a Quaker-sponsored interracial conference in New Hampshire? Did he intend simply to give me a needed break from the turmoil I described to him that existed in my home? Or did he anticipate a bigger impact? Whatever his intent, attending that conference could well be regarded as a turning point in my life—a new, exhilarating experience—blacks and whites, students and grown-ups—sleeping, eating, playing, studying and talking together—often into the night discussing such as the movement for a "world government" where all countries and peoples were equally valued and had an equal say. We dreamed that one day we would see it happen.

Two young men, Quakers, told us about the government study they'd participated in, in lieu of military service. Fifty or so volunteers had agreed to live in a simulated concentration camp—some as guards, others as prisoners. "The prisoners were given a ration of bread and thin soup twice daily, all were constantly hungry," they said. "Before long we were fighting each other over food and trying to find some means to bribe the guards for special treatment." I'm not sure what the government's purpose was, but in retrospect these peaceful Quakers were shocked at their own behavior; shocked to learn what a corrupting effect hunger and deprivation can have even on the most moral and righteous amongst us.

We met the principal of a small black school in Mississippi who described for us the appalling conditions his students faced, mostly in one-room school houses. "We have to use the torn and raggedy books that are discarded by the white schools, most of our blackboards are broken, the floors are unfinished and splintery, pot-bellied stoves heat crowded rooms, and sometimes the younger ones get bad burns when they bump against it."

For me the camaraderie, the chance to know blacks, the lessons learned, were invigorating; had offered a whole other view of the world and its possibilities. I hated for the conference to end, and in a sense I guess it never did. I had taken as my own a set of values and beliefs that would last a lifetime; that would forever guide my actions and my thinking about the alienated and the disenfranchised in our society.

Whether called a mentor or not, I know the Rev. Francis Willard Thompson was responsible for enriching my life in ways he would never know. Now I want you to meet this man who was loved by many and who influenced the lives of many, and yet died believing he was a failure.

Introduction

by

Jack Nordgaard, Pastor, Evangelical Lutheran Church in America; Director, Aid to Alcoholics, Prisoners & Family Ministry, Lutheran Social Services of Illinois (Retired)

I have known Barbara Mills for about thirty years. We met in a neighborhood that had become one of Chicago's largest "skid-row" communities. At the time, she was working in a drop-in center aptly named, A Center for Street People. Barbara was also involved in justice work with prisoners. Later she moved east to manage a shelter for battered women. To all of these ministries, she brought a passionate activism and personal sacrifices. I remember meetings when Barbara wore me out describing all of the things that needed to be done, and then beyond this, all of the possibilities that could bring hope and dignity to the people on the streets.

I never imagined that Barbara could sit long enough in one place to write a book. But she has become an author. In this book she writes about a friend and mentor, Frank Thompson, and is generous in allowing Frank to speak often and well for himself.

Frank Thompson's story is about a number of journeys that coalesce around the belief that God created his life for a purpose. And that his response to God's act—the challenge to live out God's purpose—is to be involved in a struggle to engage the world and to make a difference. Frank Thompson's life is about belief and struggle and perseverance. In response to this belief, and as stops on his journey:

he teaches and coaches Native American college students; later becomes their college's president;

he studies at a seminary, and, when ordained, serves congregations, encourages them to reach out and serve the poor and oppressed;

he is a vocal pacifist; encourages young men to resist the draft, to become conscientious objectors in World War II;

he works to build a strong United Nations; and,

he works to build cultural ties with the people of Laos.

Stories of people like Frank Thompson are important. They describe people who made a difference. They encourage and stimulate hope that we can all make a difference.

In a world that is increasingly dangerous and fragmented—in a world where we are tempted to trade freedom for security (which is always a hollow bargain)—in a culture that nurtures individualism and violence and has a dangerous disregard for the health of the environment—and in a time when there is little interest in the common good—we, too, need to engage the world, dare to be different, and seek to make a difference.

Frank Thompson persevered in the struggle to be such a person; to live out the purpose of his existence as he saw it. And his life made a difference. It made a difference to Barbara Mills, and Barbara's life has made a difference to me. This is how it happens when we are open to one another and to the world. This is how it happens when we struggle together to bring tolerance and justice and peace to the world.

I am grateful to Barbara for the gift of this story.

Peace! Jack

CHRONOLOGY: FRANK THOMPSON

11/20/1909- Frank Thompson Born in Phoenix, Arizona [brother, Lewis, 1901]

1927-1931- Worked for older brother Lewis in Los Angeles & San Francisco, CA (Loans, Real Estate Development, Construction), Golden Glove Boxing Champ

1931-1935- BA from University of Redlands, Redlands, CA 92373

1932- Student Pastor, Arcata First Baptist Church, 1700 Union Street, Arcata, CA 95521

1935 (Fall)-1937(Spring)- Bacone College, Librarian & Boxing Coach, East Shawnee Ave. & Highway, Muskogee, OK. 74401

1937- Assistant Pastor, First Congregational Church, 282 Rock Street, Fall River, MA 02720

1937-1940- BS, Andover Newton Theological Seminary, 169 Herrick Road, Newton, MA 02459

1938-1948- Pastor, Phillips Memorial Baptist Church: 565 Pontiac Ave., Cranston, RI 0291. [Married Loretta Bell Long, 7/2/1939; Sara Sue born 9/9/1940; Willard Scott (Woody) born 1/1/1942]

1948-1955- President, Bacone College (see above): Loretta returned as volunteer after Frank's death.

9/55-8/58- Pastor, First Baptist Church: 819 Massachusetts Ave., Arlington, MA 02476

9/58-9/63- Vice President of Development, University of Redlands (see above); [1961 expected appointment to head Bureau of Indian Affairs]

10/63-6/65 West Coast Director (of twenty-five chapters), San Francisco Office, United World Federalists (later World Federalist Association), Aaron Knight, Deputy Director, P.O. Box 15250, Washington, DC 20003

7/65-8/66-"Ran" bi-cultural center of the USIA Field Office in Laos (after contracting hepatitis was medically evacuated after only one year)

1967—— Associate Minister, First Congregational UCC, 1651-46th Avenue, San Francisco, CA 94122

2/25/68-1975- Minister, First Congregational Church, 1912 Central Avenue, Alameda, CA 94501
[12/68 suffered ruptured appendix; peritonitis]
[7/73- suffered a near fatal heart attack]

1975-1980- Retired to Lake Wildwood, near Nevada City, CA

1980- Fatal Heart Attack; died on November 19th (one day before his 71st birthday)

(1981-1985 ?)-Loretta volunteered at Bacone (see above)

1984 ——Scott, son, divorced (had married in 1968); "came out" in 1985

1992—— Sara Sue Thompson Nies, daughter, died in March of pancreatic & liver cancer (but *not* alcohol-related) after eight months of suffering that included surgery and chemo; was at home on couch, friends & family around her.

1994- ——Loretta Long Thompson, wife, died October 24th of heart attack just two years after moving in with Scott on farm in Virginia.

Justice, Peace and God:

A Minister's Personal Odyssey

1. The Rushing Wind: A Preview

One of the first dogs I had was a mongrel, part shepherd, part collie, mostly dog. There was nothing unusual about Gar. He was a fair cattle dog and a fine playmate, but one thing I will never forget: He loved to rush the wind! As we would set off in the early evening to round up the stock for the night, Gar would wear himself out racing the wind across these crisp prairies, head high, snapping and biting into the unseen wind. It was infectious. It made me want to race the wind, and my horse would nearly always fight the rein to follow Gar as he raced and rushed the challenging wind.[1]

† † †

This is the story of Francis Willard Thompson, a child of pioneering ancestors who became a minister extraordinaire. But despite his popularity with those he preached to and worked with, Frank seems always to have been plagued with inner doubts as to his effectiveness; his ability to make a difference; his ability to persuade others of the importance of incorporating inclusiveness and peace into their daily lives—Christ's message as he saw it. He wore himself out fighting the reins that always seemed to hold him back, challenging the winds of life; seeking the Prince of Peace. A lifetime pacifist, his search, his sermons, resonate with messages as pertinent today as then.

Frank's father, Claude Thompson, forest ranger and

---

[1] Like the book's title, this opening is from Frank's sermon, 5/20/45, based on Acts 2:2: "And suddenly there came a sound from heaven of a mighty rushing wind, and it filled all the house where they were sitting."

itinerant Methodist preacher, was in Arizona when Frank was born on November 20, 1909; had been in California when Frank's brother, Lewis, was born in Lompoc, California on October 22, 1901. Frank was still an infant when his mother, Olga Winifred Willard, left his father, and on October 24, 1912 married Paul Elbert Gano. Soon after, Frank again found himself in Arizona where he would spend his childhood on the Gano family farm near rustic Cottonwood in the Verde Valley, surrounded by half-brothers and sisters. Meanwhile, his brother, Lewis, stayed in California with their grandmother, Nannie Christian Thompson, purportedly because he was never very fond of his step-father. For Frank there had been no choice.

Given the eight years difference in ages of the two boys, the fact they were separated at an early age, were raised by different families in different states, and, finally, followed entirely different career paths, it would not have been surprising if the two had become alienated. However, such was not the case; they remained close, the two enjoying a game of golf together only weeks before Lewis's death on January 20, 1975, age seventy-three. Frank died five years later on November 19, 1980, one day before his seventy-first birthday.

2. Where It All Began

Frank's pioneering ancestors were seeking new and better lives for themselves and their families despite the many hardships they faced in the process. Frank was striving to find the path for himself and others that would enable us to make God's way our way–and his path was equally strewn with countless obstacles.

† † †

On his mother's side Frank's family can be traced back to Major Simon Willard, born early in 1605, baptized at the St. Margaret's Church in Horsmonden, Kent, England,[1] and an immigrant to Massachusetts in 1634–part of the Puritan tide seeking to escape England's bloody persecutions under King Charles I. Simon is credited with helping establish the town of Concord, Massachusetts where he served as local magistrate and commanded the militia company. He is closely associated with the Indian trade, affairs of the frontier settlements, work with the Merrimac tribes, laying out land grants, and punitive expeditions against the Niantic sachem, Ninigret. After Concord, he lived variously in Lancaster and in Grafton. In 1676, he returned from one of his expeditions to find his home destroyed and thus forced to move his family to Charlestown. He died there in the Spring of 1676.

Simon Willard married three times and fathered seventeen children, as many as twelve of whom were clockmakers. Famous for their grandfather clocks, they were commissioned to make one for the Supreme Court and one

---

[1] Ancestral information is from the Appendix of Frances E. Willard's autobiography, from http://WillardFamilyAssn.org and from information provided author by Willard descendants.

for President Adams's family. They also held the patent for the banjo clock.[2] A Willard House and Clock Museum in Grafton, Massachusetts has an extensive collection of these clocks, as well as family portraits, furnishings, and quilts made by the family.[3]

Frank's own branch of the Willard family is traced through Major Simon's son, Henry, born June 4, 1655 in Concord, died in Harvard, Massachusetts, 1701.[4] There followed Jonathan I, born in 1695 in Lancaster, Massachusetts, died in 1785; Jonathan II, born on February 26, 1720 in Lunenberg, Massachusetts, died January 15, 1799; and Jonathan III, also born in Lunenberg, on September 21, 1745, died on July 3, 1832. He married Betty Caswell and after her death married Katherine (Stevens) Stone. He served as a lieutenant in George Washington's army.

Alexander Hamilton Willard, Frank's great grandfather, was the only son of Jonathan III and Betty Caswell. All we know of him prior to his participation in the Lewis and Clark Expedition of 1804-1806 is that in his early youth, after his mother died, he ran away from the home of

---

[2] Clockmaker information from Olga Willard's sister's memoir and http://WillardFamilyAssn.org.

[3] Additional information about the family and museum are from a piece by Cynthia Dias-Reid, "Ahead of Their Time: Women of the Willard Family." None of the women she discusses seems to be in the direct line of Frank's heritage-Emma Hart Willard, who founded the Troy Female Seminary in Troy, NY; Frances Willard the noted temperance leader; Eliza Willard, wife of the clockmaker Simon Willard, Jr. who's noted for her intricate silk embroideries; and Martha Willard, wife of Major Joseph Willard and mother of the first white child born in Grafton. He lived to be 100 years old, had 12 children, 90 grandchildren, 226 great grandchildren and 53 of the fifth generation.

[4] See Appendix 1: Family Tree.

his father and stepmother.[5] Why is not explained. At the time of his recruitment, he was in the army, stationed in Kentucky; he became one of the few who followed the expedition to its final destination.

† † †

Thomas Jefferson, even before he became President, was interested in an expedition that would go Westward beyond the Mississippi River which then marked the States' western boundary.[6]

Fearing Britain would secure that land, he wanted to "open a highway for the American fur trade, to win over the Indians from Spanish or British influence, and to lay the foundation for a carefully regulated trade and intercourse

---

[5] From "An Old-Timer's Scrapbook," by Don Willard.

[6] Map found in Vol I of the 3 -vol 1814 edition of *The Lewis & Clark Expedition* by Meriwether Lewis, Intro by Archibald Hanna, Lippincott Company, NY

with the Indians that would avoid some of the evils of unrestrained competition and interracial conflict so common in American experience." Jefferson was also interested in learning about the region's plants, natural history, mineralogy and astronomy.

After Meriwether Lewis and William Clark were selected to head such an expedition, they spent most of 1803 recruiting men to make the trip (mostly from army enlistees), constructing a keelboat and gathering supplies: "mosquito netting, ink powder, thermometers, Indian trade beads, waterproof lead canisters for gunpowder, cooking utensils, and clothing"– 3,500 pounds of equipment to be carried across the continent.[7] They began their historic 2,000 mile trek across largely unexplored territory to the Pacific and back on May 14, 1804, at a point near St. Louis. Private Alexander Hamilton Willard appears often in the detailed journals kept by both Lewis and Clarke. A few of these are quoted; chosen as representative of the trials faced by Willard in particular and the expedition generally.[8]

Only two months into their trip, on July 12th, 1804, Willard finds himself facing a court-martial, his case being heard by Captains rather than enlisted men as was usual for lesser offenses. Accused of "lying down and sleeping on his post whilst a Sentinel on the night of the 11th," one can perhaps sympathize since the *Journal* entry that day begins with the comment that "our men are much fatigued." Willard pled *guilty of lying down*, but *not guilty of going to sleep.* However, he is convicted of both charges and sentenced to receive "one hundred lashes on his bear back, at four

---

[7] pp. 5 & 6- Moulton, Introduction to Vol. 2. (This and previous quote)

[8] What follows from the *Journals* are found in a few of the 13 volumes of journals, edited by Gary Moulton.

different times in equal proportion—the punishment to commence that same evening at sunset, and to continue every evening untill completed." A harsh punishment indeed, but not uncommon, the same just a month earlier meted out to John Collins for drunkenness—in Willard's case, an offense that could have resulted in a death penalty under the military regimen of the party—so categorized because it is the kind of lapse in duties that could subject the whole party to a surprise attack and the death of many or all of them.[9]

Willard is again in trouble on July 29, 1804, though not so seriously this time as to result in a court martial. The *Journal* notes that it is a cold, windy, rainy day, "two men sick and several with boils," "not Willard's day." He was on his way back to their previous camp to retrieve his forgotten tomahawk when he lost his gun in Bowyers River (perhaps in Iowa). Fortunately Fields dived in and brought it up—why Fields and not Willard is not explained.[10]

Much later, on March 24th, 1806, Willard is one of those sick. Clark wrote (spelling is in the original):[11]

> After a slight brackfast we set out at half past 9 a.m. and proceeded to the *Cath lah mah* Village at 1 p.m. and remained untill ½ after 3 p.m. At this village we purchased a fiew wappato and a Dog [they ate these] for our sick men. Willard and Bratten who are yet in a weak state. At this village I saw two very large elegant canoes inlaid with shills I took to be teeth at first view and the nativs informed several of the men that they were the teeth of their enemies which they had killed

---

[9] pp. 370-371 & 373, Vol. 2, Moulton
[10] pp. 426 & 428, Vol 2, Moulton
[11] p. 10, Vol. 7, Moulton.

> in war. In examineing of them closely haveing taken out several pices, we found that were sea shells...

Then, on April 16, 1806, Lewis writes in his *Journal* of a typical problem encountered in their trek, but one that eventually finds Willard again in trouble.[12]

> About 8 a.m. Capt. Clark passed the river with two interpreters, the indian woman and nine men [Willard among them] in order to trade with the natives for their horses, for which purpose he took with him a good part of our stock of merchandize. I [Lewis] remained in camp; sent out the hunters very early in the morning, and set Sergts. Gass and Pryor with some others at work to make a parsel of packsaddles. Twelve horses will be sufficient to transport our baggage and some pounded fish which we intend taking with us as a reserved store for the rocky mountains....

Later Lewis writes that Willard and Cruzatte returned with a note from Capt. Clark indicating that his party had been unable to purchase a single horse. Lewis sends them back with a note requesting him

> to double the price we have heretofore offered for horses and if possible obtain as many as five, by this means we shall be enabled to proceed immediately with our small canoes and those horses to the villages in neighborhood of the mussel shell rapid where horses are more abundant and cheaper...

Meanwhile, Lewis has purchased a few horses and has been invited into the house of the 2nd Chief "where he

[12] This and following quotes and information from pp. 125, 129, 131, 133-135, Vol. 7, Moulton

concluded to sleep. This man was pore, nothing to eat but dried fish, and no wood to burn. Altho the night was cold they could not rase as much wood as would make a fire."

As if they weren't having enough trouble with obtaining horses, Willard adds to their troubles:[13]

> Willard was negligent in his attention to his horse and suffered it to ramble off; it was not to be found when I ordered the others to be brought up and confined to the picquits. This in addition to the other difficulties under which I laboured was truly provoking, I repremanded him more severely for this piece of negligence than had been usual with me. I had the remaining horses well secured by picquits; they were extremely restless and it required the attention of the whole guard through the night to retain them notwithstanding they were hubbled and picquted....Many of the natives remained about our camp all night.

In most instances the *Journal* accounts of encounters with the different Indian tribes they meet up with along the way is positive. When thefts by Indians occurred, on occasion, Lewis and Clark report that the Chief generally informed them that the thieves were renegades, not representative of the relationship the Indians sought with the white man.

Perhaps representative of their contacts with Indians can be found in an entry by Clark on May 8, 1806. It mentions Willard, who often was designated to go to an Indian village, usually to barter for needy supplies. It was not

---

[13] p. 143, Vol. 7, Moulton

uncommon for those on such a mission to stay overnight:[14]

> Late in the evening The Twisted Hair and Willard returned; they brought about half of our saddles, and some powder and lead which had been buried at that place. My saddle was among the number of those which were lost. About the same time the young men arrived with 21 of our horses. The greater part of our horses were in fine order. Five of them appeared to have been so much injured by the indians riding them last fall that they had not yet recovered and were in low order....The situation of our camp was a disagreeable one in an open plain: the wind blew violently and was cold. At seven p.m. it began to rain and hail, at 9 it was succeeded by a heavy shower of snow which continued untill the next morning–several indians joined us this evening from the village of the *broken arm* or Tunnachemootoolt and continued all night. The man who had imposed himself on us as a relation of the Twisted Hair rejoined us this evening. We found him an impertinent proud supercilious fellow and of no kind of rispectability in the nation, we therefore did not indulge his advances towards a very intimate connection. The Cutnose lodged with the Twisted Hair. I believe they have become good friends again. Several indians slept about us.

An entry by Lewis on May 15th is representative of the hunting that was necessary on a regular basis, as well as their interest in the nature and habitat of their surroundings:[15]

---

[14] p. 234-235, Vol. 7, Moulton
[15] p. 260, Vol. 7, Moulton

> This morning early Reubin Fields in surching for his horse saw a large bear at no great distance from camp; several men went in pursuit of the bear, they followed his trail a considerable distance but could not come up with him. Labuish and Shannon set out with a view to establish a hunting camp and continuing several days, two others accompanyed them in order to bring in the three bears which Labuish had killed. Drewyer and Cruzatte were sent up the river; Shields R. Fields and Willard hunted in the hills near the camp. They returned in the evening with a few pheasants only and reported that there was much late appearance of bear, but believed that they had gone off to a greater distance. At 11 a.m. the men returned with the bear which Labuich had killed. These bear gave me a stronger evidence of the various coloured bear of this country being one species only, than any I have heretofore had. The female was black with a considerable proportion of white hairs intermixed and a white spot on the breast, one of the young bears was just black and the other of a light reddish brown or bey colour. The poil of these bear were infinitely longer finer and thicker than the black bear, their tallon also longer and more blont as if worn by digging roots. [He continues, comparing these to bears in other areas]

Entries by Lewis and by Clark on May 19, 1806 that mention Thompson make clear that he played the same role as many of the others.[16]

> It continued to rain this morning untill 8

[16] pp. 271-273, Vol 7, Moulton. It cannot be substantiated whether the Thompson on this expedition is or is not an ancestor of Frank's.

> OCK when it became fair. We sent Charbono, Thompson, Potts, Hall and Wiser over the river to a village above in order to purchase some roots to eat with our lean bear meat. For this purpose we gave them a few awls, kniting pins and arm bands....At 11 a.m. Thompson returned from the village accompanied by a train of invalids consisting of 4 men and 8 women and a child [They were given laudanum, an opium derivative used as a sedative, and a volitle liniment] all of those poor wretches thought themselves much benefited and all returned to their village well satisfyed.

By May 21st, 1806 the *Journal* reports that ten days earlier their tent was not adequate to keep out the rain and that their bear meat was gone.[17] The final entry quoted by the writer indicates that while they are greatly dependent on bear meat for sustenance, Clark, at the same time, is interested in the minutiae of his surroundings. On May 31st, 1806, he wrote:[18]

> Goodrich and Willard visited the indian village this morning and returned in the evening. Willard brought with him the dressed Skin of a bear which he had purchased for me. This Skin was of a uniform pale reddish brown colour, the indians inform us that it was not the Hoh-host [Nez Perce tribe's term for the grizzly bear] or white bear, that it was the Yack-kah [Nez Perce term for black bear]. This distinction of the indians induced us to make further enquiry relitive to their opinions of the deferent species of bear in this

---

[17] p. 276, Vol. 7, Moulton
[18] p. 314, Vol. 7, Moulton

> country...the white, the deep and pale red grizzle, the dark brown grizzle, and all those that had the extremities of the hair of a white or frosty colour without regard to the colour of the ground of the poil...[a great deal of detail follows].

† † †

There was also a John B. Thompson on the Expedition but it has proved impossible to determine if this is an ancestor of *our* Thompson. In an appendix to volume 2, Gary Moulton gives a brief biography of those on the Expedition. His account of one Private John B. Thompson, includes his inability to find his birth and death dates. Moulton wrote:

> His date of joining the expedition is unknown, but he may have lived in Indiana. He seems to have had some experience as a surveyor. Clark refers to him during the expedition as "a valuable member of our party." His post-expedition career is equally obscure: Clark listed him in 1825 as "killed." Speculation places him with John Mclellan's expedition in the Rockies in 1807.[19]

An internet site is somewhat more substantive, stating:

> Place of birth unknown, but he lived in Indiana. He was a former surveyor at Vincennes, Indiana, and it can be imagined that he was of some assistance to Captain Lewis' celestial observations, and of Captain Clark's map-making. In addition to other duties, he often served as a cook while on the

---

[19] p. 522, Vol. 2, Moulton

expedition. Clark notes that he was dead by the years 1825-1828.[20]

Moulton offers more information about Private Alexander Hamilton Willard than he was able to glean about Private Thompson:

> Born [August 24, 1778 at Charlestown, New Hampshire]. He was living in Kentucky when he enlisted in Captain Amos Stoddard's artillery company in 1800. [He went on Lewis and Clark's payroll as of January 1, 1804.] He was [a good] blacksmith [gunsmith, and fine hunter] and apparently assisted John Shields in the [blacksmith] work during the expedition. Lewis hired him as government blacksmith for the Sauk and Fox Indians [in Quashequema's village that became Nauvoo] in 1808, and the next year he held the same position with the Delawares and Shawnees. He served in the War of 1812 and lived in Missouri and Wisconsin. His marriage in 1807 produced twelve children. In 1852 he emigrated with his family to California [*most if not all of his children were adults by then*] and there died and was buried near Sacramento. There is some suggestion that he kept a journal of the expedition, but if so, it is lost.

At the time he married Elinor [or Eleanor] McDonald on February 14, 1806, Alexander Hamilton Willard, Frank's maternal grandfather, was described as "five feet ten inches tall, brown hair, dark eyes, dark complexion and of fine

---

[20] www.artsci.wustl.edu/~lande/html/clarke.html (8/19/2002). The following information on Willard found in brackets is also from this source. That from Moulton on p. 524, Vol. 2 supplemented by information from his genealogical sheet prepared by family members from Mormon records.

physique."[21]

Since 1806 is the same year that the Lewis and Clark Expedition ended, their marriage that same year suggests they were already engaged, or at least had met, while Private Alexander was stationed in Shelbyville, Kentucky prior to his selection for the Expedition and where Elinor was born. Even though they undoubtedly had met while both were in Shelbyville, evidence suggests they married in St. Louis, Missouri where the McDonalds probably had moved by 1806.

Alexander Hamilton Willard & Eleanor McDonald
Photo courtesy of Willard Family Association

Records confirm that at least by 1808, Alexander was working in Missouri as a blacksmith, he and Elinor living first in St. Louis and then in Gasconade, upstream from St. Louis on the Missouri River where her father had his sawmill. It's probable that the grant of 160 acres of land and the $166 (plus an additional $100 sometime later) that

[21] Willard descendants have spent considerable time tracing the Willard genealogy and their information varies slightly from the above quoted from Moulton's appendix.. See www.aartsci.wusl.edu~landc/html/clarke.html.

Alexander was paid for his two years with the Lewis and Clark Expedition helped the newlywed couple get started. However, it's not certain how much Elinor saw of her husband in the early years of their marriage; his restlessness, as indicated earlier, having led him to join Lewis on various government-sponsored expeditions among the Indians.

His extended absences may explain why the couple did not have their first child, named Alexander after his father, until February 2, 1812.

But even then, Elinor could not depend on her husband's presence since he was once more off to fight in the War of 1812, declared against Britain on June 18. However, since their next child, Martha Eliza, was born in August or September of 1813, it's possible that Alexander did not at once leave for the war. He may have been deliberately sought after by the Army a year later [in 1814], because of his extensive prior contact with and knowledge of the Indians—for it was on October 5, 1814 that the battle at Tims River, an Indian village in Canada, took place. The War itself lasted until after the Battle of New Orleans on January 8, 1815, because word had not reached the combatants there that the war had ended on December 24, 1814 when the Treaty of Ghent had been signed with Britain. The extent of Alexander's participation in the War has not been determined. It is determined that he later he participated in "various Indian wars and the Mexican War, where he preferred to be classed a common soldier than to be promoted to a higher rank."[22]

Somehow, with all his ventures, Alexander was able to be home sufficiently to father twelve children—seven sons (one named Lewis, another Clark) and five daughters. All his

---

[22] From Obituary of Olga Willard Gano, *Prescott Evening Courier*, 3/11/1942, written by Frances Willard Munds.

children were grown, he was seventy-four and Elinor sixty-two, when he, as venturesome as ever, was tempted by the California Gold Rush to leave Wisconsin for California in 1852. His son, Lewis Augustus, Frank's grandfather, had already been there and returned–clearly had inherited his father's pioneering spirit. Unfazed by the fact the trip was hard, dangerous, and full of Indian scares, in 1849, Lewis had "crossed the plains with a few other hardy spirits in the forefront of the Great Gold Rush."[23] Lewis's return to California a second time with his family continues:

"Returning east across the Isthmus a little later, Lewis again crossed the plains [leaving from Platteville in March 1852] with a great train [of forty-nine people which included all his father's family with the exception of one son], and many relatives."[24] Due to Alexander's knowledge of Indian warfare, and Lewis's previous experience, they "were able to pilot that company through the three months of their perilous journey to Sacramento, California with the loss of but one man and a few head of stock. [By the time they arrived], the gold rush of '49 was somewhat subsided and people were beginning to recognize California as a place to make their homes [a Homestead Act was finally passed in 1862 after similar bills had been defeated by Congress in 1852 and 1860]. Alexander Willard soon moved with his family to a farming district now known as Franklin and bought a tract of land which is still known as the Willard Farm."

Alexander Hamilton Willard, Frank's great grand-father,

---

[23] Quote from his obituary, Obituary Book, p. 476. Sharlot Hall Museum Library, Prescott, Arizona.

[24] Quotes are from his obituary, Obituary Book, p. 476. Sharlot Hall Museum Library, Prescott, Arizona. Handwritten notation, "June 17, 1911." Insertions from Obituary of Olga Willard Gano. The quote that follows is also from the Olga Obituary.

born August 24, 1778, died on March 6, 1865, aged 87; his wife, Elinor, born July 4, 1790, died June 11, 1868, aged 78.

Both are buried in Franklin, California, near Sacramento—his grave "marked with a historical plaque honoring him as having been a member of the Lewis and Clark Expedition." He was the next-to-last surviving member of the Expedition and the only one whose photographic likeness is known—he and Elinor having lived during the time of the discovery of photography. His grandson, Donald Willard, writes of Alexander: "He must have had a large measure of the Spirit of '76, and also of his venturesome ancestor, Simon Willard, who had left England to come to the colony of Massachusetts in 1634."[25]

California State Historical Marker located at the Franklin Cemetery, Franklin, Sacramento Co. CA for Alexander Hamilton Willard

[25] P. 18, Don Willard, "An Old-Timer's Scrapbook"

3. Homesteading in Arizona

The land, whither ye go to possess it, is a land of hills and valleys, and drinketh water of the rain of heaven: A land which the Lord thy God careth for; the eyes of the Lord thy God are always upon it, from the beginning of the year even unto the end of the year.[1]

✝✝✝

Alexander Hamilton Willard had lived just long enough to see his son, Lewis Augustus, Frank's grandfather, marry his first wife, Angeline (Ann) Billops, in Sacramento County California, in September 1860. Thirteen years Alexander's junior, Ann was born October 9, 1844 in Marion County, Iowa, to one of Sacramento's pioneer families. She and Lewis had five children: their first-born, Edward, died before he was two, and James when he was a mere 3 months old; next came Flora, born April 2, 1867, Wallace, born August 14, 1869, and Lewis Burleigh, born November 25, 1871. Ann was only 27 years old when she died on December 11, 1871, the date suggesting it most likely was from complications that followed her last childbirth. She was buried in the Franklin, California cemetery near her in-laws, Alexander and Elinor Willard.

Soon after Ann's death,[2] Lewis Augustus followed his brother, Joel, to Pine Valley, Nevada where the latter was a freight hauling contractor for the gold mines at Cornucopia. There he met Julia Ann Frost, an elementary school teacher, who by then had moved from Tioga,

---

[1] Deuteronomy 11: 11-12.

[2] Sacramento records list Lewis as a laborer who was registered to vote in 1867, 1871 and 1873, the latter, perhaps, being the year he followed his brother, Joel, to Nevada.

Pennsylvania, where she was born on November 22, 1857, to Missouri and then to Nevada. Lewis and Julia Ann married in Elko, Nevada on October 24, 1877,[3] and Lewis's three still-living children, Flora, Wallace and Lewis Burleigh, came to live with them.

At first Lewis's family lived in the mountainous mining town of Cornucopia, Nevada, 100 miles north of Elko, working with his brother, Joel. At the peak of operations, they had 25 teams hauling the mine's silver and gold. But then the veins dried up, and they, like most of Cornucopia's residents, moved to Elko, located on the Union Pacific Railroad and on the Humboldt River. During their time there, Lewis bought and sold properties in the area that included a boarding house, mines, mills, smelting furnaces, etc. He is listed in the 1880 census as a teamster. Lewis's children were in school in Elko and his and Julia's first daughter, Frank's mother, Olga Winifred, was born there on June 26, 1882.

† † †

Meanwhile, in 1878, Lewis's brother, Joel, for health reasons, decided to move his family from Pine Valley, California, where they were then living, to the warmer climate of Arizona. Joel took with him his three oldest sons, Ninian, 23, Charles, 20, and Dolph, 18, as well as his youngest, Alex, 10. He left Mack, 17, Jim, 15 and three daughters, Jennie, Nellie and Frannie, with their mother to come later after he was settled. Their herd, by then, had grown to over 400 head and included a small number his brother, Lewis, had acquired.

Regrettably, Joel never made it; he died in Dolan Springs, Colorado from pneumonia on January 27, 1879. After

---

[3] Some Willard family records put their marriage date as September 1, 1880. Julia's parents were Ruel Ufford and Sophia Ann (Allen) Frost.

burying their father and discussing amongst themselves what to do, the children decided to carry on, Charles assuming charge. It was not an easy trip; they lost, had stolen, or had to sell a considerable portion of their cattle, arriving in Verde with only 250 head–and Alex suffered through a bout of whooping cough en route. It was several years before the rest of the family left Pine Valley and joined them in Arizona.[4] After they were all settled, they recovered Joel's body from Colorado and moved it to Cottonwood.

In mid-1884, Lewis decided to follow Joel's family to Arizona, homesteading land in Cottonwood, Arizona, across the river from Clarkdale. Julia has provided us with a vivid account of their trek there. She begins by expressing her reservations about making the move, having heard that Arizona was rife with "rattlesnakes, centipedes, tarantulas, scorpions, horned toads, Gila monsters and even mosquitoes and flies in such numbers as we had never heard of." Nevertheless, on July 15, 1884 Lewis Augustus and Julia set off in three wagons, with their four children: Flora, 17, her brothers, Wallace and Lewis Burleigh, 15 and 13, and Olga, only two. They also had with them for the trip Harry Barr, who served as the teamster and handyman, and a young man who proved to be an excellent cook.

Julia was grateful to have someone else doing most of the cooking. "You know how campfires are," she writes in her account of their trek to Arizona. "When you get on one side to attend to the food cooking, the smoke comes right in your face; then you go to the opposite side and the smoke goes too. So you can easily see why I did not want to cook."

Julia usually drove the largest wagon, covered, which had

---

[4] "An Old-Timer's Scrap Book," by Don Willard, son of Mack, who had become "the man in charge back in Pine Valley." In 1885, after he joined the others at Cottonwood, Mack became Cottonwood's first Postmaster.

been modified to hold, behind two seats in front, a set of beds for her and Olga, their suitcases, books and magazines; water tucked under the seats. A larger freight wagon held their furniture and most of the other goods they were bringing with them. Six horses pulled it, plus an attached smaller covered wagon that held Flora's bed [no mention is made of special sleeping provisions for the two boys], trunks, camp chairs, and the rolls of bedding used by the men who slept on the ground. It also had in its rear a cupboard containing their cooking and eating equipment; its door hinged so that it came down, propped by a leg, to form their dining table. Most of the time Flora and the men rode saddle horses, necessary for driving the 70-80 loose horses with them; one by one taking turns riding inside a covered wagon when tired.

It took them two months to reach their destination, Cottonwood, Arizona. Early-on they stopped for a day or two to visit with old friends before starting to cross "long stretches of uninhabitable mesas and barren deserts." They also stopped for a few days at the oases encountered periodically to rest, drink the good spring water and let the horses graze on the plentiful grass. Julia writes: "I do not remember how many of these deserts we had crossed when we came to Paranagut Valley and people living all along the way. They had already decided to rest there for several days, when, unexpectedly they met the Griers's family who knew and admired Dolph Willard, his brother Joel's son. They were immediately invited in and fed a sumptuous dinner before retiring to set up camp.

The next two days they traveled mostly at night to avoid the intense heat and had depleted their water supply before finding another oasis. Finally, reading by match light, they found a small sign that informed them of a spring a quarter mile from the road. Again they rested several days before undertaking the next long desert stretch that would take them to Colorado—"not the 'Silvery Colorado' of the song—but the red muddy water that had to be put in tubs and buckets to settle before it was fit for use."

They then followed the river bank for a ways, until they came to the Scantlin Ferry, a big flatboat that took them across. There they nearly lost a half broken pony which had "jumped from the boat and was letting the current carry him down the river without making an effort to swim." Fortunately, Harry, who was collecting water on the shore, saw him, jumped in after him, and when he tried to grab his halter, the pony started swimming after him toward the shore—Harry barely able to keep sufficiently in front of him to avoid being hit by the hoofs. There were other horses that also were without "good horse sense" in crossing and floated downstream before landing on a beach of quicksand. Julia writes:

> It was getting dark by this time. Mr. Willard and Harry Barr in their B.V.D.'s crawled, for they could not walk without sinking, and tied the end of ropes to those horses and pulled them to solid ground. In the course of time they managed to pull them all out; only the last one was minus a tail, as the rope had to be tied to that appendage, and it became detached in transit. We had a late supper that night.

While they were camped in this area, nearby Indians brought roasting ears of corn and watermelons to sell them, a real treat, Julia exclaims, from the canned goods they mostly lived on—supplemented on rare occasions by milk, eggs and butter from ranch houses they came upon. After they left the river, they crossed another big desert, finally in Arizona, but not yet home. They were, however, at a luscious spring, a corral for the horses, and a hotel, kept by a man and wife, where they had supper. Julia remembers the enormous sum (for then) they paid for these amenities for their two night's stay—$40.

Sometime later when it started to rain heavily and they were seeking a shelter, they unexpectedly encountered a nephew, John Hunt, who took them to his sister's home five miles distant. They stayed with the Imus family for several days as "the most terrific rains I have ever seen came."

By the time they reached Hackberry both Olga and Julia were sick with chills and fever. They continued on to Walnut Creek, but could not go further and spent two or three weeks there, paying off the men who'd accompanied them. Lewis, meanwhile, rode on to the Verde and came back with Dolph to help him drive the team on to Cottonwood. By the time he returned, Julia and Olga were well recovered and they all resumed their journey to Jerome, going through Williamson Valley, then to Chino Valley, through the Black Hills, and then Sanders' Station to the summit, and finally down a treacherous hill with a forty-five degree slope—the freight wagon taking a longer route to avoid the steep hill. When they all finally got to Jerome, it took them two hours to get through the main street "on account of the congested traffic." It was September 17, 1884, almost exactly two months after they set out, when they arrived in Cottonwood in Arizona's Verde Valley.

† † †

They stayed with Mary and Charlie Willard (Charlie another of Joel's sons) and their four sons while they looked for a place to buy. Julia writes:

> We soon found one that had a good well. The water tasted like real water and so cool. So we bought Dave Jones' improvements, as he had not homesteaded the place, and Mr. Willard proved up

on the land. I have homestead patents signed by Grover Cleveland and Chester A. Arthur. On this place I have lived the greater part of the time for forty-five years.

Lewis planted an orchard, raised grain and hay, and tended a truck garden. Later he built a large two-story brick house near Main Street, Cottonwood that still stands as far as family knows. During this time, Julia had three more children, Frances Edna, born September 14, 1886, Lewis (Bub), born June 5, 1892 and Alexander Frost, born August 5, 1894. Four years later, in 1898, Lewis received a letter from his sister, Elinor (Ellen), whom he hadn't seen for 41 years, informing him that her husband, Major William Downing, had just died, and asking him to come to Bisbee, Arizona where they lived to help her settle up the estate. He not only obliged, but census records show that Ellen then came to live with them "in Beaver Creek Precinct [near Cottonwood & Bridgeport], Yavapai county, Arizona."

Sisters, Edna, 3, & Olga, 7, 1889, in Prescott, Arizona

26. Justice, Peace & God

Olga 10,
Edna 6 &
Lewis, (Bub)
5 months,
1892

Sisters Olga
& Edna &
brother,
Lewis in
August 1899

27. Homesteading in Arizona

Olga with her Mother, Julia Ann Frost

Lewis Augustus on his favorite horse

28. Justice, Peace & God

†††

A lengthy and informative obituary appeared in the local paper when Lewis Augustus died at age 80. He was born on December 28, 1831, the eighth of Elinor and Alexander Hamilton Willard's twelve children. It read:[5]

> L.A. Willard of Cottonwood, died at his home June 9, 1911, and was buried in the family plot at that place, June 10. The death of "Lew" Willard marks the passing of one of the real pioneers and nation builders of the great west. Sprung from the sturdy stock of heroes, son of Alexander Willard who was a member of the Lewis & Clark expedition, he lived his long life as a worthy successor of great ancestors who carved an empire from the rough wastes of the Pacific coast. As stock man, Indian fighter and rancher, he lived in the open and partook of the breadth of horizon and of the open-faced honesty of the best of such life.
>
> A man positive in his character, always knowing his own mind, tenacious of his own views, vigorous in maintaining his position and defending his rights, he made many warm friends and some enemies. As a friend he was faithful to the last; as an enemy he was a hard fighter, but absolutely fair, never holding malice nor hitting in the dark. His latter years refined his judgement and softened the sterner aspects of his character so that practically all his enemies of earlier days became his friends, and mourn the loss of a good neighbor, a strong active, square man, a man's man, a lover of all that is best in

---

[5] P. 476A, *Obituary Book*, Sharlot Hall Museum Archives

humanity.

This is attested by a small incident–the fact that for many years and until his death his neighbors on the same ditch would have no other man to manage the delicate water question among them and to arbitrate their differences on that subject.

A large concourse of people from the Verde Valley and Jerome attended his funeral, which was conducted by Rev. Phillips[6] of Jerome. All the members of his family were with him at the last. To them it is not the loss of the man of affairs, active in politics and all questions of public welfare, but of a faithful husband and a loving father, wise counselor, whose home was his castle which he surrounded with his care and watchful guardianship.

He married in Nevada, September 2, 1880, to Julia Frost, who survives him. The four children of this marriage are Mrs. Claude Thompson [Olga] of Flagstaff, Mrs. John Alexander [Frances Edna], and two sons, Lewis and Alexander, who reside at Cottonwood.

Mr. Willard lived for some years in Sacramento county, California, afterwards removing to Elko, Nevada. From there he came to the Verde Valley in 1884 and bought the ranch on which he died.

Lewis's wife, Julia Ann Frost, born November 22, 1857, was much younger than her husband. Buried in Cottonwood, Arizona, she had lived on until February 28,

---

[6] Could he possibly be related to the Rev. Phillips, after which Phillips Memorial Baptist Church in Cranston is named; the church where Frank became minister, the place he stayed longer than any other?

1938 when she was 81 years old.

Julia Ann Frost Willard about 1897

4. Frank's Parents: Olga & Claude

Frank began the following "rambling" account declaring: "It does not purport to be a documentary or a scholarly study of the area, but rather an outline for grandchildren's eyes of the newness of our great west." [He writes] "It was the worst of times; it is the best of times for our last frontier state. Arizona in 1912 moved into statehood, but there was little to commend the territory to a classification with other states. In one lifetime, however, the land of coyotes, rattlesnakes and outlaws has become one of the richest and most sophisticated in these United States. Having lived in and through this miraculous transformation, Grandpa Thompson [Frank] is attempting to weave a dichotomy between the last frontier and the present tourist trap and art center that is present-day Arizona.

"Another purpose of this woven record will be to capture much of the drama that attended your ancestors' journey from the worst of times to the best. To try to paraphrase Dickens is always dangerous but his classic bifurcation of the critical times his two cities struggled through provides a jumping-off place for this account. So much drama, so many crises, such acute poverty and suffering, will make the writer suspect of more than exaggeration." [1]

† † †

On May 10, 1942, only two months after his mother Olga died, the Reverend Frank Thompson devoted his whole sermon at Phillips Memorial Church in Cranston,

---

[1] This begins Frank's account of his early days before Redlands and Andover Newton, written for his grandchildren in 1980, the year of his death.

Rhode Island to a review of her life. He starts by declaring it "an unforgivable sin for a minister or any other public person to bring his own family into public view." But he justifies his doing so in this instance by declaring that an "inner voice" kept insisting that enough of the congregation knew his mother when she lived with him on two occasions to be interested. Frank calls her a "rugged pioneer mother," "a friend of life," who, when asked her most exciting day replied, "Tomorrow." Even though Frank may have a few of his facts slightly wrong, his account is real, and his love and respect for his mother shine through every word,[2] making this the best way to become acquainted with her life, and, eventually, with Frank's early years spent on a ranch. Frank begins:

> My mother was not very old when she died, just 60 [she lived from June 26, 1882 to March 3, 1942], and yet in that short time she moved from a crude, rough, rugged Western civilization to the polished, cultured East. She was born in the mid-west [Elko, Nevada] and went to the far west as a young girl [two years old] by caravan wagon train into a small valley in North Arizona [Cottonwood], a valley into which there was no road leading. The wagon had to be taken apart and loaded on horseback and carried into the valley [perhaps referring to the location of the homestead land they purchased], and there this caravan of people started scratching the old hard Arizona earth, the dry earth, trying to make a go of it and finally to establish great

---

[2] The account that follows is in Frank's own words with minor deletions, added punctuation, and, in parentheses, names, dates and a few suggestions and facts culled elsewhere.

cattle ranches there. As a young girl she used to ride with the cow hands; was what is called a cow girl, riding long hours during the day with the hands, cooking their meals at night, and tales of her experiences seemed to thrill us far more than some of the weird mystery stories some of our young people like to read.

I remember her telling of one instance when she was cooking for the herders, and they did not have any meat. They hadn't located the herds of cattle yet and one young man went out saying he would bring back some venison. They heard a shot and soon he came back with the meat. She cooked it and someone said that wasn't venison to which they all agreed and they didn't like it. After they had finished, the man asked how they had enjoyed the burro.

Another experience, later. She was sleeping in a tent with her sister who had a small child. Her sister [probably referring to her half-sister, Flora, considerably older than Olga] was helping with the cooking and they slept in this tent together with the baby between them. One night mother woke up and saw a hydrophobic skunk standing over the baby. One scratch would give the baby hydrophobia. Without thinking she grabbed the skunk by the tail and threw it from the tent, thus obviating the possibility of disastrous results.

As a young cow-girl Olga began to get ambitious to study. No one went to school in that neighborhood. In the valley there were no schools and parents taught their children as best they could. But Olga Willard decided she wanted to go away and study so she went to Flagstaff, Arizona, with a population of 3,200, and there she went to high school and normal school [to prepare teachers, at Tempe] and came back and organized a school in the valley.[3]

Then to that valley came a young Methodist minister [Claude Thompson] and she started teaching him how to become a better minister.

[It's strange that Frank remembers this about his mother and Claude since, according to Olga's sister, Frances Edna, there was no regular minister at their church, only itinerant ministers, like Claude himself, who came only once a month, except for revival meetings. At those, one or more ministers would preach every night for weeks. Olga was always active in church work, and so may well have met Claude at one of these services, and their friendship may have developed at the parties held in homes or the school house where games were played and refreshments served, followed by country dancing. "Everyone went, women with their babies, men, single and married, and they danced until daylight. They also may have gone together to the ball games on a Sunday afternoon or horseback riding, all forms of recreation in the area.][4]

Claude did not stay in Arizona long but went

---

[3] In her memoir, Olga's sister, Frances Edna, tells of going to the "old Cottonwood school, except when my mother moved to town in the winter so we would not have the long drives to school in the cold. Part of the time we were in Prescott and in Jerome where I [Frances Edna] graduated from eighth grade." She, like Olga, later graduated from Normal School in Tempe [in 1905] and received a Life Diploma to teach in Arizona. Is it probable that Olga shared none of this experience, was taught only at home prior to high school, even though she was only four years younger than Frances Edna?

[4] Memoirs of Edna Willard Nichols; no date.

to California and Mother with him, and they lived in the world she had longed for, in a very important church.[5]

Then Claude's health broke and it seemed her dream was not to come true, for they were forced to go back into the mountains for his health. Two babies were born out there in the rugged wilds of Northern Arizona. *[Actually the first, John Lewis, was born on October 22, 1901 in Lompoc, California.]* The second baby, they had hoped would be a little girl so planned to name her after a prominent relative of Olga's, Frances Willard. *[Some in the family believe it was after Olga's cousin, Frances Lillian Willard, her Uncle Joel's daughter; others believe it after Frances Elizabeth Willard, the prominent educator and feisty activist member of the Women's Christian Temperance Union who was related but not in Olga's direct line of Willards.[6]]* Disappointed when I turned out to be another boy [*so Frank believed*], they changed the "e" in Frances to an "i" and went ahead with the naming

---

[5] See Appendix 2 for Family Tree: Claude Thompson

[6] As noted, Olga also had a sister, Frances—both sister and cousin may have been named after the earlier Temperance Crusader and Suffragette, Frances Elizabeth Caroline Willard, perhaps a fifth cousin of Olga's who lived from 1839-1898. Olga, however, probably named Frank after her first cousin. Olga was 16 years younger than her, but from the age of two onwards lived very near her, and in their youth both were country school teachers. Frances Lillian Willard, who married John Lee Munds, was well-known in Arizona; much like her forbear, active in Arizona's politics and suffragette movement. She was elected the first woman in the state senate in Arizona in the first election in which Arizona women could vote. It was she who wrote Olga's obituary. (From the Willard Family Association)

as planned. Then my father died *[a misleading sequence that was generally believed by the family; the actual facts regarding his parent's separation and his father's death will be discussed later].*

Mother went back to the city [according to divorce records she left for San Diego] to realize her dream again, and with her two small babies she made good. She started teaching, also began a little business on the side and got going pretty well. Several years later she married a fairly prosperous business man *[Paul Elbert Gano on October 24, 1912 in San Francisco–why* there *is not explained; possibly related to the fact that Paul's job required considerable traveling].* Again it seemed her dreams would come true. Then his health broke and she was again forced back into the wilds of Northern Arizona, out of civilization.

It seemed God constantly moved this rugged little pioneer woman out where she could be carrying on the simple tasks of helping people more than she realized at the time. She dreamed of being able to be in a great church where she could be with many people, but always she was shuttled off to small areas where she had just a few to work with. There in Northern Arizona four more children were born *[Actually, Ford and Fenner (more commonly known as Lynn) were born in Sacramento, California; only Paula and Mary Jo were born in Arizona]* and the family had a hard time making a go of it in that lime stone country. Just when they got things going, some smelters moved in and started mining for copper and a fire started and all the vegetation was burned to the ground.

My mother tried to organize the families to try

and get an adjustment [from the miners] for this devastation but rugged individuals that they were, they would not organize and it was then mother used the words I often heard which have helped me thru my life. She said, "If you do not oppose an evil that approaches you, you will not only become the victim of that evil, you will lose the ability to discern what is evil."

And so Mother determinedly began to try to oppose the evils that were creeping into that community, which had no church, no school, no organizations, no unified approach to this tragedy [when their land had burned]. First my mother organized a little Sunday School and out of it grew a little day school, then a PTA–all three being organized in the three rooms belonging to the Gano family on the barren hill–all three finding their birthplace in these three rooms where seven people lived!

I remember my first real thoughts about Mother were that I never saw her sit down. I wondered how she did it. Every morning I would find her busy in the kitchen preparing breakfast after she had milked four or five cows. We kept about eleven cows and sold the milk around. *[This writer was told by family members that Olga was also responsible for a sizable vegetable garden, raising chickens, collecting their eggs, and regularly taking the eggs and milk to market in town.]*.[7] And yet she was never too tired to light a coal oil lamp and read to us kids at night from the

---

[7] The sentence following, inserted here, is from another sermon, May 14, 1972. Frank throughout his ministry often included comments about his mother, especially references to her hard life.

Bible or other great literature And she had a zest for grammar, never acquired by her brother, Dolph. He would write letters which only love could decipher, and one time after she criticized his punctuation, he wrote a letter putting a whole flock of marks at the top—periods, commas, exclamation marks and question marks—and began his letter by saying, "There are the punctuations, you put them where you want. HERE'S WHAT I GOT TO SAY."[8]

My step-father, Paul Gano, became the Postmaster there and carried mail for twenty miles on horseback, and when he got so sick he couldn't do it, Mother covered the twenty miles on horseback, did the chores and carried on the work. Of course, we children thought we were great helps, but I suppose we were more handicaps than helps.

To add to our problems we had a flood. I think everything that could possibly happen to anyone happened to that little family in Northern Arizona.[9]

It was during this same period of time that my mother started teaching children in the valley to play the piano. All the children around came to play. She also taught groups to sing. She even tried to teach me to sing. I even thought I could. I used to sing at social affairs before my voice changed. I guess I had a fair voice but it certainly changed. I remember she never took a cent for teaching. I suppose none had a cent to spend. They did not

---

[8] This recollection inserted from a sermon April 14, 1974.

[9] Frank said more of this in his sermon but the author has chosen to tell this story in the section following where it is combined with the version told by Ford in his memoir.

have any money.

I remember her telling us during the first World War about sugar, and I remember my step-father and I one day had to ride eleven miles on horseback where sugar was rationed out. We stood in line several hours and it was all gone before our turn came and we never went back for any. We had no sugar for a year and three months in that house in Northern Arizona. We had none of the comforts that seem to be taken as a matter of course today: we used coal oil lamps, had no electricity, had wood fires in old crude stoves, no modern plumbing, no running water–only "walking water." We used to run to the nearest river and bring it back with us. And yet thru all that there was time to do things for other people.

I remember that in addition to the already named organizations Mother started, she started a Literary Club and we all used to go there and say pieces and sing solos and had a great time listening to the older people tell tales of the early days there in Northern Arizona, but always she was a pioneer, pioneering into human relationships, into the betterment of lives of others, never satisfied with just the work that had to be done in her own home, which was always sufficient, I think, to have kept several women busy all day. Then my step-father was struck by lightning and never recovered from that and so at fourteen I had to leave school to help them carry on the farm after he had really broken down so he was not able to do anything at all. Mother had the knack of getting things done. I think a little better than either of the men she had married or any of the males she gave birth to. She always got things done in a grand way and finally my stepfather died [*February 14, 1931*].

Mother then moved into the city again, this time to the big city of Prescott, Arizona, then larger than Flagstaff, 3,400 people. There she made good again by herself with four little children, two of us [*Frank and Ford*] had gone away to work and study.

She made a go of it and recently when we stood around her casket we realized how much we owed to her, for all four of the children had gotten a professional standing or at least a business training, and I say it with no pride for myself but with pride for her. We were the only family in that whole valley in Arizona from which even one had gone to college; because she had a vision to want to do something more and better, wanting to do for others what she never had been able to do for herself. No matter how hard the situation was at hand, Mother always had faith that there was a better world, not awaiting after death but awaiting now if only people would let God bring in that kind of world God had ordained for man. My mother's life was good, I think; trying to bring in that kind of world.

† † †

Not as much is known of the Thompsons' roots as is known of the Willards', but sufficient records have been found for us to say with some certainty that Frank's account, above, is not quite accurate as it pertains to his father–not surprisingly since he was a baby when separated from his father, Claude, and there is no indication he ever saw him again.

Claude Thompson was born on November 21, 1870

in Muhlenberg County, Kentucky and had one sister, Mary, eight years younger than him. The two, apparently, were never close and we know little of her other than the fact she lived in Long Beach, California as an adult. The 1910 census records indicate that at that time she was teaching elocution in a private school. According to family members, the only known contact they know of that she had with her brother was a call she once made to ask his advice and financial assistance in connection with some business dealings.

The earliest information we have about Claude is the fact that for one year, in 1898, he was pastor of Bethel Church in Phoenix, Maricopa County, Arizona.[10] As an itinerant minister with the Methodist church, one presumes that he was briefly a minister in a number of churches in the area. He and Olga Winifred Willard were married in Phoenix on September 16, 1900 by Rev. L. J. Hedgpeth "in the presence of W. L. Teel and Emma Teel," presumably friends. They must have left Arizona for California soon after, for Lewis was born just a year later, on October 22, 1901, in Lompoc, Santa Barbara County, California (possibly the time when Claude was serving at a good-sized church, as mentioned in Frank's account above).

However, we learn from records of Claude's and Olga's divorce that they were again in Arizona, on November 15, 1906, living in Sedona, Coconino County, Arizona where Claude was then, apparently, serving in the dual roles of minister of the Verde district of Arizona and as a forest ranger—near where Frank was born (in Phoenix) on November 20, 1909. Frank's account indicates that Olga was not happy with

---

[10] Information provided by Harold Byrn an archivist for the Methodists, who lives in Phoenix and was once pastor at that church.

the return instigated by Claude's poor health; she was the happiest she'd ever been when actively working with Claude in the sizeable church he had been serving in California.

At the time of their return to Arizona, Lewis had just turned five and became one of the first ten students to attend a new school in Sedona. It was probably about 1907 when Sedona's families with children recognized the need for a school, and came together to build a one-room school house; all the families with wagons having gotten together, and, in one trip, hauled down from Flagstaff sufficient lumber. Then, after the first teacher, young and lonely, quickly resigned, Olga Thompson took over despite having just had her second child, Francis. But she too quit after a short time, overworked and having trouble getting someone to care for the baby.

What happened next we learn primarily from the divorce records of Claude Thompson, Plaintiff, and Olga W. Thompson, Defendant, filed on his behalf by Attorney J. E. Jones. At the time of the filing, Claude was still living in Cococino, Arizona, but with a leave of absence in hand from the Forest Service, granted for health reasons, at the time of the interrogatories in November 1912, he had received permission from the court to answer them, under oath, before a notary at Soledad, Monterey, California, where he was then living. He was still residing there when the divorce was granted on December 5, 1912.

† † †

During this same time period, Olga Thompson, as defendant, was living at 1834 "C" Street, San Diego, California, where she was served notice of both the pending divorce and copies of the interrogatories which both she and Claude could answer. Curiously, at no point do the records mention Paul Gano or the fact that Olga married him on

October 24, 1912 in San Francisco, over 500 miles to the north of San Diego and *prior* to the date Claude answered the interrogatories; the records throughout always refer to her as Olga Thompson. Also, there is no indication that Olga ever responded to the interrogatories, so we are left only with Claude's revealing answers.

Claude declares that they had continuously lived together as husband and wife from the time of their marriage on September 16, 1900 until August 17, 1911. On that day she left for San Diego, California, "ostensibly to visit relatives." [Her older half-sister, Flora (Willard) Mason, lived there with her husband John.)

> She gave no intimation of any other intention, but bade me an affectionate good bye. I did not suspect her intention to abandon me at the time. I gave her no cause to abandon me and she had never hinted at any reason for so doing except on June 20, 1911 [this was less than two weeks after the death of Olga's father on June 9], when I spoke of discharging a man in my employ whom she wished me to retain as he did the washing and relieved her of other household duties which my work prevented me from doing.
>
> After she abandoned me I repeatedly besought her to return by letter, through friends, and, on May 26, 1912, in person in the presence of witnesses. She said she had ceased to care for me and that she would not return. [*Did he not know she had met Paul Gano by then?*)
>
> To the best of my ability, I always treated Olga in a kind, affectionate and husbandly manner, both personally and financially, and gave her no

cause whatever to abandon me.

The desertion of Olga brought on a serious illness and the worry of being where the event occurred prevented my improvement. I therefore asked for and was granted, on May 15, 1912, leave of absence form the Forest Service until I should be able to resume the work of forest ranger. My health at present is such that I cannot safely go to Flagstaff, Arizona to appear in this case.

"Suffer little children to come unto Me, and forbid them not, for of such is the Kingdom of Heaven."

Cradle Roll Certificate

This is to Certify that [illegible]
born on the 26 day of [illegible] Residing at
San Diego California is now a member of the Cradle Roll
Department of the Park Place ME south Sunday School.
Name entered on Cradle Roll this 29 day of [illegible] 1911.

Mrs. R. O. Allen
James T. Branch, Pastor

On October 29, 1911, soon after walking out on Claude, Olga enrolled Frank in the "Cradle Roll Department of the Park Place ME South Sunday School, in San Diego, California.

The divorce was granted on December 5, 1912 and the court, having found both Claude and Olga suitable as parents, gave custody of John Lewis, then about 11, to Claude, and Frank, then about 3, to Olga. A supplemental decree, still referring to Olga as Olga Thompson (no indication of her having married Paul Gano by then), was submitted to the court by Claude asking that each parent be required to keep the other informed at all times as to the whereabouts of the child not in their custody. This was granted on April 19, 1913.

It's doubtful that Claude ever returned to work as a forest ranger, certainly not in Arizona. What brought him to the Monterey area of California when he left Arizona during the divorce proceedings is not known. Probably, since Claude had been given custody of Lewis, he at first went to live with him in Monterey, but Claude's obituary gives no indication that his son was with him when he died on July 4, 1914, little more than a year after the final decree in his divorce proceedings. More likely, when his father became very ill, if he wasn't already with her, John Lewis went to stay with his Thompson grandparents in Ventura, about 200 miles to the south and where Claude's body was taken for burial. [The 1920 census shows John Lewis, 18, working out as a farm laborer and living with his grandparents, John C. and Nannie G., who had become farmers in Moorpark Precinct, of Ventura County.]

Claude's obituary, found in the *Salinas (near Monterey) Daily Index*, Wednesday, July 8, 1914, reads:

> Claude Thompson, who has been stricken with paralysis [the death certificate notes that he died of encephalitis] and has been ailing for some time, passed away at 1 p.m. last Saturday, the 4th. He has been a patient sufferer and we all sympathize with the bereaved family in their hour of trial. Mr. Thompson's mother, who had been at his bedside for some weeks assisting Mrs. Thompson in caring for the sufferer, and Mrs. Thompson departed for

> Soledad Saturday evening with the body in charge of Undertaker T.B. Pettit, who prepared the remains for shipment to Ventura, where the funeral will be held and interment made in the family lot at that place.

What remains a mystery is the fact that both Claude's death certificate and his obituary indicate that he was married at the time he died on July 4, 1914. The best explanation would be that he had *married again sometime during the brief time between his divorce and his death, but this* writer has been unable to locate such a marriage certificate. *Alternatively one might speculate that a wife who would remarry before her divorce would also resume her role as wife after divorce when her first husband was dying.* Perhaps Olga was drawn there by the fact that Lewis was with him and she didn't bother to inform the local news people that she had married again—even had given birth to Ford Gano by then, on, July 7 1913—only three months after the final custody decree was handed down. Further, at the time of Claude's death, Olga was in the early stages of pregnancy with Fenner (Lynn) Gano, born February 16, 1915.

Whatever the answer to this conundrum, we *are left to wonder whether Olga was ever legally married at all; whether her children with Paul were legitimate? Did Claude, possibly, know about this marriage and file for the divorce as a favor for Olga, to legitimize her marriage—or, possibly, because he himself wanted to marry again? Or did Claude even know Olga had married again?*[11]

---

[11] Information about Claude and his ancestors that follows comes from his divorce records which include extensive interrogatories; from his death certificate and obituary, from the 1850, 1870 & 1880 censuses and from the marriage certificate of Claude's parents.

In any case, it is strange that Olga's marriage to Paul Gano is never mentioned in the divorce proceedings.

† † †

Claude's mother, Nannie Christian,[12] was born in 1849 in Todd County, Kentucky: *her* mother in Logan County, Kentucky and *her* father in North Carolina. Claude's father, John C., was born in 1841 in Logan County, Kentucky, *his* father, James, a farmer, was born in 1814, in Muhlenberg County, Kentucky, *his* mother, Mary, was born in 1819, in Logan County. At the time of the 1850 census when John C. was just 9 years old, they lived in Logan County. That same year, according to the Todd County, Kentucky census, "Nancy" was two years old, her father an ordained M.E. Minister with real estate valued at $800.

On November 2, 1869, Nannie and John were married in Nannie's home; both then living in Muhlenberg County, Kentucky. Claude was born the next year, almost certainly in Muhlenberg County.

According to the 1870 and 1880 censuses, taken in Greenville, Muhlenberg County, Kentucky in their respective summers, Nannie was a housekeeper and John a lawyer, possessing $1,000 in real estate and a $3,000 personal estate. From a Muhlenberg history we learn that J.C. was admitted to the Muhlenberg bar in 1880. Then, from 1874 to 1882, J.C. served as a Muhlenberg County judge; at a time when "the people had the active sympathy of the court in fighting what was universally believed to be 'the railroad swindle.'" Thereafter, Nannie is said to have called

[12] Her birth name, according to the 1850 census, Todd County, Kentucky was Nancy, but this is the only time it has been noted; all other references are Nannie.

her husband "Judge."[13]

The family describe Nannie and J.C., as he was commonly called, as a Mutt and Jeff sort of couple, Nannie quite short, J.C., quite tall. After J.C.'s retirement, they moved to California, the 1910 census for Ventura County indicating they lived on a farm on Foothill Road, raising "Berys & Walnuts." Later they lived on Wiltshire Boulevard near the Ambassador Hotel. It is said that Nannie, having outlived her husband by several years, and unable to drive, thereafter took a bus or walked wherever she wanted to go. The writer has been unable to accurately determine the date or place of death of either J.C. or Nannie.[14]

---

[13] See Rothert, pp. 55,353-354 & 374.

[14] This writer was sent a death certificate for a Nannie Catherine Thompson that stated she died of "pernicious anemia" on January 14, 1919 in Inglewood, Los Angeles County, California where she had lived just over four years. However, the writer believes this is not the death certificate for *our* Nannie Christian Thompson. If the only discrepancy were the use of Catherine on the certificate rather than Christian as her middle name, we could explain the difference as the use of a given middle name rather than the maiden name she more commonly used. However, the death certificate also notes this Nannie's birthplace as Ray County, Missouri, not Kentucky; and, most important, names different parents (C. Vanderpool and Polly Holder Vanderpool from Missouri) and a different husband, Andrew J. Thompson, not John C. Given these major discrepancies, it is still strange to find another Nannie Thompson, a widow, born the same year, 1849; who lived in California approximately the same number of years. A new search for the death certificate of another Nannie Thompson will be made, along with a continuing search for that of her husband, but it may prove just as elusive as finding one for J.C. has proved so far.

5. Frank's Boyhood in Rural Arizona

"In one lifetime, the land of coyotes, rattlesnakes and outlaws has become one of the richest and most sophisticated in these United States."[1]

† † †

According to the 1910 census for Camp Verde Precinct, Yavapai County, Arizona Territory, Paul Gano was at that time single; a boarder there; and a salesman in a general store working for wages. The question was not previously raised, but it's quite possible that he and Olga met at this time, since Olga had many relatives in that area whom she frequently visited. [*Is it possible that Paul's return to California is what prompted Olga to leave Claude when she did? Could they even have met up and left together?*] In any case, according to the divorce papers, after leaving Claude, Olga was living in San Diego, California; teaching, running a small business and raising her two boys, Francis Willard and John Lewis. And that's where she was living when she became serious with Paul [originally or again] and married him on October 24, 1912 (*before her divorce was granted*).

At the time Paul was a fairly prosperous employee, a salesman, with the Benner Tea Co.. His job took him to cities all over California–presumably the explanation of their meeting in San Diego, marrying in far off San Francisco, and having their first two children in Sacramento–to say nothing of the fact that the courts continued, as late as April 1913, to state Olga's address as San Diego. The rationale for Claude's having sought that amended decree in April that required their parents to keep each other informed of the children's addresses

[1] From opening of "Frank's Odyssey for our Grandchildren"

may well have been Claude's knowledge that Olga seemed to move frequently.

As for Olga, it is unlikely that even if she had known of the health problems that had brought Paul west from his home in New York, it is unlikely that she would have anticipated that they would recur and force her return to rural Arizona which she thought she'd escaped. Be that as it may, by 1915, Paul's consumptive health condition had worsened to the extent that his doctor advised him to seek a high, dry climate. Northern Arizona, where Olga had other relatives ranching, fit the need.

Claude, who had had custody of Lewis since the divorce from Olga in December 1912, had died [7/4/1914] by the time Olga and Paul decided to move to Arizona. Even so, Lewis, who'd never cared much for his step-father, chose to remain with his Thompson grandparents in Ventura, just north of Los Angeles.[2] Frank no doubt missed his brother, especially now as he was leaving California for Arizona. Lewis would not be accompanying him, their mother and their new family as they made the long and tiring trip by narrow gauge railroad.[3]

By the time they moved to Arizona, Frank was approaching six, Ford, was barely two, and Fenner Lynn was still a babe in arms. All we know of the years in Sacramento before the move comes from Ford–those presumably told him by Olga. The first, the fact he'd won a silver trophy cup as the "top specimen of spoiled babyhood." The second, the fact he'd suffered a scar over the pupil of his right eye, permanently affecting his vision in that eye, as the result of

---

[2] While living with her, Lewis graduated from Ventura High, and later attended Oregon State College.

[3] See Appendix 3 Familly Tree: Olga Thompson Gano

"creeping on the floor with a sharpened pencil in my hand."[4]

The Gano group was met in Clarkdale, the town about seven miles west of Cottonwood, by Olga's sister, Frances Edna, and her husband, Art Nichols, driving a "span of horses hitched to a sturdy buckboard." The boys all piled in back, Ford and Lynn soon snoring, but Frank began to explore the provisions Art and Edna had purchased. Frank writes:

> My surreptitious search uncovered what seemed a prize of all prizes: a whole cracker barrel of Fig Newtons. They went down in twos and threes and soon the burps were loud enough to alert the folks. When my pilfering was discovered, Aunt Edna sighed that I would have a rough beginning in Arizona for the prized cookies were alive with worms and had been purchased as hog feed. To this day I have never been able to touch a Fig Newton.

The family first stayed a few days with their Willard relatives in Cottonwood before renting a farm about four miles north of there on the opposite side of the Verde River, owned by Olga's half-brother, Wallace (son of Ann Billops and Lewis Augustus). Ford recalls how he and Frank stood behind the seat of a borrowed buggy on the drive with Lynn and their parents to Uncle Wallace's where Paul parked the

---

[4] Most of this section comes from Frank's writings done "for his grandchildren" in 1980, just before his death, and the memoirs by his half-brother, Ford Gano, found on the internet: www.csd.net/~liz/gano/la.htm (see Resources under Gano, Ford Iman). It is supplemented by selections from Frank's sermons, and from memoirs by Frances Edna Willard Nichols, his mother's sister, and Don Willard, grandson of Joel Willard, Frank's grandfather's brother.

Olga and Frank about 1915

borrowed buggy in front, gave the reins to Olga, climbed out and went into the house to make the necessary arrange-ments for occupying their new home.

Frank asserts that he and his brothers found life on the farm "busy and exciting," with chick-ens to feed, fresh eggs to gather, and "every Sunday such tasty fried chicken as to water our mouths forever."

Ford pronounces their favorite game as "roll the hoops," little round, usually metal, hoops that were pushed with a stick shaped "in the form of a handle with a cross on the end." With this, you pushed the hoop along, trying to keep it upright as you ran as fast as you could, trying to outrun the others. Mumblety-peg and marbles were two other favorites, Lynn so good at the latter that he had a huge sack full. At school breaks, there was Blind-Man's-Bluff, hide-and-seek, and Annie-Over. The latter consisted of two teams, one on each side of the school building. They took turns throwing a rubber ball over the roof and if the team opposite caught the ball they ran around to the thrower's side to try to hit someone. If hit, you left the game; the object, of course, was to eliminate one side.

During warm weather, the youngsters relished daily swims in the quiet Verde River that ran through the lower part of the ranch, and the rare occasions that Uncle Art took them fishing, "showing remarkable patience with boys who didn't know which end of a hook to bait."

Frank liked the Sunday fried chicken, though not the preparations that came before, which he may have been old enough to escape. Only Ford described them.[5] He writes about their beginning on Saturday night, in the kitchen, when they all had baths in the same galvanized tub their mother used to do the laundry—the water warmed up a *little* with hot water from the tea kettle kept on their big old wood range (that needed a lot of firewood to do its job). Then, Sunday mornings brought the hated dressing-up for Sunday School:

> [Mother] would dress us up in our stockings and shoes, which Lynn and I hated with a distinct venom,...because we liked going barefooted much better....We only had two teachers, one of them was the minister that lived there. He was a Christian, you might say one of those Holy Rollers, and he had an egg farm on the road going to town, and a big sign up in the front of his house which said, "Look to God" or "Do you trust in God?"...printed in big black and white letters, very boldly, right out there on the road in front of his place so that everybody knew that he was a Christian.

Later the children learned that the noise they heard at night was him out at his chicken house, talking to his

[5] All the quotes that follow regarding Sunday School and church-going are from Ford Gano's memoir.

chickens in "his holy roller language, which was entirely different from the English we spoke.

> He would yodel that out loud and clear to those chickens. I think maybe, or at least we surmised, that he did it to make them lay eggs [which he sold to Cottonwood and Clemenceau stores], because it wasn't very long after that that the lights would come on in the chicken house, and the chickens would start crowing and cackling, and start in their business of producing eggs for their good chicken man.

Despite all this, Ford described him as a good man and a good Sunday School teacher, as was also his wife. "They were very serious folks, very good, just loved us kids, and tried their best to make us good Christian kids." Dad Gano was something else again. He rarely went to church or to the revival meetings that came to town with some regularity. All these sermons ended with an altar call [to be saved] and kids generally responded each and every time. On one occasion that Ford writes about, Olga had enticed her husband to come, and the minister ordered him [Ford] to go to the back where his dad was standing and bring him up to the altar.

> I pleaded with him, but no, he just stood there, never cracked a smile, stood there very sternly against that call [to accept Jesus as your Savior]. I think all the neighbor people standing there had kind of a smile on their face, smirking....Well, I went back up there without my dad, and I don't think the minister got anybody else to come up that night. ...I remember this vividly because of that situation.

55. Frank's Boyhood in Rural Arizona

†††

School itself was a long trek up the hill to a typical one room school house where Aunt Edna was the teacher. En route we passed the house of Mrs. Petschen,[6] who was "the crossest woman in that whole section. She was a German who lived in a vine-covered cottage half-way up the hill to the school."

> As we kids would go past her house, we would yell obscenities and dare her to come out, which she usually did, wielding a mop like a baton, shouting back to her little tormentors. Those of us who came to her house on any errand were afraid of the great dog that guarded her house and we remember her looking out and saying things in German we did not understand but had a good idea what they were.

Frank explains that it was a time when "war clouds were gathering over the western world and anti-'Hun' feelings were spreading," especially after the sinking of the Lusitania, without warning, on May 7, 1915.

And then came the winter that "saw the heaviest snow in history" and the spring that brought thaws up river causing "the casual Verde River to become a raging torrent." Augmented by Ford, Frank writes:

> As the climax of the flood approached, Uncle Art [who seems, because of their own father's poor health, to have been something of a father figure for the children and a resource for their mother] ordered

---

[6] The story that follows combines the version found in Ford's memoir and as told by Frank in a sermon and in the story he wrote for his grandchildren.

everyone–family, workers and nearby neighbors–into the largest haywagon he owned and whipped the span of two mules and four horses up the muddy grade toward the school house that by then had been built some miles away.

We were half-way up the hill when 'Ol' lady Petshire' came screaming out of her cottage shouting German words that all of us knew meant "Help!" and frantically waving to be picked up, but the teamster swore back at her that we couldn't stop [without getting stuck in the mud]. Two ranch hands, gallantly having temporarily overcome prejudice, reached down to help her on the back end, but she slipped away. Her multiple skirts caught on one of the belts at the back end but the mud was too deep to stop. By the time we got to the school, she was so covered with mud nobody was able to recognize her, but knew it must be her because she was the largest person we could see.

We all found refuge at the school and watched as the flooding Verde swept everything before it in the brightly shining moonlight. That night I remember my mother standing over by the fire with the little children telling funny stories about her experiences in the past, keeping their heart up, and yet her home had been washed away.

When the flood subsided and we went down to the farm next morning, we found the farm house still standing but all barns, sheds, fences and animals were gone. Gone too was the gigantic stack of wood that Paul Gano, not well enough to do much farming or range tending, had cut with a dogged passion....For several years we picked wood, clearly from his cutting, from bends and boulders in the river miles below.

While viewing the disaster, they heard a peculiar "oink."

> We looked around and couldn't see anything at first, then we looked up and saw our pig up in the tree. This pig weighed about 140 pounds and the water had raised it up. It had swam around and gotten into the crotch of the tree and stuck there and we had some time getting her down. We first borrowed a block and tackle to try, but without success. Eventually we were able to roll her down into a wagon loaded with hay that had been pulled up below the old cottonwood tree.

Eventually this sow must have provided the family with more pigs because Ford writes of how they butchered at least two hogs each fall in a kind of butchering place they had on their farmstead.

> It was a place where we could hang an animal up between two poles, and then while they were strung up with their head down, their throat could be cut, and they could be bled good, and the hide stripped off of them, and then the two sides separated.

Olga wouldn't allow them to watch the actual butchering, even though they wanted to. Ford does, however, go on to discuss the delicacy of the brains and tongue which they liked, and their getting a good price at market.[7]

> In general, we would store our meat, we'd smoke it and store it in a smoke house. Salt it down and try to keep it as long as we could, eat off it as we needed to. That's the way we got a little meat in the wintertime. It

---

[7] Ford Gano's memoir

> seems to me like we always had a good table of food to eat. My mother would have various vegetables that she had brought out of our garden, seasonal vegetables like corn or turnips, beets or radishes. We always had potatoes and gravy. I think that was part of every dinner, along with biscuits and gravy. That was part of our growing up. I learned to love them.

† † †

The regular slaughtering of pigs that Ford recalls must have come later, since the immediate losses from the flood were so great that the two families agreed the Willard-Nichols ranch land they'd shared until then could no longer support them both. Only a year after the Ganos' move to Arizona, they were forced to move to far less comfortable quarters. Of necessity the Ganos accepted the offer of Dolph, Uncle Joel Willard's son, of "his homestead spread five miles down the Verde River." It was only a three room shack with a large tent attached; had no indoor plumbing, only walking-water. Frank writes, "We walked three quarters of a mile to draw our drinking water from the Smith's deep well. Other water was carried from the river two hundred yards down and up the river bank. The ranch had a few head of range cattle, a milk cow, one strong work team, a mule, and one riding horse."

Fortunately, during that first year, Arizona's climate had revived Paul Gano's health, enabling him to perform much-needed "miracles" at their new home. Frank writes:

> Out of the rugged alkaline soil he grew crops that were the envy of neighbors, and, in fact, provided many neighbors with the only vegetables and hay they had during the tight war years. One of

> our best years was 1917 when the war had taken all the young men of the valley who were old enough to lie their way into service. Nearly all the farms hired any school boys available to do men's work. Had Mother Gano not been a teacher, it is unlikely that any of us three boys and later our two sisters who were born on the farm [Paula Elberta, born June 9, 1917, and Mary Jo, born January 19, 1920], would have gotten any schooling.

One of their best crops was watermelon, which was so plentiful they sold it up and down the river for five cents a piece. And its juice came to the rescue the year (previously mentioned) they had no sugar.

> When faced with the dearth of sugar, Dad Gano boiled watermelon juice into rich strong molasses and peddled it to sugar-hungry neighbors. To boil that liquid, 98% water, into usable syrup took all the wood we could gather from five miles of river banks. I am sure we regained at least ten cords of Dad's wood, he'd so carefully cut and stacked—before the flood, described below.

Olga was boiling too—water for the old galvanized tub she used to do the laundry. She used a scrub board for rubbing the dirt from clothes, and big old yellow bars of soap, homemade from tallow gotten from their hogs, and lye from ashes off the stove. The whole process was conducive to red hands and scraped knuckles. Frank's half-brother, Ford, describes it in detail:[8]

> [Mother] would very faithfully clean our

---

[8] Ford Gano's memoir.

britches at least once a week, and any of the rest of the clothes and household goods that needed washing. And it was an all day job, believe me, it was quite a chore for her to do. Nobody else ever volunteered to do it. Lynn and I [and no doubt Frank too when he was there] carried the water up from the river, maybe 75, 100 yards from the house. We always thought it was quite a job, and protested quite loudly, but we did it. We did it in two steps. We'd take the tub down and set it up on the embankment, before it went down into the river. And then we'd go down a trail that had been built down the embankment, get to a deeper place in the river where we could dip our buckets in, and carry them back up the embankment, and dump them in the tub. And then we'd get a hold of the handles on the tub and carry it back up to the side of the house where mother did the washing. She had to hang the clothes out on a wire clothesline that had been built there for that purpose.

† † †

But hard as ordinary life was on the ranch, the Ganos suffered what Frank called "a series of unmitigated tragedies." First came the drought conditions that caused Dad Gano to invest his last penny in "blooded hogs and purebred cattle" as the only way to go.

His dream seemed near fruition: the herd of jersey hog had increased to the size that omened a cash return sufficient to pay off all loans. On the day the appraiser for a southern buyer was due, we found the hogs lying on their sides in the pens with legs extended and all but three stricken with cholera. Those three had to be destroyed and the other two dozen carted away and buried in ditches not less than twelve feet deep.

They'd hardly gotten over this tragedy when a cloud burst and washed away all their fences, feeding sheds and cattle. Unable to retrieve most of their heifers, they faced bankruptcy.

Fitted into all this gloom, before the next tragedy would descend, was an exciting visit by Frank's cousin, Blake "Blacky" Mason,[9] who was sheriff of San Diego County, "one of the last of the gun-toting lawmen whose exploits had been written about in magazines and journals across the country."

> He rode with us, fished with us and taught us how to grip, draw and shoot from the hip. His renown was such that even in our backward area where the only news media was the "Country Gentleman" and "Farmers Almanac," neighbors came to see and meet the fabled Blacky Mason.

But then, when Frank was twelve, he recalls the next tragedy, leaving Dad Gano feeling himself a modern Job.

> Dad and Ford and I were in the southern section haying when the blackest cloud ever loomed over us. Quickly we unhitched the horses and started home. We had learned from experience that horses can seldom be trusted when ridden into a thunderstorm. The wind was so fierce that we grasped each other's arms, bent low and struggled to keep on our feet. Suddenly there was an ear-splitting explosion and each of us landed flat on the hail-

---

[9] He was Flora Willard's son: Flora, the daughter of Lewis Augustus and Ann Billops; Julia Frost Willard's step-daughter; Olga's half-sister.

covered ground. There's no way of knowing how long we lay prone to Mother Earth, but when I recovered, I saw that Dad was completely out beside me, and Ford had blood gushing from his upper arm. Quickly I bound my bandana around his arm above the spurting blood and sternly ordered him to the house, about two hundred paces away.

Ford's account differs somewhat and emphasizes the role played by the strong wind that had blown off the top of the barn as they were running toward it for shelter.

> One piece came up flat-wise and knocked my dad cuckoo;...and another piece that came by, kind of edge-wise, and hit me on the arm, and made a real deep slash in my right arm. My brother Frank wasn't hit....With the rain just beating down on us and the wind blowing, Frank was a little bit unsettled. He didn't know just what to do. My dad laying there on the ground, me with my arm that looked like it was going to bleed me to death, and finally, Frank said "Hold your hand over this, and run for the house!" So I did that. And the house was probably a good 150 yards away.[10]

Frank continues his version of the incident:

> I was twelve years old and certainly not a husky westerner, but somehow I lifted Dad and struggled to the house where mother determined that something very critical had happened. She made us comfortable and then set out to find help. One of our nearest neighbors drove his model T to

---

[10] Ford Gano's memoir

Cottonwood [all the way to Jerome, 10 or 11 miles away, according to Ford, a trip that then took about 2 hours because it was before a bridge was built across the Verde River where they lived] to bring the doctor back. The medic took one look at Dad [who, according to Ford, had revived somewhat and could talk] and reported he had been struck with a splinter of the lightening bolt that had struck the galvanized roof of our barn. Ford's arm had almost been cut off by a flying piece of the roof. Dad lay in critical condition for several days.

As for Ford's arm, he writes that the doctor took out his needle and catgut, washed his arm with alcohol and sewed it up. "I think he put about 9 or 12 stitches in it. Seemed to me like he sewed on it all day. But anyway, it stopped the bleeding, and, I guess, outside of having a real sore arm, I was fixed up as good as new" [but with a permanent scar].

Before this last event, when Frank was nine, he suggests for the first time in his memoir that there was a growing conflict between him and Dad Gano; as he put it, "as a stepchild and the oldest of five at home, I had failed to assume all the responsibility expected of me." In retrospect, Frank says he regrets the conflict, and recognizes that his Dad's health, patience and perspective were being affected by his efforts to "wrest a living from land that Uncle Dolph had given up on five years before, plus the unspeakable traumas and continuous hardships that bedeviled them." Be that as it may, some have suggested that this early feeling that he was never quite good enough to get his father's blessing was at least partially responsible for his life-long feeling that his efforts (e.g., his sermons) were never quite good enough, and, ultimtely, his feeling that he'd been a failure.

64. Justice, Peace & God

Frank on the Arizona Ranch

65. Frank's Boyhood in Rural Arizona

In Ford's account of how the boys had to collect cedar trees in their wagon, haul them back to the ranch and cut them up for their wood-pile with "a little old hand saw," he suggests tensions also existed between himself and his half-brother, Frank:

> We got plenty of exercise doing that. ...Lynn [the younger brother] and I got our turns quite often. Now Lynn was a little smaller than I, and it seemed to me like he got off a lot easier than I did. But of course when brother Frank was there, he got a large part of that. Maybe that was one of the reasons he liked to go back to Los Angeles to live with his brother [Lewis], which he did quite often.[11]

In his memoir, Frank never suggests, as Ford did, that he went often to Los Angeles, nor that Lewis visited him at the ranch with any frequency. But Frank does describe a visit when he was nine and Lewis seventeen that perhaps stuck in his mind because it was the most memorable. During his visit to the ranch, Lewis was sufficiently concerned about the tensions he observed between Frank and Dad Gano that he urged Frank to return with him to California for the rest of the summer. (As we've noted, Lewis had lived with his Grandmother Thompson in California since the court awarded Claude custody of Lewis in 1912.)

But before they left for California, Frank tells of a scary adventure they had that grew out of Lewis's interest in Indian caves and relics. With their Uncle Alex (their mother's brother who lived in Cottonwood), they were crawling on their hands and knees, Lewis in front, in a cave on the far side of Mount Sugar Loaf when Uncle Alex whispered in a stern tone,

---

[11] Ford Gano's memoirs

"Squat." Lewis did, and Alex shot the head off a four foot rattler not three feet in front of Lewis.

Looking back at his summer in California, Frank describes it as one of "hard work in the walnut grove and lima bean fields" that gave me "a heap of maturing," wise counsel from my brother and the sharing of many exciting events. The most dramatic involved an adventure in the rugged Santa Cruz Islands that Lewis was planning with four of his school buddies.

Believing his "little brother" unable to hold his own with five athletes in a wilderness inhabited only by "a few sheep herders, numerous bootleggers and escaped prisoners," they allowed him to come along only after he agreed to stay in camp while the others were hunting wild sheep and deer. Apparently they were not adverse to bootlegging themselves since they defied both prohibition and teetotalling grandparents to make a midnight stop at a still to collect "refreshments" (beer, wine and other spirits), before embarking for the islands on a little tramp steamer whose pilot had no license to carry passengers, let alone illegal beverages. Frank writes:

> The night trip over was routine except for the violent sea sickness that lay me out before we had gone more than a mile in the tossing Pacific. On the rugged island we fished, hunted and imbibed as only young celebrants can when freedom from school and uncertainty about future plans grant fleeting freedom.

Frank especially remembers the close call he'd experienced when they'd gone to a cove two miles away to try some different kind of fishing.

> I was in a row boat with one of Lewis's friends, Howard, when a violent storm struck, tidal waves began to lash the boat and one of the oars broke. I passed out with the dread wrath of the sea while Howard jumped in and tried to push the boat toward shore as he swam in its wake. Those on shore watched with little hope we would make it, but after several hours, Howard's unbelievable effort brought us to the mouth of the cove where they were able to swim out to relieve and rescue us.

But there was yet another "dramatic and almost fatal escapade" that Frank recounts which occurred while "the others were off hunting and I, according to pretrip agreement, had stayed in camp. I could see from my bunk a ferocious-looking 'pirate'...starting to forage among our fast dwindling supplies.

> I aimed and pulled the trigger of a German Luger, the bullet didn't fire but the fellow heard the snap of the trigger and whirled to grab the gun away. Seeing it was only a small boy, he let out a curse, telling me what he would do to me if I tied any more shenanigans.

All in all, the six of us were ready to leave when the planned-for ten days ended, but we had to wait another three for the tardy boatman; living on potatoes, the only supplies left, plus the meat and fish we'd acquired through our own efforts.

† † †

Though there was much hardship during Frank's childhood in Arizona, there were also fun times, carnivals being one. In a sermon on February 2, 1941, Frank tells of one carnival event he obviously enjoyed:

> Contestants would bring their teams of horses to see which team could start a freight car. Now there were some grey stallions and everyone thought it would be easy for them, and they would strain and start but couldn't move it. Then after awhile, they brought in the buckskin mules. Now these mules were probably very good at pulling but for this kind of job those old buckskin mules always won the prize. They would rear back in their harness and both hit the shoulder pads together and just jerk together and yank the car loose. It is the first jerk that starts it, then it rolls easily. It was a matter of considerable humor to see those little tiny mules whose driver had learned the secret of how to move that great freight car. [In his sermon, Frank added] It was not the size of the animal that is the thing we need: the power to start. If you would do good, start where you are. Don't wait till you have overcome all those little evil habits before you start being a Christian.

After Frank graduated from the one-room Willard school that had replaced the more distant little Cottonwood school his mother and her sister Edna had attended, he entered Clarkdale High, by comparison gigantic with nearly 100 students. In a brief memoir written for the family, Edna described the old Cottonwood school's long wooden benches that held four or five children.

> The desks were so high that only the tops of heads of small children might be seen and their feet dangled, not being able to reach the floor. The

> blackboard was a piece of canvas with some black paint on one side. When the wind blew, it rattled the doors and windows and much cold air came in. The school term was six or seven months.

In a sermon on November 21, 1940, Frank spoke nostalgically and approvingly of a time, during his school years, when his parents had the "courage and strength to discipline."

> I want to let you in on a little secret. I remember when we were told that for every whipping we got in school, it would be duplicated at home. I imagine it was when whippings were not against the law at school and I can remember the one or two I got. One led to the second, but I am thankful it was only one. One in each place, I mean.

In another sermon in 1947, Frank spoke, not so nostalgically, of having "to be displayed in those ridiculous pantaloons with long stockings and circulation cutting elastics until I was 12 years of age." Perhaps what was then common apparel for boys until they reached their teens ended for Frank with his start of high school in Clarkdale, Arizona.

Then, Frank traipsed seven miles on foot, or, occasionally, horseback, to reach it, and on very stormy days, Dad Gano would take him in his old Ford, with chains he'd managed to secure. During his three years there, he claims his chief pleasure were the weeks he played hooky; spent rounding up the cattle for the trek out of the heat of the valley; and another spent deer hunting with his cousin "in the beautiful Garland Prairie near Flagstaff." Frank preferred this even to playing football, track, the many dramatic productions he was in, and the honor of being selected as class president.

> I bagged but one buck during the three year effort, and have always regretted killing that beautiful denizen of the forest. We couldn't carry it on our skittish horses and so hung it from a tree limb, little expecting the carcass to be there when we returned. But two days later, we found it as fresh and eatable as when left.

Despite this downplaying of his interest in football, it nonetheless had a sufficient impact that he was impelled to recount one experience at the very heart of a sermon on July 16, 1939 at Phillips Memorial Church in Cranston, Rhode Island. He declared:

> The power of morale was first brought to me in high school in a football game. We had been badly beaten by our bitterest rival in an early season game, and our last game was to be a return with them. Just the week before the titanic struggle was to take place our star player, about the whole team himself, was out hunting and accidentally shot his arm off. We didn't have a chance from all logical viewpoints, but just before the whistle blew, in that most breathless of all moments, the coach read a telegram from our hero in the hospital. I don't remember what it said, but I do remember we won that game. We all played ourselves out; we were truly supermen that day.
>
> Literature is filled with the records of such power from that little thing called morale—a faithful few holding the pass of Thermopylae [in Greece] until help came [during Persian Wars], a little girl [Joan of Arc] rallying the defeated armies of France, the bleeding barefooted soldiers at Valley Forge.

> Charged with that power called morale, men become supermen.
>
> It is much easier to say that we need this morale than it is to help us find it. But just as it is such a little thing itself, I wonder if it isn't, after all, the combination of a number of little things that makes *real* morale.

For his final year of high school, Frank went to live with his Uncle John and Aunt Edna Mason (his mother's sister) and attended San Diego Union High where he encountered three thousand students, "something else for a country hick." That year the young "hayseed" also had a cultural introduction to the world of art—heard the famous violinist, Jascha Heifitz, saw the most popular ballerinas dance, and watched Fritz Reiner conduct, as well as any number of other stars of the era. He was so impressed with the poetry of Francis Thompson, an Englishman who lived from 1859-1907, he began to claim him, rather than Frances Willard, as the person after whom he was named.

† † †

After graduation from high school, which would have been about 1927, Frank went to work for his brother, Lewis, who was part-owner of a loan and investment company in Los Angeles. In his memoir, Frank describes this as a time to compare "the spartan existence" of life in Arizona where they made one trip a year to see a 10¢ movie, to "the sprawling culture of the burgeoning city of angels" with movie stars, ice skating, baseball games, the Rose Bowl, and world championship boxing matches, "almost more than I could comprehend." His half-brother, Ford, writes:

> Lewis would take him in to Los Angles to the

> Olympic Club gymnasium. There he really learned to box and to do all kinds of exercises, and he would make friends of all kinds, and he really enjoyed that part of his life, growing up.[12]

In the 1920s when Frank became enamored of the sport, boxing had just been legalized and was beginning its golden age. And if, in fact, it "suited the ethic of a frontier society," as it has been described, then it certainly would have been attractive to a young man such as Frank who was just making the transition from the frontier to the big city.[13] No longer required to physically exert himself as he had on the ranch, he no doubt relished the running, rope jumping, bag punching, sparring and all the rest that went into becoming a boxer. He kept at it for four years, at least until he left for college, even keeping up his training during the winter months at a lumber camp in the High Sierras.[14] Frank became good enough to become a Golden Glove champ, good enough to consider boxing as a career.[15]

---

[12] This excerpt from Ford Gano's memoir that puts the Olympic Club in L.A. is more accurate than the 1950s article in the Muskogee, Oklahoma newspaper that put it in San Francisco. The writer was referred by the Boxing Commission (310-641-8668) to an old boxing enthusiast, Jerry Bildermain (310-452-1164), now 80 years old, who affirmed that the Olympic Auditorium was at 18th and Grand in LA, famous for boxing. He also affirmed that there was no Olympic Club in San Francisco; any boxing Frank did there would have been at one of the city's many gyms. The famous Cow Palace in SF only did promotions.

[13] Anasi, Robert.

[14] From an article from the Muskogee newspaper, undated, but content would put it in 1950.

[15] A national Golden Glove tournament has been held annually since 1928. Originally it was between boxers in NY and Chicago. Now regarded as the most prestigious of amateur boxing events, the national Golden Glove competition is preceded by a series of local and regional

73. Frank's Boyhood in Rural Arizona

Family legend has it that Frank fought with Max Baer immediately before Baer's bout on August 25, 1930 in San Francisco with Frankie Campbell, a fight that ended with Campbell's death. Baer was cleared of the resulting manslaughter charge but California suspended him from fighting for a year. The death is said to have affected Baer's boxing, especially psychologically, but, nonetheless, only three years later, in 1933, he became World Heavyweight champion. Prior to that fight in San Francisco and beginning in July 1929, most of Baer's fights had been in Oakland, one on April 22, 1930 in Los Angeles. Since, during those same years prior to his starting college, Frank is known to have lived in Los Angeles and then Berkeley, and, at some point, attended church at the First Baptist in Oakland, it is quite likely that he did fight Baer at least once; probably in a training bout rather than one approved by the Boxing Federation.[16]

An article that appeared on February 20, 1948 in *Bacone Indian*, Bacone College's student newspaper (only months before he became President), suggests that Frank, while a coach there, had had a team active in Golden Glove Boxing and had sent one of its members to the National semifinals in Chicago. Two years later the newspaper has two pictures, found in Frank's scrapbook, of Bacone's sizable boxing team entries in "Muskogee's 1950 Golden Glove tournament." The caption suggests that boxing has continued since Frank's early days as coach. It states, "Baconians are consistent winners at the annual fisticuffs festival" which is "opening Monday at the City Hall."

---

competitions. *Frank's championship was almost certainly at this level.* There is no record of him as a national champion, nor any indication that he ever traveled out of California to fight.

[16] Information about Baer from *The Ring* and from *Boxing Register...*

74. Justice, Peace & God

In the long run, it is of more significance that Frank was affected by his job during his time in L.A. with Lewis– "passion impregnated itself in my inner being" he writes:

> How to equalize the conditions between the poverty stricken youth of Arizona, including my own siblings, with the lush existence of West Los Angeles. In my job with Lewis's firm I had to collect payments from the indigent of West Los Angeles. I saw children eating rats and mice and knifing each other for a slice of bread or meat. Later, as the depression grew more acute, I saw families sacrificing sons or daughters to provide food for their famished families. Such conditions must not exist in the most wealthy nation of all time.

This passion for the underprivileged, be they individuals or countries, never left Frank. Perhaps it deepened as the Depression saw Lewis having to close the doors of his loan and investment company for the last time, both he and his brother leaving with nothing but a typewriter between them. However, according to Lewis's wife, Marie,[17] whom he married in 1938, Lewis must have quickly recovered for he was the West Coast Collector for a loan company, later president of the Builders Association, and Frank continued to work for him until he left for Redlands.

† † †

Herbert Hoover was President on October 24, 1929, "Black Thursday," when thousands of Americans lost their savings on the stock market. Hoover took several steps to try

---

[17] Though Lewis died in 1975, Marie, born in 1912, was, in November 2002, still alive and well, corresponding with this writer.

to prevent a depression, but by the time of the election in November 1932, things had gone from bad to worse, banks were closing right and left. Franklin Delano Roosevelt won in a landslide; one of his first acts after his inauguration on March 4, 1933 was to declare a National Bank Holiday. Then, taking advantage of the radio which had begun regular programming only a decade before, he spoke to the American people in his first of many soothing "fireside chats."

Frank, at the University of Redlands by then, writes in his memoir:

> As a sociology major, I saw thousands of arms pilloried in basements of homes waiting for the time to use them against the opulent social leaders who seemed to ignore the need for equalization of opportunity and property. We were within a month or two of such a revolution as would have beggared the Bolshevik uprising of 1917 [in Russia] had not a strong voice [President Roosevelt's] come over the squeaky little radios assuring us all that we had "nothing to fear but fear itself."

6. Self-Proclaimed "Country Hick" Goes to Redlands

Time was when a person was born upon this old earth in a lonely sort of fashion. A few individuals stood by him in his infancy, but the trees, the hills and the stars were his most common companions. He climbed the steep hill of maturity alone and stretched his soul toward whichever distant goal he longed to reach. He felt the world waited for him to help his soul find its way up the paths of space. But now it's the mass that counts. Only as he makes a mark upon the latest statistical chart or the Gallup Poll is the individual important. Keep the turnstile moving--that's our motto.[1]

† † †

It's not clear when or where Lewis relocated when he became the West Coast Collector for a loan company, but Frank, on registration at the University of Redlands in the Fall of 1931, gives his address as 801 Carmel Avenue, Berkeley, California;[2] his religious affiliation, the First Baptist Church in Oakland. But however apart the two brothers may have been they kept in touch.

Just shy of twenty-two, Frank, by then, was far from being a country hick, but that's how he still thought of himself. And maybe it was a lingering country-boyishness,

---

[1] From an undated sermon titled, "Chain-Reaction: the Greatest Peril to Freedom!" It's an adaptation of words found in his prize-winning essay, "A Link or a Chain" written while a Freshman at Redlands University.

[2] a clipping dated April 1933, states this also as the residence of his mother, Olga, by then 49 years old. She apparently had moved there from Arizona after her husband, Paul, died on February 14, 1931. Whether she or Frank moved there first has not been determined.

Frank (on left) & Lewis (date unkown)

combined with his socially conscious beliefs, a vibrant dynamism and an appealing persona that initially attracted Beulah Parker. They most likely met sometime during those early years after Frank left the ranch for the big city, still a teenager, perhaps still homesick for the country he'd left behind. For her part, Beulah, ten or fifteen years older than Frank, had been early-widowed by a much older wealthy man and had no children of her own. On meeting, some sort of chemistry must have been triggered between them for a friendship was sparked that lasted a lifetime. And it was Beulah's financial support that made it possible for Frank to attend college. Who or what influenced him to choose the University of Redlands we don't know.[3]

---

[3] Tuition at Redlands, seeming miniscule compared to today's charges, could then be a real detriment even to the upper working/middle class. It was $115 per semester with various other charges that ranged from $5 to $20 each. Also, unless living with relatives, living in a college

78. Justice, Peace & God

† † †

What is now the Univer-sity of Redlands was founded in 1907 as a Christian college after authorization by the Southern California Baptist Convention and the approval of the State legislature on November 25th that year. The city of Redlands then gave a campus of forty acres and $100,000. However, classes for its first students, who arrived on September 29, 1909 (the year Frank was born), were held at Redlands First Baptist Church. By the time Frank entered the university in 1931, it had a "beautifully landscaped campus of one hundred acres," owned 725 additional acres in the San Bernardino Mountains, and had fifteen well-equipped buildings.

Although founded as a Baptist college, Redlands has always welcomed students of any faith. Its stated purpose:

> To help its students to attain their best, to become men and women whose wholesome bodies are fit temples for the indwelling of the Holy Spirit, whose social graces make them welcome where gentlefolk congregate, whose keen minds enrich scholarship, whose reverent souls worship God in spirit and in truth, whose loyal lives exemplify the teachings of Jesus Christ and serve to advance His kingdom and His righteousness. Motto: "Ye shall know the truth and the truth shall make you free."

† † †

Frank died too soon after he started writing his memoir

---

dormitory was required, room rent ranging from $40 to $47 per semester depending on its location. Meals were extra, perhaps served and charged cafeteria-style. These charges remained the same through Frank's four-year stay.

to tell us much of his life at Redlands or thereafter. But in his final paragraph, written in 1980, he does clue us in to his interests–at least as he assessed them looking back. He writes:

> My first year of college had been a heady one for a rube from the last frontier. Oratory came easy to one who had grown up under the memoried [sic] spiels of William Jennings Bryant and the emotional speeches of the World War I bond raisers, Chautauqua troubadours, and yearly evangelists. It was the frenetic debates and oratorical contests that brought me to plan for a career in politics or international affairs.

Frank was a master with words, whether in writing or in oratorical contests, the force and eloquence of his delivery capable of mesmerizing his audience.

The campus newspaper reported on May 18, 1932, his first year at Redlands, that he won first place in the Colwell essay contest, a prize given annually for the best essay on American Ideals. In the opinion of the judges, Frank's entry, "A Link or a Chain," a copy of which still exists in his files, "revealed logical thought, personality and genuine originality." During the commencement exercises that year he was given his award of thirty dollars.

The "chain" that concerned Frank was the growth of monopolies that were spreading across the country, "linking" communities, destroying the humanness of the old corner store, the bank that knew its clientele. He wrote:

> [No longer could man] stretch his arms, and ask the earth what she held in store for him. [Nor] nature in all its glory beckon to him and the voices of life call, "Come! Come and See!"...We find [now] that the great problem of living in this world is not

how to make a living but how to find room in it to live.

He concludes his five-page essay on a hopeful note:

> If those who control our great chains will realize that each individual has a right to be pleased in his own particular way, and will meet those desires by adapting this system to the needs of each section of the country, to each individual, and to each ideal, a great problem will be solved without the loss of that so important inalienable right of men—individuality.

Time-out for Tennis

During the summer after his first year at Redlands, Frank served as a student pastor at the First Baptist Church in Arcata, a small town in the far northern part of California, far from Redlands, Los Angeles, even Berkeley. His files contain a small clipping that appeared in the paper on July 30, 1932, a week after his arrival. It read:

> If you are a pessimist, don't attend the morning services at the Arcata Baptist church Sunday, as Frank W. Thompson, student pastor of the church, will have a real message for the depressionists and no doubt will

have something interesting to tell those attending the services....[He] held his first services last Sunday morning and evening in which large congregations attended. He has a pleasing personality and is a versatile speaker with real messages in his sermons.

Two sisters, Mary Catherine and Isabel Wilson, who were then part of the church's young people's group, still remember Frank and credit him with having held the church together at a time when their old minister had left. I heard from them in May 2002; a follow-up phone conversation eliciting no additional information. They wrote:

I believe we are the only members who have any remembrance of Frank. We remember him as a handsome young man who served as interim pastor for a short time to our very small congregation....He was well received by young and older members alike. The young people especially appreciated some of his innovative ways of presenting the Gospel, such as through drama. [And] since we are situated just a few miles from the ocean, beach parties were fun for all when he was here. All the girls were happy to have Frank as our pastor and so sorry when he had to leave. I think that he can be credited as being a link in the process of keeping the tiny congregation of 30-50 members alive and helping it to grow into the vital church body that it is today (about 800).

The Wilsons included the above picture of Frank taken in 1932 in front of Mrs. Ripley's house where he lived while in Arcata. "She was one of the pillars of our church," they wrote.

† † †

When, or for what purpose, the eloquent essay "The Quest" was written, it comes across as an ode to Redlands. It is a very personal account by Frank of a religious awakening that purportedly occurred while a group of young college men are listening to a devotional speaker at a conference [he does not note the location]. Frank writes that "the speaker seemed to fade away," as his eyes beheld the rear of the platform.

> A great plate glass window reached from floor to ceiling, [disclosing] a portrait of nature in all her majestic grandeur. Afar off the white-capped ocean tossed with incessant restlessness, catching the eye and holding it until the gaze dropped with restful joy upon the smoothly rolling sand dunes, and then presently to the rugged wind-blown pines which framed the picture and protected the chapel from the heavy storms that pound upon the shore...In the center of that display stood the figure of Christ with one arm raised pointing the way up the trouble-strewn path to a higher way of life, and the other hand reaching down to beckon all to follow.
>
> In a second my mind traveled five hundred

miles to our Memorial Chapel [at Redlands] where I had many times watched the same Christ reaching downward for me with one hand as the other pointed to the heights above. A sudden ineffable pride told me that it was this same Christ who had inspired the leaders and founders of the University of Redlands to surround its students with all the beauty possible, giving them every opportunity to fill their lives with the appreciation of beauty....

As the exquisite stained glass painting with its story of eternal beauty and perfect knowledge became ever more real to me, I saw a band of older people striving to follow more closely the devout principles of this clear-thinking man of Nazareth....A new flush of pride raced through my veins as I realized the sublime leadership which all are encouraged to follow at our University....For two years I had been blessed with the privilege of sitting at the feet of leaders who are not content to be teachers only, but followers of the supreme Leader of all mankind. But the full realization of those blessings had never formulated until in this far-off beauty spot beside the sea....

As I sit now in Memorial Chapel writing these words, a shadow passes over, and the Master is almost obscured from view. Throughout the world a shadow is apparently obstructing the view of this Prince of Peace, and something seems to whisper that this shadow will not lift until the world follows the ideals so exemplified in Christ and followed by our great University.

As Frank so often did later at the end of his sermons, he closed this essay with a poem. "As our heads bow in rededication of our lives to the ideals for which the

University was founded—to portray beauty abundantly, to give knowledge freely, and to serve always joyously—may our hearts whisper the 'Prayer of the Quest'." He quotes the first and last stanzas of the poem:

Take us on the quest of Beauty,
Poet seer of Galilee,
Making all our dreams creative
Through our fellowship with Thee.

All along our quest's far pathway,
Christ, our Leader and our guide,
Make us conscious of thy presence
Walking always by our side.

† † †

In the spring of his second year at Redlands, Frank's oratorical skills were rewarded when he first met a fellow debater, Richard Nixon, then a student at Whittier, a Quaker college near Los Angeles. Curiously, neither college can find any record of this contest, but Frank's files contain a clipping from the *San Bernardino Daily, The Sun*, dated April 29, 1933. It reports (along with a photo of Frank) that Frank won first place for the University of Redlands; their first win in four years. This was no small accomplishment since Frank was competing against participants from Pasadena College, Occidental College, California Institute of Technology, California Christian College, La Verne College, and Whittier College, the latter hosting the annual Southern California conference oratorical contest. Frank's award was a silver loving cup, "presented each year to the winning college" to be kept by them for at least a year. For himself, there was "a small gold award." The newspaper goes on to say that his "oration that captured first place was entitled 'The Voyage of Our Shipless State'." It notes Frank as a sophomore "preparing himself for the ministry," and as "a member of the student-faculty committee on public events," and "particularly prominent in Christian activity and forensics [debating]."

It was in the fall of 1933, now a Junior, that Frank again met up with Nixon at Whittier. This time Nixon was the winner, having given, according to his campus newspaper, "a well-delivered speech" on the topic "Youth of 1933." The Redlands' campus newspaper on November 22nd had this to say of the occasion:

> Frank Thompson, a prominent junior in campus speaking circles, placed second in the Southern California extemporaneous speaking contest held in the Student Body Auditorium at Whittier College. Richard Nixon of Whittier was first place winner. Frank's topic was "Imagination and the Machine Age."

The contestants knew the topic would be selected from the October and November issues of the Reader's Digest, but the subjects were not distributed to them until the hour before the contest started. Both Frank and Nixon were awarded gold medals, but the cup with Nixon's name engraved on it went to Whittier. However, rules required that a college must win first place for three years in a row in order permanently to retain possession of the cup.

A year later, in November 1934, Frank was competing on his own campus to be named to the team of debaters and orators which would participate in the annual convention at Salt Lake City. The question the national honorary debate fraternity to which Frank belonged, Phi Kappa Delta, had selected as the topic to be debated was

"Resolved that the nations of the world should agree to prevent the international shipment of arms and munitions." In the local contest Frank came in second, his oration titled, "Where There is No Vision, People Perish." It has not been possible to determine if he went to Salt Lake City, but he did win two of the University's prizes, in his junior year, possibly again as a senior:

> (1) The Mattison B. Jones Prize for the best original oration delivered by a regular student of the University at the annual Oratorical Contest on the third Friday of January, a gold medal or a prize of twenty-five dollars.
>
> (2) The W.H. Fowler Prize for the best extempore speech delivered by a regular student of the University at the annual Contest in Extempore Speaking on the first Friday in December.

Photo by Jim Sloan; copy provided by U of Redlands News Bureau
Frank, George Armacost & then-Vice President Nixon

87. "Country Hick" Goes to Redlands

The University cannot locate the cup Frank won for Redlands, but they did produce an undated photo, probably taken between 1961 and 1963, of Frank and Nixon on either side of University President George Armacost who is holding the cup. Frank was then Vice-President of Development at Redlands, and Nixon was Vice President of the United States.

One might surmise that forensics and academics would have been enough to keep Frank busy, but they were only part of what he was involved in while at Redlands. He was a guard on the football team for at least three years (the Frosh team undefeated, the next year the Varsity team also undefeated, and then missed out on the title his junior year by just one game); was a half-miler on the track team; joined Alpha Gamma Nu, a social fraternity; was an associate member of Sigma Tau Delta, a national professional English fraternity; was active with the YMCA, for two years its president; and was a member of the Cosmopolitan Club which was made up of students, active alumni and faculty. It had been founded in 1924 by a Chinese and a Russian student to promote the brotherhood of races. They planned special get-togethers, such as an India dinner, Chinese night, Persian tea, and an All Nations party. They also arranged contacts with students abroad. As if all this didn't keep him busy, Frank also acted in the University's plays. In his senior year he had a small part in the class's farce hit, "Pigs," "an uproar of mirth for three acts." Staged March 10th in Redlands' High School Auditorium, Frank played the consulting veterinarian for Celestia, "herself," the pig ideal.[4]

Apparently with all that extracurricular activity, Frank still found time to study. The campus newspaper, dated March 20, 1935, named him as one of four seniors making the honor

---

[4] From the University's yearbook, *La Letra*, 1935

roll (out of how many unstated).[5]

[5] Unfortunately school policy prevented this writer from getting copies of his transcript.

7. An Indian College's Boxing Coach & Librarian

> *We have been broken up and moved six times. We have been despoiled of our property. We had schools for our children and churches where we listened to the same gospel the white man listens to. The white man came into our country and drove away our cattle and our horses, and if our people followed them they were killed. We try to forget these things but we would not forget that the white man brought us the blessed gospel of Christ. The Christian's hope: That this more than pays for all we have suffered.* Anonymous.

†††

Of all the extracurricular activities Frank was involved in while at Redlands, there is no mention of boxing, so why now? Was he still enamored of it as offering a possible career? Why not the ministry? Why Bacone? Apparently it was settled by the time he graduated for immediately afterwards he informs the alumni office that his address is Bacone College, Bacone, Oklahoma; his occupation, Librarian and Boxing Instructor. The closest we come to an answer was given some years later in his Ordination paper for the Rhode Island Council.

> Through four years of college the conviction grew ever stronger that God had a special task for me to fulfill. Nothing but the obstructions of my own sin and inadequacy stood in the path of that fulfillment. From college I felt a desire to be a missionary without further schooling and so went to Bacone College to work with the Indians.

Possibly a number of factors were at play here. In that same Ordination paper, Frank credits his minister father, through his mother, as having had a lasting influence on his conversion to Christianity and on the "ideal in my heart," even though he died before Frank was old enough to know him. But Frank also expresses a "subconscious fear of the ministry that haunted my youth, due to the poverty and hardship and finally death which my Methodist Circuit-riding father had undergone in the wilds of Northern California." On another occasion Frank characterizes his father as having been a missionary to the Indians, the reason for the family's being in Arizona when Frank was born—a characterization this writer has been unable to substantiate. Whether correct or not, the fact Frank believed that his father was a missionary to the Indians, and his own life-long interest in the Indians, may go hand-in-hand with his belief he was 1/16 Sioux Indian—a belief he passed on to his children, despite, so far, its having proved impossible to trace in his genealogy.

† † †

Bacone College began in September 1880 with just three students and one instructor, Almon Bacone, after whom it is named. A monument of him on the present-day campus reads: "A Christian school planted in the midst of a people becomes one of the most powerful agencies in the work of civilization...." Bacone was an enlightened educator from the American Baptist Home Mission Society serving with the Cherokees in Tahlequah, Oklahoma. It grew quickly, open from the beginning to all the "Civilized Nations"—Choctaw, Chickasaw, Cherokee, Creek, Seminole, and Delaware—these seen as "more cosmopolitan than most of their Anglo-American neighbors in the surrounding states of Arkansas, Kansas, and Texas because of their strong cultural heritage, their contact with Christian churches, their sophisticated struggle to retain their homelands, and their cross-cultural understanding. Each of these nations had been uprooted and forced to move westward to a new land" where their fortitude and resourcefulness had enabled them to renew their broken institutions.[1]

Initially, classrooms, boarding and sleeping rooms were all located in a two-story brick building provided by the Home Mission. Then, in October 1881, they received permission from the Muskogee-Creek Nation to locate on 160 acres of their land, near the site of the Union Indian Agency. Classes continued at Tahlequah while funds were sought for building the new college; the first bachelor's degrees awarded in 1883.

Bacone College is situated in the western foothills of the Ozark mountains — the Green Country of Oklahoma!

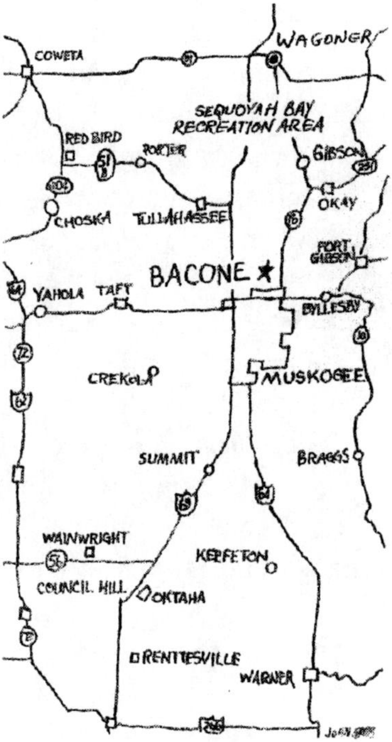

[1] pp. 6-7 for quotes and information, Williams & Meredith

Construction of the main building on its new site three and one-half miles northeast of Muskogee, started in 1884 after an especially generous contribution from John D. Rockefeller, who then controlled much of the petroleum industry through his Standard Oil Corporation. By the time the college moved to its present site, there were 109 students, and by the mid-1890s, 703 students in a system that included primary, preparatory, and a full-fledged, four year academic program. But their move coincided with years of turmoil for the Indians whose republics were being destroyed by banking, railroad, and petroleum interests seeking their land.

Things changed markedly for the college in 1906 when Congress declared that both the Indian and Oklahoma Territories would enter the Union as a single state. As a consequence, after statehood became a reality in 1907, Indians lost control of their schools, even though their system, until then, had been highly successful, achieving an 80% literacy rate using bi-lingual materials. The Cherokee Academy that had been a student-feeder for Bacone closed, and enrollment at the latter declined accordingly–its courses dropped from those leading to a four year college degree to those at the high school level only.

About this same time, the American Baptists who owned Bacone, in order to cut expenses and improve the orphans' educational opportunities, moved the Murrow Indian Orphanage from Unechuka to Bacone. J. S. Murrow had opened the orphanage in 1902 to care for children left destitute and helpless during a period of government mandated allotments. The orphans, made wards of the courts, were regularly swindled out of their inheritance by their non-Indian appointed "guardians." This reflects Theodore Roosevelt's 1901 edict that Indian land should no longer be held by the tribe, the very foundation of Indian life, but should be divided up amongst its individual members; and by the nation's economic depression that preceded WWI.

The children were taught on campus until 1946 when elementary courses were eliminated. Since then the children have been bused daily to Muskogee's public grade and junior high schools. At first hesitant to accept this new arrangement, the townspeople soon learned that the Indians were making the honor role in the same proportion as the white kids, and the appearance of Indian boys on the school athletic teams led to championships.

Between 1911 and 1916, Bacone offered few courses beyond the high school level; not again offering college level courses until 1927. However, it never again offered courses at the Senior college level; hence never again was able to give degrees beyond the Junior College level. Despite this, Bacone again began to grow both in student enrollment (by 1936, 40 tribes were represented) and in physical plant. "By 1922, the student population had again risen to 234, drawn from twenty-four tribes in five states," and "by 1923, the demand for space was so acute that Bacone had to restrict entrance to those of Indian heritage."

A major construction campaign followed, the buildings erected to form the shape of a Christian cross; and college level courses again appeared in a big way. And despite the 1929 Depression, Bacone continued to grow, reaching 306 students in 1932; by 1936 having representatives of forty tribes on campus; and it "made one of the most important contributions to American culture by creating an Art Department which focused on and fostered what has come to be called 'the Bacone School of Traditional Indian Art.'" From 1935 to 1938 Ace Blue Eagle, who had just completed his studies at the University of Oklahoma, headed the department. Because of its impact on campus, "a large new stone structure was erected in 1937, to accommodate the department."[2]

†††

Those exciting years of growth at Bacone that occurred between 1935 and 1937 were the very years that Frank Thompson was there as boxing coach and librarian. They must have been exciting ones for a young person just out of college, but regrettably there are no records to tell us of Frank's experience. Boxing is never mentioned in the Williams-Meredith history of Bacone; football is mentioned twice: once, as introduced in 1895; and again, as of particular interest to students in the 1920s.[3] And it was a major sport when Frank was again at Bacone from 1948 to 1955.

The only record of this visit by First Lady, Eleanor Roosevelt, is this un-dated photo found in Frank's files. Frank is standing on the right behind three unidentified women.

---

[2] See pp. 57, 60, 64, 74, 75, 78 & 80 for above information and quotes, Williams & Meredith

[3] pp. 31 & 61.

95. Indian College's Boxing Coach & Librarian

Despite the lack of information regarding Frank's time at Bacone as boxing coach and librarian, there is no doubt that while there he developed a deep and lasting love of the Indians and an appreciation of Bacone's emphasis on developing their natural talents for art and handicrafts rather than just teaching them a trade. He was unusually sensitive to their culture and the significance of their ceremonies, something that shines through in the account that follows.

Near the end of his two years at Bacone, Frank, illustrating his gift with words, wrote a very moving account of a Kee Too Wahs day-long annual ceremony. He drove fifty miles over rough country trails to attend, accompanied by Tom Raincloud, President of the student body, football star and leader of Christian activities on campus. Effectively counterpoised are the quiet dignified Indians calling to the Great Spirit, and the noisy, intrusive, rude behavior of the whites who seemed to expect, indeed hoped for, such raucous behavior by the Indians that would lead to their arrests. Frank's story begins:

> "White man all time be where he not wanted."
>
> Inwardly I cringed backward as the tall, full-blooded Sioux boy uttered these unexpected words....But even as thoughts of flight flashed through my mind, the realization came that Tom had not meant me, for my two years of work among his people at Bacone College had entitled me to share the free thoughts of an unguarded moment.[4]...All around I could see the real causes for

[4] It's curious that in this account Frank never mentions his belief that he was part Indian, and, according to his son, Scott, never did in his

> that bitter epithet. It was not yet noon; the Indians had gathered in the early morning hours, yet the unwanted whites had begun to push in and around the sacred council fires....
>
> Quietly, from the midst of a group of passing braves, young Groundhog Squirrel, alumnus of Bacone, welcomed [Tom and me] to the ceremony and offered to interpret for our foreign ears.
>
> "My father come early this morning....They hold fire ceremony then."...That fire was a symbol of the eternal reverence of America's first born for things elemental. "That fire burn for all time back in hills. No one ever see it, but Kee Too Wahs find it on morning of sacred dance." The ceremony gives the seven clans of the Cherokee Nation a "chance to make new clan fire from main fire of eternal."

After the picnic lunch the Indians gather in the woods around the grave of Redbird Smith, "old chieftain who had established schools and had held the Cherokees together when crop failures and swindled fortunes had threatened to disintegrate his peaceful tribe."

But meanwhile Frank has been stuck with two white women who are collecting material about the Indians. Squirrel facetiously says:

> "White women stay in Indian camp meeting one day, mebby two; go home to write book, Life and Customs of Indian People." I laughed inwardly at young Squirrel's dry commentary on a sad truth, for weren't the shelves of our library at Bacone, of

---

speeches or sermons regarding Indians. Perhaps he felt too insecure about the status of his claim. In a later letter, written while traveling, he alludes to plans to do some research regarding his claim.

> which I was custodian, filled with books about Indians—compiled and written from funds of appalling ignorance.

The graveside ceremony was a long one, starting with John Redbird Smith, the present chief of the Kee Too Wahs, explaining at length the traditions of the Cherokees, his voice rising in a monotonous pitch. He was followed by shorter speeches by each of his seven sons; then Cherokee hymns sung in the "dirge-like six-note scale of the native music." After about an hour Frank writes:

> Every muscle in my back and hips ached from the long period of squatting on crossed legs in pseudo-Indian style, but not a fullblood had moved so I was determined to prove my right to be at this ceremony by being Indian in form if not in fact.

But little did he realize that the foregoing had been "Introductory remarks." Like young thunder, Uncle Billy Rogers was to make the annual speech. He ended it with a call to young Indians not to forsake the old customs; "to realize that white man would soon burn himself out with his fast pace, that the Indian way of life was more lasting."

By the end of the graveside ceremony, darkness was descending, it was near time for the stomp dance to begin, and a stream of cars had circled like "birds of prey ready to swoop down when the victims emerged. Earlier Groundhog had informed me that the dance was part of sacred ceremony, but had a bad name because 'sometimes Indians get liquor. That make them very wild, very bad.'" Groundhog continued:

> Two years ago somebody bring liquor to ceremony. Many Indians get very drunk; make much

> hell. Officers say no more ceremony if one drunk Indian come to town! [The next year] floods wash out road: no white people come. Indians have fine ceremony.

Tonight's dance began with a summoning by Chief Redbird of all clansmen to join the sacred dance of the fire bird. For five minutes he stood with his arms upraised, his eyes joining those of the night. Frank writes: "Never have I witnessed so potent a prayer."

> With coiled suddenness a serpent of glistening-backed braves circles the fire. Shapeless crowds flowed into a rhythmic stream. Five gourd shakers followed by two drummers formed the inner circle. Quickly the two hundred Kee Too Wahs coiled and uncoiled, gliding to the plaintive notes of the native music makers.
>
> The splendor of the night was enhanced as the rhythmic chant of the encircling dancers rose in a tone of symphonic grandeur. Weary muscles became alive with the infectious spirit of harmony which reigned supreme. This was the appeal to Great Spirit offered in joyous gratitude for the past and reverent optimism for the future. This was the dance of the firebird.

The only discordant note that jarred the rhythm were the hordes of white men and women who stormed from their cars to push the circle almost solid, yelling rude and crude remarks at the dancers.

† † †

Frank gave no hint in this story that he was about to leave Bacone, but he did leave after two years. Maybe the ceremony itself had inspired him to seek further fulfillment as a minister. In his later ordination paper, he merely says: "the call for more adequate religious training was loud within, and so to seminary I came." In a recent conversation with this writer, Ginny and Dickson Kenney, who became close friends of the Thompsons after Frank became pastor at Phillips Memorial Church, suggest a more dramatic, if more mundane, event that may have elicited his "call within." They had this to say:

> Frank talked very little about it, but once made the comment that he'd intended to make boxing his livelihood, **until the car accident**. He told us that in his earlier years [they could not offer a date], when he'd had a car accident and almost died, he had an epiphany: he'd declared that if he came out of it he would dedicate his life to God.

His son, Scott, also felt that the car accident had been a traumatic event in his father's life, one he often referred to within the family. But like the Kenneys, he could not fix the date or exact nature of the accident, other than recalling he had multiple broken bones that required hospitalization; paid for by Beulah, who more than once helped him out financially.

Since we only know this accident occurred "in his early years," (but after he met Beulah), it's probable that it happened during his time at Redlands, or soon after, and that the "religious awakening" it had evoked, reinforced by the Indian ceremony he witnessed, led him to believe he had to move beyond the role of "boxing coach" if he was to fulfill his promise to dedicate his life to God.

8. Called to Christ

As a child, God had seemed to me a mighty tyrant in the sky reigning with vengeance and cruel force over the world. His wrath had robbed me of my father and had sent my step-father to Arizona with broken health. I believed if I didn't do right he would strike down my mother. Some Pentecostal enthusiasts had filled me with the terror of the Almighty. As high school training and some attempts at independent thinking assured me of the fallacy of these concepts, there grew up within a desire to forget about God. I came back to God through Jesus Christ–"to wit, God was in Christ, reconciling the world unto himself...and hath given to us the ministry of reconciliation." [1]

† † †

After Frank heard the call for more religious training, as previously noted, there is no explanation available as to why he chose to go all the way across the continent to Andover Newton, on the outskirts of Boston, Massachusetts, rather than return from Bacone, Oklahoma to the more familiar state of California and attend a theological seminary there, such as The American Baptist Seminary of the West, founded in 1871. All Frank tells us is that he arrived on "Newton Hill the day the man who had called me to Christ left this earth to rejoin his maker," referring, I believe, "to the inspired preaching and close friendship of Harold Camp[2] of Oakland, California," whom he credited as having been a great influence in his

---

[1] Bible quote from II Corinthians 5:19. Passage found in Frank's "Ordination paper for the RI Council"

[2] Frank belonged to a church in Oakland prior to going to Redlands. Harold Camp, probably was his minister. There is only one other reference to him, the second, later, suggests Camp is dead.

religious growth. He continues:

> Though infinitely smaller and more insignificant [than Camp], I felt much as Elisha must have felt when the mantle of his beloved master fell upon him. Since that day there has been a terrific urgency about life, a dynamic that will not let me rest.[3]

† † †

In 1808, Congregational leaders founded the Andover Theological Seminary in Andover, Massachusetts, an American pioneer of schools devoted wholly to ministerial education. A century later it briefly removed to Cambridge and affiliated with Harvard, but dissolved their relationship in 1925. The pioneer school among the Baptists, the Newton Theological Institution was established in 1825 at Newton Centre, Massachusetts by men desirous of pastors who were "deeply religious and well-instructed." "Newton shared with Andover the same theological tradition of loyalty to the evangelical Gospel and zeal for its dissemination," and regarded their uniting in 1932 as a "contribution to our divided Protestantism, one of the signal exemplifications of the spirit of Christian unity."

After 1932, until 1965 when the merger was complete, the two schools shared buildings, courses and faculty, but students still registered in one or the other, as they preferred, and received their degrees from either Andover or Newton.[4] Frank received his Bachelor of Divinity from Newton in 1940. However, whether registered

[3] From Frank's "Ordination paper for the RI Council"

[4] Information from "Historical Heritage" section of the Schools' 1939-1940 Catalogue.

with Andover or Newton, students took the same courses and had the same professors, and Frank had comfortably served in both Congregational and Baptist churches even while a student.

In an article about Dr. Everett C. Herrick, President of the Seminary when Frank was there, Herrick is quoted as saying:[5]

> The Baptists and Congregationalists of New England were a decade in advance of their denominational cousins in coming together to build a strong cooperative theological faculty. New buildings appeared on the quadrangle, but the greater goal has been men.... [Prior to coming to head the Seminary, Dr. Herrick] spent 25 years between two parishes which gave him a pretty good view of both sides of track. The First Baptist in Charlestown took him among the tenements where he would see many human needs [a reminder of Frank's experience in Los Angeles]. The First Baptist in Fall River ran the gamut between mill hands and mill owners.

† † †

The 1937 recession cost four million workers their jobs–the year Frank started his studies at Andover Newton. That first year he took six or seven courses per semester, including "History, Literature, and Religious Ideas in the Old Testament" "History, Literature, and Religious Ideas in the New Testament," "Preaching," and "Public Speaking" amongst others, and he received grades ranging from 80 to

[5] The clipping in Frank's files is dated Sunday, January 17, 1943, the article, "Profile of a Man Who Would Avoid Paganized America," by Herbert Allen. The newspaper is not stated other than "Boston."

97. Simultaneously, during that first year, Frank served as Assistant Pastor at the First Congregational Church in Fall River, perhaps as a "field placement." There's no indication he was ever involved in any extra-curricular activities at Andover-Newton, but obviously he found time for a social life.

Where Frank met his future wife, Loretta Bell Long, is not disclosed, but during that first year at Andover Newton both these lively, good-looking, young people were taking the courses, "Ethical Theory" and "How [To] Teach Life of Jesus." Loretta was classed in the seminary's official records as a "Special Student," and left at the end of her second year. Until then, Loretta had continued to take a full range of courses; her choice of classes, however—music (a member of the Choir all four semesters), psychology, dramatics and the educational work of the church—suggest she never was interested in preparing to be a pastor. In fact, seminary had always been her brother's idea; Loretta more interested in developing her beautiful contralto voice. Lack of interest would at least help explain why her seminary marks were consistently lower than Frank's, ranging in the 60s and 70s—except for choir (100) and dramatics(90). She was undoubtedly much happier after she left Andover Newton and began studying at Boston's New England Conservatory of Music under the tutelage of the school's most illustrious teacher, Royal Dadman. Her roommate and fellow student at the time was the soon-to-become-famous Eleanor Steber (an operatic star at the Metropolitan in the 1940s and 1950s).

† † †

During the summer after completion of their first year at Andover Newton, letters began to flow regularly between Frank and Loretta; a few are in postmarked envelopes; the dates of others had to be approximated from the content.

In the first letter, postmarked July 18, 1938, Frank is temporarily at Phillips Memorial Baptist Church in Cranston, Rhode Island. He writes Loretta in Seabrook, New Hampshire where she has some sort of hostess job. He wrote:

> It was so grand to have had that short time with you last week, it must have gone quicker than a moment.... Here it is Monday and the rain is falling fast, does it ever go for a week without a lot of rain here?... [He thrills over a lobster dinner he had on Saturday, but feels rather guilty to be so enjoying himself.] I am constantly too tense, too anxious to fill the place Harold Camp left vacant, and yet no human can do such a thing, it is only as God is able to use us that we become effective...
>
> I got back to Cranston mighty late to prepare for the next day's sermon. It was installation day in the church and the summer pastor was installed for a brief ministry there [I believe referring to himself]. How I wish you could see that fine group and how wonderfully they have rallied around. You see any young man would have been perfectly set there because the older pastor has sort of lost contact with the youth. I wish it weren't so far from Newton. I would try to stay on there and do school work too. They need someone to build them up a little more and then build a great new church. They have nearly everything except the little spark that such enterprises take.

Frank then goes on to write about the Hingham church as bigger, with a bigger split, feeling being there will be "one big rushing strain every minute of the time." He then writes of yet another church in Northampton where there's only a small salary but a great need. In making a choice, he admits he's most concerned about not being near Loretta. "I can't begin to think of losing out with you, though I understand that real friends don't need quantities of time together in order to keep alive the vital spark." He closes with a request that she "help me solve it and tell me the answer Friday. Love, Frank."

The next available letter is postmarked July 29th and addressed to Camp Ataloa in Ocean Park, Maine.

> Sunday is almost over, so this note will go out as a last benediction to a great day. The rain stopped during the evening and now there is a glorious symphony of the stars,.... While the rain was displaced by such beauty, I hurried down to the Park concert. It was one of the most delightful programs of symphonic favorites that I have ever heard—how grand it would have been to have shared it with you, but since that was not possible there was nothing to do but sit and think of you and hope that we might someday enjoy just such a program together...[He describes the music and then] after the concert I sat on the south steps—of the hill—and said a little prayer for you and "us."...
>
> [As the letter continues] Dearest Loretta I want you to know that you are very near my thoughts at all times and will continue to be more so as these busy days hurry on. [Alluding to what seems to have been a recent disagreement, he continues]...This much I will say, there will be no more declarations of love on my part until that time when you want them.

> You see I too believe that if it is God's plan then there will be such a strong bond between us that no words will be able to affirm or deny the reality of it. And so until you are convinced that my actions and desires are all that you would want them to be I shall be a fairly silent lover....
>
> [Returning to an issue raised in the prior letter] It was raining black cats and pitch forks at Hingham this morning and yet there was a goodly crowd, and fine music. It really was a new thrill to be there and realize that those people are so loyal to the interests of that church and its future. They have not given me the written call yet, but there was verbal assurance that it will be forthcoming. ...Everything seems set, unless that strong pull of guidance that often comes when we least expect it, comes to pull me towards Cranston. I am open and only too anxious to take either one that seems to be in His great plan of things.

Frank closes with praises of the job he feels Loretta is doing with the girls at camp, and implores her not to look back at the apparently better-paying hostess job she left. "How proud I will be of what you can do for those little girls, and how proud I shall always be of your unselfish devotion to our God and our fellow men—'men' in the general not generic terminology!"

There are several undated letters, most filled with sentiments such as this:

> My very own Darling, How can I ever find words to tell you how precious your letters are to me, and the surging thrill that sweeps over me when I pick it up and read of your busy life and your loving

words. Well, it just makes me know that it has all been the most glorious plan in the world and worked infinitely beyond comprehension.

But there is one that's full of self-flagellation and apologies; following an obviously major "fight" that appears to have been verbal:

> I can't expect you to want to read this or to listen to me again, but I have been in such anguish and disgust with self for twelve hours that something must be said. There is not one thing that can be said to right the terrible wrongs that I did you last night, but if remembering forever that I have broken a sacred trust, and regretting it more each time I think of it and working hard each time to make up for the injustice will in any way ease your mind, and make you feel that God hasn't been so cruel to you by making you cast your lot with me, then perhaps someplace in your gracious self you may find means to forget and forgive.
>
> You will never understand that it is because I love you and you alone so much that I make the mistake of wanting you to love me as much as I have asked......If there is one speck of manhood in me you shall never have occasion to blame God for throwing you with me again. Those words are seared so deeply in me that I shall never forget them, and if you still mean them, it will be far better for us to say goodbye forever, or else get out of the Christian ministry.......Loretta, every act, every attempt to lead people upward now is done because I am so proud of you and so eager to become more worthy of the you that God blessed my life with....

108. Justice, Peace & God

> Mother has planned so many fine things for you that we should have been talking over last night, but now I have forfeited the right to ask you to do anything with me until I hear that one word that will change this worst of all miseries into hope that something lasting and worthwhile can be salvaged....If you knew how much I depend on you, long for you, plan things for your pleasure, look forward to seeing you and feel miserable when not around you, then surely you might know that my love for you will either make you the happiest person in the world or the most miserable--yours is the choice....I shall be out of reach for a time, but as there is a Good God in the heavens, you shall never again see the Mr. Hyde that tormented your tired self last night.

Hints questioning Frank's love, or its manner of expression, was raised in more than one letter, perhaps at least in part due to fears Loretta harbored that Frank might still have feelings for the girl he was serious about when they met. Though it doesn't really sound like it, maybe these feelings were behind the above fight, indirectly if not directly. In any case, there is another lengthy letter dealing with this issue; whether written before or after the above, there's no way to determine. It begins like most of his letters, praising God for so much more than he deserved in finding her. Then, half through the letter, Frank writes:

> This is told only because I know you want things to ever be on the very frankest and most honest level between us. There is no use going over and over old events, you know only too well how I felt, why there was the constant reticence to proceed more amorously. I knew full well that I no longer loved

Margaret with a healthy love, and yet each time the confidence would become sure in me, a letter would come from her that would make me upset and not certain, because of the strange attitude which she seemed to take regarding our future—but this summer it was all worked out, and even with the memory of her last letter fresh in my mind, I knew that I didn't want to go out to see her, and then the absolute assurance came to me that I loved you, with a greater and more lasting and more God-guided love than I had ever had for her, and I declared that fact to you in person and in writing BEFORE I HAD THE SLIGHTEST IDEA WHAT HAD HAPPENED TO HER, yet just about the time that you were being assured of my love, she was discovering that she didn't love me hopelessly after all and the first word that I received of that glorious news was the other day when a card came from Munich, Germany, with this glorious sentence in it, "Just as you predicted, Frank, I met him and loved him at once, we were married in record time, and are having a glorious honeymoon in Europe!"

Can you see why I am so gloriously happy and released and anxious to see the one that God has planned for me since the beginning of time? Loretta, I can take you in my arms with the confidence and faith that I have done His will, that though I may have been unfair to you at times that it was all for the best, and that my love was truly free even before the facts from California were known. You mean more to me than can ever be expressed, and my only way of truly expressing my love for you will be in pouring out greater and more worthwhile service for our people.

> THE LIGHT IS GREEN AND WE ARE GOING THROUGH! But along with that assurance is also this further one that you will be with me in whatever the circumstance...
>
> Truly life does become a growing adventure when we believe and trust in Him. You are finding more and more the truth, and not just the statement of that fact, aren't you dearest one, that is the eternalness of this cosmic adventure—the more we experience Him the more we yearn for more of the same, and the freer our lives become, the fuller they are realized in others....
>
> Tomorrow I am trying the difficult subject of giving a picture of the Bible—not as a relic to be dusted from the shelf occasionally, but as a guide to each day's activities, business and pleasure. There is so much that we miss in the Bible by trying to find a "RELIGIOUS" lesson in every chapter, instead of finding the everyday instructions and practical applications in it. ...
>
> Love from all my soul, Frank.

Frank seemed almost uniquely able to do just what he said he would attempt in that last paragraph. And it was that ability that made him such a great, and greatly appreciated, pastor. He had been at Phillips Memorial since July when he'd been appointed to assist in the daily Vacation Bible School and to conduct the Sunday services.

In a later undated letter, Frank writes of his attempt to do justice to the great theme, "A Grave in a Garden."

> There have been several tragedies here within the year and the subject is one of the most tremendous that we can attempt. I am doing the church up into a

garden scene, with artificial grass mats on the pulpit and lots of flowers to go with it. All that will be needed is one gracious person with a beautiful soul-filling contralto voice to sing "My Beautiful Garden of Prayer" [*referring undoubtedly to Loretta*].

That this sermon made an impact is clear since it's one of the first memories of Frank that was recalled recently by both Louise Anthony Green and Lucille Spooner Votta, two former members. Louise said, "We were so impressed;" Lucille said, "It was absolutely unbelievable." Lucille called Frank's sermons inspirational as she recalled others that expressed his belief that there would be just one world, that we'd all be one color, and that if Jesus should come today, he might not be let in because he was too black–"something I'd never thought of before," she added.[6] Lucille also remembered what she believed to be Frank's favorite hymns: *Are You Able?*, *Living for Jesus*, and *He Leadeth Me.*

† † †

Both Louise and Lucille went on to say what an immediate impact Frank had on the church's young people. Lucille recalled how he arrived the first day of Vacation Bible School laden with boxing gloves around his neck, and how, on the very first day, he taught them the Lord's Prayer in Indian sign language. And she's still amused by Frank's

---

[6] Frank's interracial concerns were reflected in the church budget after he came to Phillips Memorial. Not only did it include an allocation for Bacone, but also for Storer College, the first higher educational institution for blacks in West Virginia. It was founded in 1867 by the Home Mission Society of the Free Baptist Church, named in honor of John Storer, a prosperous businessman in Sanford, Maine. Unfortunately it ceased operation in 1955, its campus now part of the Harper's Ferry National Historic Park.

recounting of the time, on his eleven mile daily horseback ride to school, he, along with a group of boys, witnessed baptisms taking place at a creek they passed en route. They all stopped and laughed at the spectacle, and some threw stones. Frank made sure in the telling that the young people understood that he was not a Christian at that time.

He was so popular with the young people that everyone wanted to ride with him to the outings he planned at Goddard Park or Carpenter's Beach for picnics and swimming. One time he got in trouble when he had sixteen people in his van and the axle broke. He didn't have much money and it was an old car. Louise's sister, Dorothea, recalled one outing when Frank went in swimming with them even though he hadn't brought a swim suit. Goddard Park was the usual site of the church's annual picnic and in one of his announcements of the event, he wrote:

> Buses leave the church at 10 a.m. All church school pupils through the Junior department ride free, others for 25¢. Clam chowder and many delicious tid-bits will be for sale. Free rides on the Merry-Go-Round. Of course we want the children to come, BUT WHAT WOULD A PICNIC BE WITHOUT A GANG OF ELDERS. Every family ought to drive down for part or all of the day (a Saturday).

Louise also remembered the plays Frank encouraged; one, *The Bishop's Candlestick*, when she played the lead, merited a letter from Frank, which she's preserved. It expressed his "deep appreciation for the honor which you helped bring our fellowship by your fine performance." Louise also kept the program; their play performed during Youth Drama Nights, February 24-25, 1939, in competition with youth groups from a dozen different churches. Frank kept the program for another play he'd written himself, "Indian Blood," which was performed on December 9, 1941 by the Grace Baptist Church Young People.

Another of the then-youngsters, Neil Ross, remembered his mother talking about how cute Frank looked when he dressed up at Halloween and had a whole gaggle of kids with him as they made their way through the Eden Park neighborhood. The newspaper, too, was taken with this new kind of minister and wrote a long article about his approach to Halloween—quoted, in part:[7]

> Police officer Bill Olafson, cruising around in his scout car last week on Halloween, spied a large group of youngsters on a street in the Eden Park neighborhood, apparently mischief-bent. Jamming on his brakes, he jumped from the scout car and gave chase to a boy dragging a long rope, and to his considerable surprise ran right smack into Rev. Francis Willard Thompson of Phillips Memorial Church, who seemed to be one of the gang....
>
> Once or twice a pedestrian walking along a neighborhood street encountered the lively group of kids, warily skirted around the ranks, and found himself face to face with a big, broad-shouldered young man wearing a grin of amusement. "Well, I'll be darned! It's the minister! How are you, Mr. Thompson?"
>
> Eden Park's unusual Halloween doings—lots of fun, but no broken windows, no clotheslines cut, no rowdyism, and no harmful mischief—were the result of an idea. A couple of weeks ago Rev. Frank

---

[7] Copy found in his files is not dated nor is the newspaper noted.

Thompson, conceived the notion of going out with the boys on Halloween. Up to that time the prevailing theory was to barricade one's home, call the police, and return nastiness for nastiness. But it seemed to Frank Thompson that Halloween pranks are not deliberately spiteful, but are rather—like juvenile delinquency itself—the result of improper supervision, or the complete absence of supervision.

The pastor decided his idea was worth an experiment. On Halloween he called together the young boys of his own parish and told them simply that he was going out with them to have a good time. They were told, too, that if they met any kids from "tough" neighborhoods, to invite them to join the expedition. And that is exactly what happened: before the evening was over, Mr. Thompson's gang had swollen to impressively large and variegated proportions. The so-called "toughies" had just as much fun as Mr. Thompson's own boys, and nobody got hurt, and nobody called the police, and nobody made any complaints afterward about Halloween vandalism.

It worked out beautifully: the kids were high-spirited but responsive. They had a good time, but no better than I had....It was a manifestation of practical Christianity—the kind of Christianity Frank Thompson likes best, and the kind his young people understand best....The pastor's Christianity is an unusual kind: It is a progressive Christianity and it is also a muscular Christianity as befits the Man who was a carpenter and a fisherman, and who drove the money-changers from the temple.

The idea was so popular that a succession of community Halloween parties followed, sponsored by the YMCA.

115. Called to Christ

† † †

Louise Anthony Green, Shirley Gallup and Lucille Spooner all shared memories, sometimes differing slightly, of trips they made with Frank up to the Baptist camp, Hazeltine, in Ocean Park, Maine. Only Louise remembered how he got car sick on one trip and how funny they all thought that was. Shirley, not surprisingly, remembered the summer she got appendicitis while at camp and had to go to the hospital in Biddeford to have the appendix removed; how wonderful Mr. T (what everyone called him) was in coming to visit her.

But one trip they all remembered. It was when he'd stopped en route and they'd wondered why. Frank said he was picking up a lady-friend [they differ as to whether she was to be a counselor or waitress]. "So we were the first to know he had a lady-friend and when we went back and told everyone, they were jealous of Loretta, because we all, including our mothers, were in love with him. He just had such a neat personality."

Louise preserved the letter Frank and Loretta wrote them at camp, August 2, 1940. It began: "Dear LouiHelluciSherlseenleey"—the running together of Louise Anthony, Shirley Gallup, Helen Phillips and Lucille Spooner. It still amuses Louise. The letter expresses the Thompsons' pride at having "such a grand delegation from our church," and asks: "Are there any other churches with as many leaders there as from ours?" The letter concludes with these paragraphs:

> Drink deeply of the air that mixes so perfectly in the salty pines; study hard at the fine courses, take a quiet stroll with some understanding companion into Guild Hall and sit down for five minutes and

> see what happens; gather enough rhythm from the waves, joyousness from the gang, wooing from the boys, and challenge from God's messengers to fill us all when you return.
>
> If the 'Princess' [referring to Loretta] behaves, I will arrive in plenty of time to bring you all back to Eden where we'll park until it's the Garden of Eden."

In one of his undated letters to Loretta, Frank writes of the young people:

> They are begging the church not to wait until October to begin the young people's programs. Can you imagine such enthusiasm? Our trouble will be to see that the fire that has been kindled so quickly doesn't dwindle correspondingly.

† † †

Several letters to Loretta in late August and September 1938 reflect the fact the church is considering "calling him" as their permanent pastor, something he clearly desires. They also suggest that the differences that previously had concerned Frank and Loretta about their expressions of love for each other have been resolved, and they plan to marry. In one letter, Frank writes:

> The Phillips Memorial Church of Cranston, RI is in the very midst of a great campaign to call a new minister to their church. He [referring to himself] is a man that knows he hasn't any right accepting such a flattering call, and who knows that he will never be able to do the work without the constant and ever present help and guidance of God, but he is one that is willing to be led by God ANY PLACE, and also who feels that

there will be a lovely helper come to add her most gracious personality and music and soul to His work in a reasonably short time.

In another, Frank writes:

The glorious stars above, the wonders of God's ever present love and guidance and the love of a marvelous girl like yourself makes me wonder if there is any possibility of ever being able to live up to it all...Truly I feel terribly humble, and recognize without question or doubt that it has only been the unsearchable goodness and loving kindness of Our Master that has given me so much.

I have been working on sermons for the future, and a great wave of optimism swells over me so that I can hardly contain practical sense on the pages. I seem to see this great community united as never before, and soon a wonderful new building going up that will house the worshipers in beauty and an inspirational setting so that out from here will go the very "beacon of life." Roger Williams brought religious freedom as a reality to Americans in Rhode Island, but that religion has almost faded into a nonentity, but perhaps God has a plan for "religious reality" to be reborn in Eden Park. I know this all sounds egotistical, but knowing that you will understand this is just the outflow of my love and optimism to you, I can't but write it....

If on top of all that outburst the church votes not to call me tomorrow night, won't that be quite a let down–but truly, if they do, I shall feel only too relieved that God showed me His will before I had gone too far.

118. Justice, Peace & God

The third letter in this group suggests the church has called him, and indeed they did, planning for him to take a two-week vacation, then start as their full-time minister on September 11, 1938 and on September 20th additionally resume his studies at Andover Newton.

In that third letter to Loretta the summer of 1939, written after his appointment and before their marriage, Frank writes:

> I hope you will be full of life and fun to make this weekend a real joy to all we come in contact with. Remember they [church members] are going to be looking at "us" with new eyes now—critically looking to see if we really are happy, or if my somber self is making a pessimist of you, or if your influence is greater and I am becoming human. You know that lots of your friends think that you are throwing your affection away on an old bear, so you help me to live that reputation down, will you?

September 1938, coinciding with Frank's call to Phillips Memorial and the start of his second year at seminary, in an effort to "appease" Hitler, Great Britain and France signed the now infamous Munich Pact which sacrificed the western Czechoslovakia region known as the Sudetenland to Germany.

September 1939, coinciding with the start of Frank's third and final year at seminary, Hitler invaded Poland, starting World War II.

9. "Called" to Phillips Memorial Baptist Church

> *I was reared a Methodist but was converted into a Baptist church; and though I still believe in the fundamental concepts of the Baptists as originally intended, nevertheless I am very loath to feel that the Baptists have any corner on truth. The great doctrines of Soul Liberty and Voluntariness and independence of church and state are principles which I shall try to teach and strengthen with every ounce of effort–not in any spirit of smug conceit that Baptists first proclaimed them but because they are concepts which should be universal and far transcend any denominational boundary.*
>
> *The church to me is not limited by any boundaries–national, racial, denominational or social....One of the greatest needs we Baptists have, I feel, is the need for a world view. Isolationism, selfish individualism, should be forgotten words in our language.*[1]

†††

Frank had been pleased to be "called" by Phillips Memorial to be their minister while he still had two years to complete before graduating from Andover Newton Seminary. From the beginning, he had been impressed with the friendliness of the church's members, and, perhaps especially, the enthusiasm of its youth. Years later, he could still recall the "carefree summer" when his "yellow rattletrap beachwagon first appeared in Eden Park."

> A fancy-free young westerner made his first appearance around Phillips Memorial. A gang of enthusiastic young people gathered on the church lawn

[1] From Frank's "Ordination paper for the RI Council"

to plan a Vacation Church School. Then followed picnics, beach parties, garden scenes in church–an unusual California windstorm followed by much chopping of wood [as a result of the hurricane soon to be described at length].

Even though Phillips was far too small–especially as their new minister kept attracting more and more new members–Frank must have admired it as a typical New England church, white with a spire.

It was in a 1940 sermon, "A Sanctuary for Security," that he said:

> As one approaches most New England cities and towns the eye is caught by the slender spires that rise out of the smoky haze. Out of the confusion of varied architectural conglomerations, one will see the

> symbols of that upward reach. Go to any old world city and above the smoke and confusion of war torn tragedy, there tower the giant cathedrals, gaunt symbols of what some men have felt. Some of these cathedrals so old no one knows who started them and still not finished, man searching for security, cries "Sanctuary!" And then by sacrifices and untold cost he builds a sanctuary where he may come in search of security. And so we have that symbol here—this little building where devout souls have gathered for nearly half a century to find security.

Frank collected a whole scrapbook full of pictures of steepled churches.

† † †

Clearly Frank was in awe of Phillips Memorial's history and in a later sermon, said, "My head is bowed in humility when I think back on its history." He wrote of its history for the church newsletter, the *Trumpeter*:

> This church was ...an outgrowth of a Sunday School which had its inception early in 1897. A recognition service for the new church was held at the Peoples "Free Baptist" Church in Auburn on June 25, 1900. There were 15 charter members representing nine families. [It continued] its association with the Free Baptists until [merging] with the Baptists in 1913....
>
> Our church was named "Phillips Memorial" in memory of the late Dr. James L. Phillips [who] spent most of his life in Sunday School work in Bengal-Orrissa [India]. He was well-known in Cranston where he served as pastor of the Peoples Church and also as chaplain of the State Institutions during a stay

in the States, after which he again returned to India.

The cornerstone was laid in 1901....[It] now has a membership of 378; the Bible School, 450. Our parish is made up of 300 families who are affiliated in some way with Phillips Memorial.

[In keeping with the view he expressed in his final thesis at Andover Newton, he said here] While we are affiliated with the Baptist denomination and baptize or convert by immersion, we have for many hears welcomed into our membership, as "affiliated" members, people from all Christian denominations [by "letter" or declaration of the Christian experience]....Affiliated members are not eligible to serve as deacons or deaconesses but enjoy all the other privileges and duties of members.

Today, Phillips Memorial stands as a lighthouse for truth and righteousness in Eden Park and is endeavoring through the preaching and teaching of the Word to win souls for our Lord and Master, Jesus Christ.

It's amusing to learn from his half-sister, Mary Jo, who, with their mother, Olga, would soon come to live with Frank, how he prepared for performing his first actual baptism. Mary Jo tells this writer she had never been baptized by complete immersion, "so we practiced in the kitchen with mother as our congregation."

He placed a folded handkerchief over my nose and carefully leaned me back just as if we were in the water. I couldn't help it, but I giggled. At which time he told me, "Little sister, if you as much as smile during your baptism, I'm gonna hold you under!" Even though that was a fun experience, it was a serious time

> for the both of us. I had attended all of the classes that he taught, so I felt the seriousness of it.

In a recent interview, Neil Ross recalled seeing his sister baptized, as did the writer see her sister, Freda. Freda described her baptism as "no big deal." Having donned white robes provided by the church, we were "quickly dunked in and out," in a tub of water underneath the altar; the tub filled and opened for the occasion.

A letter from Frank to Loretta, postmarked September 13, 1938, states that Olga and Mary Jo had "finally arrived about midnight last night, and are still sleeping the sleep of the exhausted and innocent." Loretta is back in Missouri visiting with her parents where everyone is not entirely pleased with her plans to marry Frank. He writes:

> I know just how mothers can feel towards those that try to take their loved ones away from them, but tell her to remember "a daughter is a daughter all her life, but a son's a son till he gets a wife."

In his letter, Frank goes on to talk of the previous Sunday's church service, then ends on a personal note. Of the service, he writes:

> We had to bring chairs into the aisles for people to sit in, and during the communion we ran out of glasses and elements, the first time in the history of the church that the service has failed to care for all....
>
> This is a busy week preparing for the installation and reception of next week [his, on the 18th] and then after that will be school [the 20th]. And

> the rush and grind will be on....You are constantly in my thoughts, and though busy as I am there are moments when a peace and calm seem to come over me and a strange sense of being with you, so as long as there is such sweet communion, I don't feel bad in just taking enough time for this short note.

† † †

September 21, 1938: this is a date Frank most likely would have remembered even without the help of nature. It had been less than two weeks since his call to Phillips Memorial, only a day since his daily drive to Boston had begun again with the resumption of classes for his second year at Andover Newton; *and* his Mother, Olga, and sister, Mary Jo, had only recently arrived from California to keep house for the newly called, so-far-bachelor, pastor. At the time Frank asked them to come stay with him, Olga and Mary Jo were living in San Diego with his sister, Paula. Mary Jo had just graduated from San Diego High School, so, as she put it, "it sounded like a great adventure to be with one of my older brothers, especially one who was a minister." Mary Jo had never really had a chance to know Frank since she was still an infant when he'd left their ranch home in Arizona.

Nature intervened that day in a big way: it made sure Frank would never forget it! And we're fortunate he left us a copy of the vivid account he wrote, soon after, of his personal encounter with the "roaring wind and rain" of the 1938 Rhode Island Hurricane "that, it was thought, couldn't happen here."

> Occasional warnings from the weather bureau had indicated the possibility of winds with hurricane intensity. The word hurricane meant little

to most Yankees, and especially little to such a recent arrival from California as I was. If there had been tornado or earthquake warnings, I would have been alert to danger.

The ancient model car that was helping put me through theological school just wouldn't steer straight as I headed south at 3 p.m. My first realization of the terror that was upon us came when opening the door to check on the tire I was sure must be flat to cause such hard steering. The door was ripped from my hand and car and driver almost tumbled into the ditch at the opposite side of the road.

Roaring wind and rain were like nothing heard on land or sea, but the thought of turning back didn't occur. The usual stream of traffic had ceased. Soon it was apparent why. Trees began to go down like corn stalks before a scythe. One fell so violently across my blurred pathway that only a skidding sideways prevented disaster. Frantically I backed to escape the power lines that were snapping and hissing amidst the mangle of limbs, only to have the projecting rear trunk of the seven year old model sliced off by a falling telephone pole.

An old Inn near North Attleboro seemed to offer refuge. The huddled tourists hysterically gave added forebodings as they shouted disconnected reports of devastation in and around Providence. "Could I get through Providence to Cranston?" I shouted to one of the drenched refugees. "Are you crazy, nobody gets through, all of Providence is gone, God knows where. We got out just in time!" There was still that single obsession in my mind, to meet my loved ones from California to prove to them that "unusual weather" didn't interfere in Yankee land.

Shingles were ripping from the breezeway of the old building and flying debris crashed like Gattling guns against the windows as the proprietors wrung their hands and sobbed, "Mon Dieu, Mon Dieu." They were obviously recent arrivals from some French area and had invested heavily only to be standing helplessly at the dismemberment of their fortune.

My ministerial concern was called forth as I noted their panic. I handed them my last three dollars, telling them to let it apply to repairs as my payment for the refuge they had provided.

The reluctant old Plymouth chugged into the raging gale. How I ever made that last ten mile obstacle race against fallen trees, torrents of water and sagging power lines is more than a mystery, it is a modern miracle. My mind was mesmerized by the overtones of high wind, my muscles were so rigid from fixation on the wheel that my biceps ached for days.

A tottering billboard brought a cynical smile as I caught the words, "Nature in the raw is seldom mild." This was nature on the loose, anything but mild, with no regard for works of man or will of God. Soon I found that even untamed nature has a junior partner even more terrifying. It is human nature gone berserk!

Haltingly, but with that possessive obsession pulling incessantly on my entire being, I drove my sputtering steed of tin, iron and oil around trees, poles and flooding embankments. Blindly I ducked behind houses, across fields, through torrents of wind-whipped flood waters until I reached Fox Point.

Slums and alley hovels had emptied their crowded contents into a mass of whirling dervishes in the middle of the street. Windows were being smashed, cars pilloried, and suddenly a sight that shall always haunt me. A shrieking mob tipped over a car and when the occupants tried to climb to the top-most window, the frenzied gang dumped the car another turn, pinning at least one rider beneath. "Should I try a rescue or attempt escape before the same fate befell me!" The odds were so overwhelmingly against me that even though my conscience will always accuse me of cowardice, I ground the car's unwilling gears into reverse to back out the stubble-strewn old street. As I skidded around the corner seeking a street that appeared clear, a smaller flank of the marauders headed in my direction with a bellow that could be heard above the unearthly roar of the storm.

It was obvious they were heading for the only car still on four wheels, which was mine. My only hope seemed to be to abandon ship and run for it, but suddenly there lurched from the door of a saloon a half drunk giant with a large bottle in one hand. "Jump on my running-board and help me through that gang and I'll give you my watch," I shouted at him. "Hell, I'd do it for free," he shouted. With one arm holding himself on the ancient running boards [then found on cars], he waved his bottle menacingly as the frightened driver gave the old crate all the gas she could gurgle as we slashed through the on-coming hoodlums. Never was a man more grateful for alcoholic courage and old fashioned running boards.

Progress was only momentary. A cordon of students from Brown University had been thrown around the flooded mall and all moving cars herded back. I recognized Gavin Pitt, a Brown student leader. "I gotta get through to Cranston," I yelled. "No can do," he snapped. "The city is flooded and all roads blocked."

The next three hours found me winding in and out of debris and flood- filled streets, in areas that I had never traveled before [and would never again be able to locate]. Somehow I reached the Capitol grounds on the other side of the city. The rain had abated and only the moan of the wind reminded me of what night it was until I opened a window to try to locate the name of the street. An eerie sound that will echo in my dreams forever greeted me. It sounded like a horrendiferous choir of gurgling, squalling, choking children gasping for breath; or the choir of the damned from over the river Styx. Later, I found it was hundreds of horns on flooded cars, shorted into gasping horror.

I edged around the foaming swirl of streams that poured through the industrial plants on Valley Street looking for a safe retreat. From the unfinished roof of a half-flooded building emerged the drenched figure of a girl waving frantically. It was another of those dilemmas that give no warning. "Should I try to help her?" The motor of my car decided the issue, for with a rusty cough it died. I located a floating plank in ebb water and reached the ledge from which the girl had appeared. She wasn't alone. Just above the mucky water within the abandoned walls, a younger girl was plastered against the fire escape with the hopeless look of one from whom the spark of life had gone. Both girls were soaked and seared into insensibility.

It took some ungentlemanly tugs and loud shouts to get the two over the sharp edge of the unfinished wall and into the foreboding swirl of the flooded street. Trembling they told me they lived in Olneyville and asked me to drive them home because their family would be mad with them for being so late. The younger sister revived enough to babble incoherently about the ordeal that had held them captive for five agonizing hours.

My own storm-stressed obsession to meet my family returned as we reached the still drenched auto, with little hope that it would start. Miraculously the heat of the engine had dried the wires enough to revive the motor. We chugged along a circuitous route vaguely outlined by the shivering girls.

The blessed unseen guide returned to steer my course after I deposited the girls near a crowded block of tenements. With absolutely no rational sense of direction, I pushed along alleys, over vacant lots and through any apparently open streets in the general direction of Cranston, and what I faintly hoped would be my family.

Parishioners later helped me in a vain search for the route of that weird journey. They didn't like to dispute their young pastor's solemn statement given as fact. But no one truly believed I made that run against such insuperable obstacles thrown up by nature on the loose. They couldn't honestly dispute the smashed trunk or the dented fenders of the car, nor would they ever forget the pale and weary look on that pastor's face when he reached home at one o'clock that next morning. No more can I ever forget the joy and relief I felt as the door opened and Mother grabbed me in her strong western embrace. Her words of welcome were, "You didn't have to arrange unusual California weather for us, did you?"

† † †

By December 11, 1938, when Frank preached the sermon he titled, "Pathways to God," things were a bit more settled in his life. Beginning the sermon by quoting two versions of an old nursery rhyme, he reminds us how science and technology have displaced many of our old superstitions.

Traditionally:

Twinkle, Twinkle little star,
How I wonder what you are
Up above the world so high
Like a diamond in the sky!

Instead, reeking of science, devoid of mystery:

Twinkle, twinkle little star
We need not wonder what you are
For seen by spectroscopic lens
You're naught but helium and hydrogen!

But science has not solved all our mysteries, Frank says. At times "when tidal waves of grief and trouble sweep all this petty knowledge away like chaff before a hurricane,...our body strains toward God" and, he reminds us, "our inability to see God is not sufficient reason to lack faith." Frank asks:

> Have you ever thought how many valuable things in the world have never been seen? Have you ever seen a germ, an atom, a blood corpuscle; have you seen friendship, love; have you ever seen a golden sunset...? In time, faith is betting your life that there is a God in the world and then living so that God will be at the very center of your life. But shall we never forget that faith without works is dead? A religion that works on Sunday and Friday night only is truly an opiate.

Frank names any number of things we can't explain, concluding, "All we can do is bow in awe before the God who created us and placed us here." Finally he points to "Love of God as the pathway to Him."

> If we could truly love God for himself first—wars, strikes, poverty, hatred, turmoil—would all vanish in the warm sea of that kind of love, as snow flakes vanish when they hit the warm sea.

Years later, on September 9, 1941, in a sermon he titled, "The God We Don't Understand," Frank again approached this subject in a slightly different way. He chastises us for blaming God for the evils of the world; disagrees with Oscar Wilde whom he quotes as having said, "There is enough suffering in any lane in London to prove God doesn't love the world."

> I am constantly amazed at some of our people saying that God sends sickness and death as punishment. Well, we don't claim to know the mind of God, but we at least understand Him well enough... not to accuse him of being capricious and

> cheap, taking his spite out on lonely old ladies and little children—that's paganism...Even though we don't understand this God that started all this, and sent our universe spinning down the hall of time, we at least have to start with a presumption. We must assume that somehow this all makes sense in the total pattern.
>
> It's not all bad. Humanity is "not a scrap of useless refuse on the dung heap of a lunatic asylum" as someone has said. If that were the true state of man, we'd have a greater mystery than we have now. ...Did you ever try to explain good without God? Or did you ever try to imagine what a dull and commonplace experience this would be if there were nothing but good, no risk in life?...If there's no abiding purpose in life calling to man to come up higher, then explain away the Christian church and its centuries of record....We can scoff all we want at the mystery of the incarnation, but when Christ shares our pain and sorrow, we begin to feel a kindred companion with him....somehow we get the feeling that we can make it too—this pain, this disappointment, this ordeal—for He's part of it, not causing it but sharing it....

† † †

The final letter in this writer's possession from Frank to Loretta *Long* is addressed to her at Chase House in Newton Centre, Mass, postmarked April 16, 1939, less than three months before their wedding, sparkles with his love. In part it reads:

> This is just to tell you that I deeply love you and can hardly wait until time to see you. It didn't

> seem possible that time could ever drag so much with you away, but now I feel as though life does not go on when you are away, and when with you, it seems that all life stops and rests in your presence.
>
> This is truly a glorious day, and maybe it is a good thing you aren't here for we would probably be compelled to slip off to some lovely grassy spot and there thrill to the glorious of the Master architect....We have a couple of tickets for *Tosca*. It won't be as good as the Met, but darling I will never forgive myself if you didn't get to attend some opera this year....Blessings on you, my sweet, Love Frank

Less than three months later, on July 2, 1939, the headline of the Sunday church bulletin reads, "Happy Wedding" and a drawing of a couple taking their vows is underneath. It had been exactly a year since Frank first came to Phillips as a summer appointment. On this day, the Bulletin announces:

> We are proud and honored to have Dr. Charles N. Arbuckle with us today to preach for us this morning and officiate at the wedding this afternoon....It was [at Andover Newton] that Miss Long and Mr. Thompson learned to know and love him as teacher, pastor, and friend.

On the back of the Bulletin, Loretta and Frank express their feelings about Phillips Memorial:

> Miss Long wishes to express her deepest appreciation and heartfelt gratitude to all the members for the grand help and friendship she has received from ALL.... Each person has made her feel as though she had always been a member of "our

> church family...."
>
> May, I, as your pastor, add my dittoes to the above and say further that you have given me many many occasions to rejoice in the past year, but you have out soared all possible expectation by the manner in which you have taken this dear girl to your hearts; and by the splendid "wedding" which YOU have planned for us....I am the proudest and happiest man alive and can only offer you my life more fully dedicated through Him whom we call Lord and Master.

The church, decorated with white flowers, palms and ferns, was filled to overflowing for the wedding that afternoon; included was a large group from the first Congregational Church in Fall River where Frank had briefly served as a student intern. Loretta looked beautiful in her white Princess taffeta gown holding a bouquet of orange blossoms and baby's breath, her veil flowing from a wreath of orange blossoms. Frank's mother, Olga, was there wearing a dark lavender dress and white hat with roses, [2] and his sister, Mary Joe, one of the bridesmaids, was wearing a rose gown and picture hat–looking quite different from the "cool cat" who smoked, as she was recently described by a parishioner who knew her–"nice but more like someone you'd meet at a club than at church." Loretta's brother, Lincoln Long of Kansas City, gave her away. Following the couple's exchange of vows in a double ring ceremony, and while still kneeling at the altar, Mrs.

---

[2] The Providence *Evening Bulletin*, Monday, 9/3/1939, had a write-up of the event with accompanying large, beautiful photo of them leaving the church. Fortunately, even though the *Journal* (the *Bulletin* defunct) does not keep photos that far back, Scott found a copy he loaned to this writer.

Mildred Burnett of Northampton sang the hymn, "O, Perfect Love."

Lucille Spooner Votta recalled how her family had gone early in order to get a seat. "It was just a wonderful,

wonderful wedding," she said. The reception was held at the newlyweds' beautifully decorated home on Colonial Avenue, after which they departed for a honeymoon in Maine. Shirley Gallup recalled that they returned from their honeymoon

while we were having the church picnic at Goddard Park. "Everyone was so happy to see them and welcome them back."

† † †

In his sermon on December 10, 1939, "Pages from Life," Frank has much to say about the Bible, beginning with the observation that too many think that just owning one is all that's necessary. "The Gideonites felt if they placed a Bible in every hotel room the problems of the world would be solved." But, Frank assures us, "these pages are not esoteric formulae, they come from life," and include God's instructions on how we are to live. Frank goes on to enumerate many of the issues it deals with. "Then," he asserts, "there are those who have used the scriptures for evil purposes....There has not been a crime in the world that cannot be justified by a verse of scripture....I beg of you to be thoughtful and intelligent as you read these pages from life because that is what they are."

Perhaps it is Frank's belief in the need for "thoughtful and intelligent" use of the Bible that inspired him to include in the sermon his rationale for "what you call the profession of the ministry:"

> So that you would have one person in the community that could give time to help go over our eternal problems and try to find the best that life has to offer. Yes, to try to find God's answer to these problems and bring them to you, inadequate as they

> are....He does not speak just to hear himself talk, tho [sic] some of us may sound as tho [sic] we do. He speaks out of a heart that is yearning to make people find the more abundant life! He gives himself to a profession that has very scant rewards in many ways and yet is the most blessed of all professions because he is trying to help you to live. But all his efforts, all his ministrations do not help you one bit if you don't help yourself to use these things, if you don't share with him these things.
>
> One of the ways a minister can be helped most is to find hearts that are tuned, trying to find the message of God, the heart that is trying to unite with others, to make an attempt to find truth, the truth that makes man free. And when the minister begins to feel that sense of strength that comes from a worshiping audience, then his words are not his own. They are words of God using him to speak to your hearts, and if the minister fails, it behooves us all to search our hearts. If we fail it is because we have not the right attitude, are not keeping our hearts tuned to the heights, and it is your job as well as his. We must apply ourselves to find the way to help ourselves to help others.

It was in another sermon that he talked about the common symbols we find during a church service: the *processional*–choir and minister heading for the chancel, "Let us go into the house of the Lord"; the *pulpit*–a place that is sacred for God's word; the *gowns*–adopted to show the difference between the old traditional formalized church and the new Protestants. But in this same sermon, Frank warns that "symbolism becomes dangerous when we allow it to take the place of true inner worship." The Church as a Sanctuary "should be a place to recover the basic patterns of life—to adjust our hopes and habits."

Frank closed his sermon on the Bible, as he may also have closed the one on symbols, with a beloved benediction he used often:

> Take us on the quest of knowledge
> Clearest thinker man has known,
> Make our lives sincere and patient,
> Satisfied with truth alone.
>
> Take us on the quest of service,
> Kindly servant of man's need.
> Let us work with Thee for others
> Anywhere Thy purpose leads.
>
> All along our quest for pathways,
> Christ, our Leader and our Guide,
> Make us conscious of Thy presence,
> Walking always at our side.

† † †

After his marriage in July 1939, Frank still had another year at Andover Newton before his graduation on June 5, 1940. Somehow, during the two years between his "calling" to Phillips Memorial and receiving his Bachelor of Divinity degree, he had managed to perform his full-time ministerial duties, court and marry Loretta, and still carry a full load of seven courses each semester, receiving grades ranging from 80 to 95, most in the 90s.

He wrote his final thesis on "The Baptist Tradition and Community Needs." It has a very ecumenical overtone, stating that "the desire to keep the denominational flag flying has resulted in unwise competition between churches." Concerned, especially, that immersion should be voluntary, not demanded, as a prerequisite for membership in the Baptist church, Frank outlines a program for making the church central to the community. In it he acknowledges that the pastor has to proceed slowly in making changes, but he envisions a church that would reflect the unique nature and population of each community and have meaning for its members in their daily lives, not just on Sundays. "If people feel confidence in a pastor's teachings, they will know he is trying to lead them to even greener pastures than they now occupy. He will be careful, of course, to enlarge his teaching into the ideal at first, before narrowing it down to the specific." In a concluding sentence near the end of his 27-page thesis, Frank asserts: "A nation which is becoming 'community minded' needs a guiding influence which only the Christian Church can give."

† † †

Commencement exercises began[3] on Sunday, June 2, 1940 with President Everett Herrick giving the Baccalaureate sermon, "The Unseen Column," at the First Baptist Church, Newton Center, Massachusetts.

Tuesday, Alumni Day, was "bright and clear with a gentle cooling breeze," pleasant for the talks they heard in the morning, and the luncheon served in Assembly Hall. The afternoon was filled with class reunions and a supper in the Commons. But for the graduating class, Wednesday was the big day, and it was hot—"a blazing sun and sultry air"—as faculty, alumni and members of the Senior Class gathered at Colby Hall for the processional to the First Baptist Church

[3] All information regarding the commencement weekend is from the Andover Newton publication reviewing that event.

where President Herrick and Dean Dabney conferred degrees on forty-four candidates. This was followed by an address to the graduating class given by Winfred N. Donovan, Professor of Biblical Interpretation, Old Testament.

Throughout his final year, there had been reminders that war in Europe had become inevitable, and rising fears that the U.S. would soon be drawn in. Professor Donovan opened his talk to the graduates with a reference to the Nazi war machine. All knew that if we entered the war, some graduates of Andover Newton would certainly participate as Chaplains; Frank, a pacifist, would not be among them. Donovan's anti-war message was very much in tune with Frank's own personal beliefs.

> There are many grounds for considering this the darkest, most tragic hour since the calendar has carried the words *Anno Domini*. Do not ascribe that darkness merely to the smooth running of the Nazi machine. The awful feature is that the use of mechanized destruction is not peculiar to any nation. All over the earth reigns the war madness; and war is the antithesis of the spirit of Christ. We abhor the Nazi war machine; but ...the massacre of innocent children is no more Christian if the explosives are made in the U.S.A. than if they bear the swastika emblem.
>
> Yet war is not the most terrible evil, horrible as it may be. Worse are the breaches of moral order that occasion wars. Back of war lies ruthless selfishness. No nation is today without fault, certainly not our own....The tragedy is that all nations, whether at war or not, are frantically seeking

to pile up material resources and make physical force the deciding factor, the arbiter of ethical issues....

These are days that may be turning points for centuries for civilization and Christianity. The two are not identical; but neither can be destroyed by mere force. Yet the course of both may be changed by the passions of our time. At such a parting of the ways are we ministers of Christ thinking in terms of money, munitions, might, or in the language of justice, service, even to suffering as our Master served and suffered? We may have very hard thinking to do....

To be a minister of Christ...is living with a sense of the eternal God, creative, orderly, purposive, and communicating His purpose to men....God is ever breaking through into human life and thought to disclose His purposes and using us to make known a message which is not of our production, but is given to us....You have felt this call laid upon you. You feel the impact of the necessity to communicate. But may we all refresh and renew our convictions as we stand together in this solemn moment before our paths diverge...

Let us expose ourselves to the Scripture, expose ourselves to the pervasive influence of the consciousness of God's presence and purpose in daily life....Amid all the din and horror of the world in your graduation year may you miss no note of the trumpet that shall never call retreat, sounded by the Christ who counted not His life dear if He might fulfill the purpose for which He came into the world.

I give you the greeting of the ancient church, "The Lord be with you and with your spirit in all your ways!"

† † †

On June 21' 1940, two weeks after his graduation from Andover Newton, Frank's ordination to the Christian Ministry took place at a 7 p.m. service at Phillips Memorial.

The church was filled past the rows of seats, back to the doors, for what was an impressive ceremony. Present were not only church members but a whole array of prominent persons eager to participate and to observe. The Rev. Everett C. Herrick, president of Andover Newton, delivered the ordination sermon; the Rev. Arthur W. Cleaves, pastor of First Baptist, Providence, performed the act of ordination and gave the ordination prayer; and the Rev. Charles N. Arbuckle, pastor of the First Baptist Church, Newton, Massachusetts, gave the charge to the new minister. The service opened with an organ prelude, "Sonata in A-minor" by Rheinberger, and a full choir, under the direction of Floriman Hathaway, sang during the service. It is believed that the photo found in Frank's files was taken at this time.

In the June 22nd article in the *Providence Evening Bulletin* describing the occasion, it noted:[4]

> During his pastorate 145 new members have been added, double services inaugurated, the church redecorated and refitted with repainting and repairing, a new chancel and fixtures installed, and a new pulpit and drapes provided. The grounds have also been landscaped with new walks and lawns. Mrs. Laura Spooner recently gave to the church a hand-carved communion table with marble top, in memory of her husband, Deacon B. Franklin Spooner. The church school now requires the use of the parsonage for intermediates, the enrollment being 450, with an average attendance of over 300.
>
> The 40th anniversary of the founding of the church is being celebrated in conjunction with this ordination service.

In his "Ordination paper for RI Council," presumably submitted prior to his ordination, Frank clearly sets out the faith and feelings of inadequacy that later drove his sermons and his life. And despite the sermon, quoted earlier, that rather justified "evil," here he expresses his doubts:

> I must hasten to say that I have not solved the problem of evil to my own satisfaction as yet. It

---

[4] *Evening Bulletin*, 6/22 & 6/24/1940. The earlier article was accompanied by several pictures.

seems to me that I need not lessen the reality and adequacy of God to say that he is self-limited. ...This self-imposed limitation of God's is at once my greatest opportunity and my deepest regret, for were God utterly omnipotent in the traditional sense of the word, I would have nothing to do but walk the grooves His Absoluteness had decreed. But in the true sense of the word, I am the son of a Heavenly Father, a Father whose heart I must have many times broken, who suffers that most poignant of all pains, the pain from parental impotency in the face of childish waywardness.

...His patience that should long since have run short were He man and Not God; His Love passes understanding. And yet co-equal with this Love, or perhaps as an integral part of it, there is suffering....It is this duality of sorrow and Love that forever calls forth our best and frightens us from ever relaxing until Hell itself shall be emptied of its victims....

When I realize that God's plan rests upon man's initiative, I wonder if there might not have been a better way, and then I am challenged again with the opportunity that is mine to help God and to share the travail of progress with him....

I believe that the historical Jesus grew to manhood under the influence of a strange and powerful sense of destiny...He pulled God into the range of human understanding and he lifted humanity to the point where it could view God. He was the physical manifestation of the eternal Love and compassion of God....

...I believe that the church holds the one

answer to the world chaos today, and if it can keep from capitulating as it did 25 years ago, it will yet have the opportunity to transcribe God's remedy for this world chaos....I bring this paper to a close with the assurance that God is our hope for every phase of life....

[*As he states again in one of his sermons, he states here*] I feel without hesitation that the ministry is at once the most blessed and the most tragic profession in the world. Most blessed because it gives us an opportunity to work with God's good people wherever we are,...most tragic in that we are human and through the frailties of human nature we see God's purposes distorted and perverted. I feel that the days ahead are to be the most heart rendering days of tragedy that the ministry has ever seen [WWII imminent], and yet I wouldn't change places with anyone else of any time or profession, for I expect to see God active in History again in my lifetime.

† † †

Tied to Frank's opposition to the impending war was his strong belief that the country's growing militarism was undermining liberalism, especially religious liberalism, and accordingly devoted a whole sermon to "The Retreat of Liberalism."

This is a day of strategic retreats in the battle areas of the world. What may appear to reporters one day as a complete rout, or tragic defeat may turn out the next day to have been but a strategic retreat to gain time, or to draw the enemy out, or to play possum. But in other areas of life there are failures

> and moments that are not preludes to great advances; they are retreats that are nothing short of disastrous to future hopes and possibilities of true and lasting progress.

After discussing political and economic retreats, Frank turns to religion's retreat from liberalism to fundamentalism; refers to the great world conferences in 1937 and 1938 in Oxford, Edinburgh and Madras where a true ecumenical church seemed near reality. But then, he notes:

> Man did not have time or energy or desire to pioneer in the spiritual while continents were being consumed in global conflagrations. So there came the inevitable retreat of liberalism. Folks flocked to the reactionary type of mystical escapism....Failing to find faith adequate to solve the dilemmas of the confused old world, we withdraw and find faith enough to drown out the cry for progress....
>
> Well, to a certain degree I am in sympathy with them. We liberals have failed to mix religion and life–not because we tried to modernize religion, but because we were satisfied merely to modernize its clothing without changing the inner man...
>
> Today, fundamentalism's escapists have caused splits in several denominations, and have stymied for a time the movement toward world religious unity. In our Baptist denomination, for instance, the fundamentalists have split many churches over such apparently little things as the wording of creeds. They are breaking every tenant of Roger Williams' great doctrine of soul liberty by demanding that their members sign a creed....

Today the fundamentalists have five major grievances with those who call themselves liberals. They demand, first, that all sign creeds...; second, the Virgin Birth of Jesus; third, the blood atonement; fourth, the physical resurrection of the body; and fifth, the second coming of Christ....We, the so-called liberals (though it seems strange for me to brand myself a liberal, in Seminary I was known as a rank conservative) we, I say, do not disbelieve the spiritual implication of a single one of these five teachings. We merely object to being forced to say that we believe that ancient words and terminologies are adequate to express dynamic, forceful on-going movements of life.

Now, if you go out from here saying that the pastor is a rank liberal with no fundamental beliefs, you will have completely missed the point. If you go out and forget this sermon, you will disappoint me terribly. But if you go out and say, "This tide must be turned, this volcano of conservative reaction must be stopped," we will build philosophies that can fly right over the lava flow of destruction and locate new lands of hope and opportunity.

† † †

The Thompsons offered a welcoming home to this writer, then in high school. Unhappy at my own home and befuddled about my religious beliefs and the value of church, they were good listeners. I still recall the time I spent a whole day with Loretta; gave her a home permanent; and, for the first time, ate popovers she made for lunch, oddly fascinated by them. And I remember her urging me to consider the church as the place to nourish the mind and grope with issues together, just as the bakery was the place you went to buy bread [*once upon a time*].

Feeling it would be helpful, Loretta urged me to read biographies of famous people, and to read books like *The Magnificent Obsession* (playboy turned surgeon cures woman of blindness he caused), *The Keys to the Kingdom* (life of 19th Century Scottish priest in China), *The Robe* (in Roman times, concerning Christ's robe, at time of crucifixion), *The Big Fisherman* (based on story of loaves and fishes), and C. S. Lewis' *The Screwtape Letters: A Devil's Diabolical Advice for the Capturing of the Human Heart* (a fascinating series of letters from Screwtape, an important Under Secretary in Hell, to his nephew, an imp, assigned to negotiate a young man "patient" into the infernal regions).[5] I was intrigued by *all* these books, and those she recommended by Pearl Buck, ironically, made me want to become a missionary in China, even as my doubts about the honesty and value of religion and of the institutional church continued.

Many of these books, no doubt, were ones read in the Book Club Loretta started. According to Virginia Droitcor, a member, she had told them: "I didn't want my mind to stagnate." Perhaps only slightly exaggerating, "The only time I have to read is while washing the dishes, my book propped up on the windowsill."

Though the Thompsons never entirely appeased my doubts about religion, there is no doubt that their influence, and especially Frank's, made a lasting impact on my life, shaped my belief in non-violence, my interest in government policies and foreign affairs, and inspired my life-long concern for the dysfunctional and disenfranchised in our

---

[5] Lewis was an Oxford scholar who actually believed in a Heaven and Hell.

society–juvenile delinquents and prisoners, minorities, the poor, the homeless, and abused women and children– all issues that were of concern to Frank and about which he preached.

And Frank's concern extended beyond just preaching. His half-sister, Mary Jo, recalled that there were times when Loretta would ask Frank for money for groceries or whatever and he would tell her that he didn't have any– because the young couple whom he'd just married, or someone who had come into the church, needed it more than they did. Scott, in future years, called his father "an altruistic and idealistic educator and conscientious objector who never saved a cent and often did give people in need the shirt off his back."[6]

Shirley Gallup is another who talked to this writer about Frank's influence on her; about how his sermons inspired her. After high school she'd gone to Brown University with the intention of being a Math teacher, but, in her words, "he inspired me to become a doctor" and "to face the challenge of being a member of the first class at Harvard Medical School that included women." After Frank had left Phillips for Bacone, he was always hoping that some of the church's young people would join him there after they completed their training. But as far as this writer could determine, none did, though many served in ways Frank would have approved. Shirley, for instance, after becoming a psychiatrist, quit private practice and did what she regarded as "a sort of missionary work"–she went to work at the state hospital where they badly needed good doctors. She was still in medical school in 1948 when Frank left Phillips. In the case of this writer, she had intended, after graduation from

---

[6] Scott, *Price of Achievement*, p. 117.

Brown University in 1950, going to work in the Murrow Orphanage associated with Bacone, but got married instead.

There was one member of Phillips who did join Frank at Bacone. After her husband died, around 1953 or 1954, Mildred Holberg, lonely and bored, came to Bacone as Frank's secretary.

† † †

At the beginning of 1941, on January 12th, Frank's whole sermon revolved around Roger Williams, whom he clearly admired and often referred to in his sermons. He began with a lengthy historical account of Williams, in England, in Boston, and finally in Rhode Island. Midway through, he begins to recount the three lessons he believes Roger Williams would teach us today: "Briefly, first, the lesson of the infinite worth of the individual. Second, the need for absolute separation between church and state, and third, the tremendous truth that the church must be the training ground for the soul of men." Frank then deals with each of these at length. But of the third, he states that Roger Williams "set up Rhode Island as a little experiment in the midst of a lot of chaos to see if he couldn't work a Christian brotherhood here...."

> When Rhode Island grew popular and began to be a little stronger, the other colonies wanted to take her back, but Roger Willliams said, "No, I will stay with my Christian savages rather than come back to savage Christians." I think we can find some savage Christians and some Christian savages today. The church should ever be the place for the training ground of the soul, the place where reconciliation can be brought about.

> We have a beautiful cross in our church. It does not look like the old cross from which it gets its symbol. The cross stands for reconciliation, it stands for sacrifices. In each of us dwells forgiveness, forgiving love will be that cross's symbol and forgiveness and forgiveness again and again. It will be that willingness to sacrifice itself if need be, that Jesus may come and live and reign.

As was so typical, Frank concludes this sermon with a challenge to his parishioners: "You and I will decide whether our cross will or will not shine brightly against a dark background in proportion to the way we let that cross affect our lives and our inner being now.

On February 2, 1941, Frank preached a sermon titled "Hitching Your Wagon To a Star," derived, he says, from a quote by "the great essayist," Ralph Waldo Emerson: "If thou woulds't attain a good life, hitch thy wagon to a star." After discussing something of the conflict between good and evil, he asserts that "Good is what we make of it with our habits, our experiences, our lives."

> ...The psychologist says one of the most important things in the acquiring of a new habit is to START....Without that important START, breaking of the old inertia which holds us where we are, we never do acquire the habits that will lead us toward the good life.

Frank then recounts a wonderful adventure of his own, beginning with the question: "Have any of you ever gone into any particularly cold water?"

> Three years ago on New Year's Day some of us decided we wanted to be able to say we had

> broken the ice and gone in swimming. There was not much ice, but a little ice or much, it is just as cold. We broke in the edges of the ice around the pond but did not go in by degrees. We did not wet our toes, our knees, and then a little more and more. We took a big breath and went in all over and it wasn't so bad. It left us with a glow, a thrilling feeling after we got out of it....
>
> It would do good to start where you are. Don't wait until that day when high resolutions are reached to a certain point before you start to help God carry on his work....We never become anything by waiting....

"The next thing is to put ourselves on a train," Frank says, and he then alludes to both drinking and war as examples:

> We might use those who are drink addicts, those who are called liquor fiends, or drink fiends, getting to a certain point where they are really serious about curing themselves and finally go and get on a train that is going to some distant sanatorium ...where they are kept away from the drink; in fact, they get into new habits when they are not given any of the things which are harmful to them. That is putting themselves on a train and so start a chain of events.
>
> If you would start the good life put yourself on a train so you cannot help but follow each good event with another....Avoid testing your strength. Don't go near saloons, night clubs or other things dangerous. I think mine is second hand book stores [or athletic stores]. I don't dare go into one, the

> family will suffer. They cannot eat books or good-looking athletic equipment.
>
> Be careful of the first step in the wrong direction. This applies to individuals, nations, institutions....The overwhelming majorities that are undoubtedly against the involvement of the United States into this war does not mean we will stay out. When we are involved in this war our young men will pay for the first step for those who wanted to involve us for other reasons. When we start it is hard to stop.
>
> We cannot live in a high tower. We cannot shut ourselves away from the world and say, "I will live a good life, I will be an isolationist." We do not get very far with this, we must be out in the world...The main thing is to have an ambition that will carry you above petty things. Aim high, let your grasp out soar your reach if you will be worthy of the name of man....
>
> Let's put ourselves on a train by hitching our wagon to a star and aiming for that high place where Christ would have us, where Paul beckons us. Except your religion exceed your righteousness and you aim higher, it will do you little good.

It's uncanny that Frank would himself eventually fall prey to the addiction he so opposed in his early years. His opposition to drinking is apparent in a number of his sermons and in 1945-46 he participated with a Cranston church group that had united to fight against a move by the City Council to liberalize restrictions on drinking in dine-and-dance places.

An *Evening Bulletin* article states, in part:[7]

> Six of the city's 31 Class B liquor license holders signed a petition announcing they were under a handicap competing with Warwick, Johnston and Providence cafes where professional entertainers and public dancing are allowed.
>
> Mr. Thompson said he visited Mayor Hoyt W. Lark yesterday and made known his objections to any move to permit dine and dance places in Cranston.
>
> "The city," he said, "is residential and such places have a bad influence...."

The article continues, quoting Frank at some length. Another article, hand-dated January 1946, indicates that a "Citizen's Committee," opposing any change in the current law, had submitted a petition to the City Council signed by American Legion, the Cranston High PTA and hundreds of residents. Frank held a public forum at Phillips Memorial and a delegation from the Church planned to attend the Council hearing urging Council member to deny the liquor establishments' request.

Frank's discussion of the issue in a sermon on March 31, 1946 suggests that the opposition was successful, but that the road-houses were ready to simply defy the law. Frank said:

> I heard through the grape-vine this week that some city officials are asking if the churches are quieted down enough so that the road-houses on the outskirts of our city may go back to their unlicensed,

---

[7] The exact date on the clipping found amongst Frank's papers is not included.

> illegal dining, dancing and drinking in their saloons. Well, who's going to keep everlastingly aware of these moral conditions and have considerations for the moral standards of our city if it's not the Christian church? I hope the Christian church is going to do something about the leprous growth of filthy literature, salacious magazines and disgustingly dirty plays and movies. Before long, I hope we're going to do something before some good old-fashioned virtues have been forgotten.
>
> If your church is a church of Christ, it's not only helping the blind to see and the lame to walk, but it's cleansing the leper.

It's unclear whether *this* Citizen's Committee is the same as that recalled by Lucille, her mother as it's head, or if there had been an earlier similar fight in the late 30s, when the issue was outlawing alcohol sales in Cranston. She recounts that over 100 lawyers, ministers and others were part of the committee, and that her mother went door-to-door, helping to collect the signatures that put the issue on the ballot. Lucille also noted that her mother was not treated very nicely, having forgotten that the big Narragansett Brewery Company was located in Cranston.

† † †

Frank's sermon called "Busting Out All Over," like many others, stressed the obligation of Christians to help the poor, and to combat prejudice, issues still of concern today. He believed that the church had the solution.

> It's the Christian church that has the message of hope in a day of despair for the poor. To the destitute share-croppers of the south the Christian

> church is shouting "Hold on, fellow men, the Christian church is coming." The conscience of America is awakening.

Earlier in the sermon Frank declared the world blind to existing prejudice, and asks: "What other groups of the world [other than the church] are trying to break down the prison wall of prejudice that separates race and classes, creeds and colors?" Though acknowledging that the church is not doing enough, Frank then asks: "Can you name any institution that is doing as much as the Christian church?" [It's ironic he should even ask the question of an institution known as the most segregated in the world on Sunday mornings. *If they're doing the most, what does this say of the rest?*]

† † †

In his sermon, "Flag Sitters," Frank exhibits his gift that endeared him to so many (including this writer)–a gift for making the Bible, religion itself, relevant to the everyday issues that are still with us–poverty, peace, crime, bureaucrats, political corruption, selfishness, love. Unfortunately, the written word cannot begin to convey his other endearing gift–a charismatic personality and a deep, resonant voice that gave his words a special penetrating power.

This sermon begins with a reminder of the flagpole sitters of a few years back: "men with strange penchants for high places would sit on top of flag poles for 29, 30 days. Finally, Shipwreck Kelley became champion by sitting up there for 50 days in a row." Frank continues his sermon by alluding to a poem by Tennyson.

> Years before that craze hit America, Lord Tennyson wrote a poem about a flag pole sitter which he called St. Simeon Stylites, a self-styled martyr. He

wanted to do something great so that he could be called a s saint. For many weeks he wore about his wrist a rope so tight that it caused a great ulcerous sore; but that wasn't glorious enough so he lived high up on a mountain for three years with his leg chained to a crag, drinking the dews and depending on handouts from occasional visitors for food. But that still wasn't enough, so finally he devised the method of living high up on a pillar, year in and year out, until the world would recognize him as the saint he thought he was. [Frank continues by quoting Tennyson's poem.]

> Am I to blame for this, that here come those
> that worship me?
> They take me for a saint,
> Some bring me offerings of fruit and flowers;
> And I, in truth–thou wilt bear witness here–
> Have all in all endured as much, and more
> Than many just and holy men, Whose names
> Are registered and calendar'd for saints.
>
> God only through his bounty hath thought fit,
> Among the powers and princes of this world,
> To make me an example to mankind,
> Which few can reach to.

Well [Frank says], Shipwreck Kelley was up there for 50 days, but St. Simeon was up there on his tower for 32 years; up away from all the evil of the world, away from temptations which bedevil the ordinary man. At last he thought he was a saint because people came see him, and some even fell down to worship him.

Frank goes on to declare that withdrawal is not part of the religion of Jesus. "He was one with the people; he was their champion, their comforter, their critic and their savior....He had a vision for society, but that vision depended on individuals... ...Jesus was a radical. Old customs, old traditions, old rituals didn't mean a thing to him if they stood in the way of bringing the more abundant life to individuals and society."

Jesus told the people that gifts placed on an altar were not enough, but rather had to be given "because the heart was purified by a passion for righteousness, and a willingness to pay any price for that righteousness to come. A passion that sends one to the altar to complete an act of adoration and worship." Today we see again, Frank says, the tendency to have a flagpole sitters' religion: we seem to believe that victory in war, whatever the cost, will bring us freedom and peace, while continuing to shortchange the task of real peace which must include feeding the hungry; uplifting the poor.

In another sermon Frank explored the question, "What is Religion?" In noting the five necessary characteristics for it to be "real," Frank is giving us the five pillars of his own faith.

1. Enhancement--lift life up; give it altitude, crescendo. Exalt life. Intensify its worth.

2. Enthusiasm--betting your life there is a God and you really believe you can find His will for your life.

3. Vision--vision of real service; the kind that interests people and changes lives.

4. Freedom--believing in a universal God and worldwide brotherhood. He created us all, and therefore we are all his.

5.-Community-Building--spreading the fellowship; passing on the enthusiasm which we have. Seeing all people enhanced with the maximum that life can

> bring them. A passion for spreading, never stopping, never turning aside until all have gotten the opportunity to realize the most of religious reality.

† † †

The Thompsons liked to vacation in Maine and it was there that Frank found the inspiration for his sermon, "Expanding Circles of Growth." He was in Mr. Stuart's cabin on his lake, looking for the formula for successfully landing a fish. It was then that he came upon "a large map of that area of Maine" nailed to the reverse side of a door. "On that map were a series of circles–concentric circles–with their center at the camp. The first circle took in the camp and pier and some woods, the second circle took in the camp, lake and several other camps."

> Suddenly I realized THAT'S A MAP OF LIFE. GROWTH BEGINS FROM WITHIN. The center is given, its right here, but where the outermost circumference is depends on us and our growth. Growth starts from the center–the kernel of life–going outward, taking in wider expanses in a series of concentric circles, each taking in new areas of activity, and new attitudes of expression.
>
> So the first consideration I would call you to make is THE LARGER THE CIRCLES OF OUTWARD EXPANSION, THE RICHER THE EXPERIENCES OF INNER EXISTENCE....
>
> Let us assume that all can draw that first circle around self; now move on to wider circles. Most everyone can draw a circle around family, and say each is as dear as my own life. But now the circles spread outward and the number who can truthfully INCLUDE ALL WITHIN decreases.

160. Justice, Peace & God

Frank suggests that as we go from neighborhood, to business associates, to office and shop employees, to those of different political positions, those with different accents, different color, different race, from different states, different nations, different economic classes, the numbers of us able to draw circles that include these groups gets smaller and smaller. But this shouldn't be so, he insists. Here, as in so many of his sermons, *inclusiveness* is insisted upon as an integral part of religion [Matt: 43-48]. Near the end of the sermon Frank states:

> It is not by chance Christ, at the very center of his teaching, told the story of the poor despised foreigner of a different colored skin who performed an act of mercy that threw the searchlight of scorn on the institutionalized religionists of his day. The poor Samaritan, rejected and despised by his fellow men, becomes the good Samaritan of eternal example to the compassionate. [Luke 10:30-37]
>
> It's not by chance that the climax of Christ's earthly life comes there on that mountain where he lifts his arms and makes a circle around the world, "Go, make disciples of All, Everywhere."...
>
> When we draw those circles out here beyond the natural horizon, we begin to call in the very essence of God's strength and help.

† † †

In recent interviews with this writer, the first thing remembered about Frank by several of his parishioners was Frank's "fantastic memory." As one of them explained, "I was so impressed that Mr. T (as most everyone then called him) never (or rarely) read the scripture [a passage from the

Bible being an integral part of every service], but each week *recited* the scripture FROM MEMORY!" "Verbatim, without notes," said another. "An amazing feat!" One of those occasions, most likely, was a recitation of the above-noted cites from Matthew and Luke to introduce that sermon. He might well also have concluded that sermon with one of his prayers:

> O God we invoke they blessing upon all who need Thee, and who are groping after Thee...Brood in tenderness over the hearts of the anxious, the miserable, the victims of phantasmal fear and morbid imaginings. Redeem from slavery the men and women who have yielded to degrading habits. Put Thy spirit within them that they may rise up in shame and sorrow and make confession of their brutish and ignorant nature. Let all have the glad assurance that Thou art with them...Console with Thy large consolation those who mourn for their loved dead...Inspire them with the firm conviction that the dead are safe in Thy keeping, nay, that they live unto Thee....Teach us all that Thy hand is on the helm of affairs, though unseen and unfelt at times. In the faith that all nights of sorrow and suffering and mysterious uncertainty shall be turned to the golden sunshine of day in time, we pray.

As with most ministers, Frank shook hands and greeted his congregants as they left the church, but in his case, perhaps unlike most, there are again memories of his "fantastic memory"–how he greeted everyone by name, asked about their families–and even remembered them years later when he returned to Phillips Memorial as a guest.

10. A Lifelong Pacifist

"Back of war lies ruthless selfishness...The tragedy is that all nations are frantically seeking to pile up material resources and make physical force the deciding factor, the arbiter of ethical issues."[1]

"We who are Pacifists wish some people would stop mixing up the two words 'pacifist' and 'passive.' Pacifist comes from two Latin words, pax and facio, and it means peacemaker. It is a positive word, being true to which involves all the strong, intelligent, morally combative faculties we have. Passive, however, comes from another Latin word altogether, patior, passus sum, meaning to suffer, to submit. These two words have no kinship! They are poles asunder."[2]

† † †

The drumbeat of war and its aftermath haunted Frank's time at Phillips Memorial–challenged his commitment to pacifism–but he never wavered. Not surprisingly many of his sermons reflect these times and will be emphasized here, but remember this was never his exclusive concern.

September 1, 1939, Germany invaded Poland, ending appeasement policies and leading to a full-scale war.

December 7, 1941, Japan struck an unprepared U.S. at Pearl Harbor: Germany's declaration of war against the U.S. followed soon after.

May 7, 1945, Germany surrendered.

---

[1] From the address to Frank's graduating class from Andover Newton. A message that resonated with Frank all his life.

[2] Frank is quoting Dr. Harry Emerson Fosdick, pastor of Riverside Church in New York from 1929-1946.

163. A Lifelong Pacifist

August 6, 1945, U.S. dropped the first atomic bomb on Hiroshima; on August 9, the second on Nagasaki.

August 14, 1945, Japan surrendered.

It is estimated that over 50 million men, women and children died in WWII, most of them civilians, many of them Jews who were killed in Germany's crematoria.

† † †

In an undated sermon but before Pearl Harbor, Frank offered this warning of impending war, and of the propaganda machine that goes to work to convince the public of its need, but the drumbeat of war was too great for the opponents to be heard:

> It won't, it can't, be long before we will be faced with the direct alternative of war again. Already the subtle propaganda is starting in newspapers, theaters and radio. Already we have forgotten the pledges to peace that were made a few years ago [at the end of WWI], but all I ask is that we study authoritative sources to find out as much of the truth of the world situation as we can. Newspapers and sensationalist weeklies can only confuse us.
>
> Jesus said, "Know the truth and the truth shall make you free," and though it is all too hard to learn the truth, still that truth can be found. Jesus found it even though it cost him his life. The truth is still the hardest thing to accept, but those who stand upon the brink of another world catastrophe can well afford to search diligently and to remember that "Where there is no vision, the people perish!"

164. Justice, Peace & God

You young women who stand ready to lose your loved ones and yourselves, study the facts, learn the truth, then go to the polls and make your voice heard above the cheap ballyhoo of the war mongers. At the Century of Progress [an exhibit in Chicago], we learned that black man and yellow, white man and red, could live together and be happy and proud of each other. Today, reactionary bullies of Italy, Germany and Japan are forming alliances, not of friendship, but of fear, and you and I must answer them. Are we to answer them in the old-time war-way of a blow for a blow, destruction of all that is beautiful, or shall we say to them, we have found a new way—a new way that is 2000 years old, the way "the Prince of Peace" taught us. No one can hurt the part of us that really counts if we have found the truth; though they take our lives, still will that truth eventually win, and mankind will progress.

† † †

Frank pasted in a scrapbook a clipping from an unnamed newspaper, dated only May 25, no year, perhaps 1942. The headline reads, "Baptists Adopt Stand on War."

The Northern Baptist Convention in session here today adopted a resolution expressing its attitude toward the war.

The resolution says: "We do not pray for man's mere triumph over his fellow man, but God has a stake in the war and we dare not wait until we achieve perfection before we rise to defend freedom and to battle for a righteous cause. We do pray that justice shall prevail, that human personality shall not

> be sacrificed upon any altar of dictatorship, and that freedom shall win over tyranny.
>
> "We do pray that men do not lose their souls; that in all our seeking we shall seek no good we would not share with friend and foe alike; that our sons may be adequate for their high hour and that we with them shall bring even that last full measure to win the war and to achieve Christian ideals in the peacetime relations of the peoples of the earth.
>
> "We will not bless war, but we will not withhold our blessing from our sons who fight and from our country's cause in which they and the sons of the allied nations now engage.

† † †

When asked by a reporter, along with a number of others, what he thought about the war with Japan, Frank is quoted as saying:[3]

> War was almost certain to come sooner or later. Evil always begets evil, and the whole international scene has been so clouded with injustice and corruption that the outbreak of war was only a matter of time. Nevertheless, we are shocked and saddened with it suddenness and horror. The one ray of hope I, as a minister of God, see is that this war will be so globular in its extent and so all-inclusive in its terrible effects that all men will rise up and demand that God's ways shall be tried for a change."

This was, indeed, his hope, expressed time and again

[3] From a clipping in Frank's scrapbook, paper and date not given.

in his sermons, but were we listening?

† † †

On September 24, 1939,[4] shortly after Germany's invasion of Poland, Frank preaches on "Re-Union in Hell," making a number of references to Hitler and Stalin and the dangers of seeking power.

> ...Of all the disgusting things, one is to hear someone say he must make friends with a certain person for someday that person will have power and be able to help him. That is the horror of totalitarianism—from childhood up, the youth of a total state are taught that they count for nothing themselves. It is only as they are able to serve the state—the symbol of power—that they are useful...
>
> What a foolish goal these builders of power have, and how ridiculous they will look as they take their place in hell to await the judgement with others. What an interesting conversation will be that between Hitler and Kaiser Wilhelm, and Napoleon and others. But remember power as a goal is not limited to dictators and despots. How many are there in homes, homes that look strong and sturdy from the outside; lives that appear well tailored and seem headed in the right direction and yet within is that frustration and struggle that comes from a longing for power and glory and self-aggrandizement.
>
> Remember the world powers may fall, the super structures of today will crumble, but life will not cease, and Christ will not die, and after the

---

[4] The dates written on sermons that have dates do not always coincide with a Sunday, so may be the date written rather than the date delivered.

> smoke has cleared away and the shouts have ceased, there will be opportunity once more to build, and though all the fine cathedrals have fallen and the paintings have been ruined and libraries destroyed, there will still be in humans that love God and desire to interpret him again. These four words will form the substitutes for the present temporary word POWER; they are truth, beauty, love and Christ.

Frank ends the sermon with quotes from the Bible: Isaiah 35, 42, 43 and 61. From the latter:

> And they shall build the old wastes, they shall raise up the former desolations, and they shall repair the waste cities, the desolations of many generations.

† † †

Not everyone was pleased by Frank's objections to the War and his urging young people not to enlist; instead to seek conscientious objector's status. For example, Louise Anthony Green, who praised Frank in most respects, who admitted to having had a crush on him, and being jealous of Loretta, as were so many others, nevertheless had this to say of his stance on the war.

> Only one thing bad I can remember about him. My father was very patriotic. Overseas in WWI, very active in the American Legion; my mother too. And all their friends were service people. Patriotism was a big thing with them. So when Mr. Thompson talked against the war, my father wasn't too pleased. He got kind of upset with some of the things he said. Nobody likes wars, but somebody has to fight them. We'd be in a terrible mess if everyone said they didn't believe in wars.

168. Justice, Peace & God

Another parishioner, Lucille Spooner Votta, who graduated as a nurse from Rhode Island Hospital in February 1944, recently recalled how Frank had tried to persuade her to continue in school rather than joining the Army, but eventually she joined.

Nonetheless, Frank remained consistent in his opposition to draft laws, and to new laws regarding conscription that were being considered in 1947. In one sermon he referred to conscription as totalitarian. He said:

> I believe it is especially insidious because it gives a false sense of security. Pass that law, send youth off to camp and then let democracy rot and tragedy reign because we are so secure. And it is those times that the dread enemy of Bolshevism will walk right in. J. Edgar Hoover has put it so well when he says that the only real alternative to Bolshevism is a strong democracy and a strong democracy begins in your street and mine; in your heart and mine.

Despite Frank's strongly held anti-war sentiments, he was such a caring person, said Virginia Droitcor in a recent interview, that when he read in the paper that her brother had been killed in action, he immediately came over to see her. Virginia was especially impressed because she'd only recently moved to Eden Park and joined Phillips Memorial. Now in her 90s, still active and spry, and still attending Phillips Memorial, this was the first thing she recalled about Frank as we talked. But soon, she also added, "He was a marvelous speaker, not only at Phillips Memorial, but was much sought after by other churches and organizations."

† † †

169. A Lifelong Pacifist

On September 9, 1940, the Thompsons welcomed a new addition to their household, Sara Sue, and around this same time Frank's half-sister, Paula, a successful business woman in San Diego, became ill. Frank's mother, Olga, who'd been living with them for some time, left to care for Paula. Paula recovered but Olga was never able to return to Cranston, because soon after she came down with an attack of pneumonia. Her son Ford, who was a vocational education teacher in Gilbert, Arizona, brought her to his home, hoping the Arizona sun would restore her to health. But "all that loving hands could do was of no avail and she passed peacefully away [on March 3, 1942, just 60 years old], with but one request: that her son Francis preach her funeral service, and he came from Cranston, R. I. and paid her a touching and beautiful farewell."[5]

Lewis & his wife, Marie, with Judy & Linda about 1943

She was survived by her six children, all of whom attended her funeral with the exception of Lewis, who was unable to come from his home in San Francisco [his absence not surprising, since even though Lewis and Frank kept in touch, Lewis had barely seen his mother since his early childhood]. Olga's half sister, Mrs. Flora Willard Mason, of

---

[5] Obituary for Olga Willard Gano, *Prescott Evening Courier*, 3/11/1942, written by Frances Willard Munds.

Maywood, California and her two brothers, Lewis and Alex of Big Park, also were unable to attend. Her sister, Mrs. Edna Willard Nichols, attended with friends from Prescott." Olga was buried in Mesa Maricopa County, Arizona.

The Thompson's second child, Willard Scott (called by all, at the time, "Woody," later Scott), was born January 1, 1942, barely two months old at the time of Olga's death.

Frank's mother, always proud of her son who had become a preacher, would have appreciated his immediate return to preaching. In this undated sermon directed at young people, Frank is less concerned about the war per se than the clamoring for power. He ends this sermon this way:

> When will we learn that all this striving for power will never get us progressively ahead. Shouldn't this present world tragedy prove to us once and for all that power is not the answer to the riddle of life. How easy it seems for the nations to unite for power, but so hard to unite for peace. It's time we stopped trying to gain and hold all power ourselves. It's time we started sharing with each other, and being willing to submerge ourselves; to run some interference for the world. When I think of the power Christ Jesus might have used, and yet he took the unlovely, yes, the horrible way of the cross, but by that fact he became the most powerful figure in the universe—he became my savior. He poured out his blood for me, and by the shedding of that blood I have been freed from the bonds of sin—my place was taken by him, he ran interference for me.

In keeping with Frank's assertion that it seems so much easier for nations to unite for power than for peace, he had this to say in his sermon, "When God Uses Us," dated May 15, 1940—well before the Japanese attack on the

U.S. at Pearl Harbor, but only a month before France signed an armistice with Germany. After criticizing our callous attitude to the poor in our own country, he turns to the situation in Germany before it started WWII.

> Back there in the twenties when the representatives of Germany's struggling republic sent representatives to the League of Nations and to individual nations telling them their children were starving and the nation was in danger of going Bolshevistic, the people of the world folded their hands and said, "There is nothing we can do about it. If we give you back your colonies so that you can feed your children, you will grow strong and we can't have a strong Germany." And every day those young German men grew more hungry and more desperate and finally a young leader came with a promise of food and a place in the sun–and you know the answer–civilization is being pushed back another century–because we love to argue about problems and haven't vision and courage to believe something can be done about them....
>
> There are those who said, "Well, an international body like a League of Nations would solve all this problem and keep outlaw nations in line." Yes, that is fine, but "No," we don't want to get involved in foreign affairs. We who proposed the League crushed it with our indifference and complacency, and now we are preparing to pay for that attitude with the blood of our youth...
>
> Perhaps you feel there is a small chance to unify our purposes even with so much conflict and chaos in the world. What chance is there now? God is waiting to use some of us to draw the world back to sanity. There have been darker hours in the past. It's

> been right in the very darkest times that God has acted to start the constructive purposes of life going—not that he has sent the dark hours, but because it has only been then that anyone would turn to him—sort of out of desperation they do it.

In an undated sermon, "Youth in Search of Wings," given to a group of youth, Frank returned to this same theme. But first he refers to the fact that with school commencements now over, wings should carry the youth "out of their little worlds into the vast realms of scientific, literary and spiritual expanses." ...He tells them "the two wings that I would wish for you above all other possessions as you go off in search of knowledge and training are these: Imagination, and Faith in a world beyond this world." Frank then refers to what he calls France's "hallucinatory imagination," appalled at what may have saved us from WWII.

> Poor old France and her mistaken imagination. Believing she could find security and peace behind a mighty fortress called the Maginot Line—while her people starved within and intrigue went on. Poor old France today must realize that she was practicing hallucinatory imagination when she thought God could be mocked, his laws broken and her integrity remain. Pierre Van Paassen in his shockingly frank and honest book, *Days of Our Years*, tells of the visit of Herr [Heinrich] Bruening[6] from Germany to France to seek help for the struggling Weimar Republic.
>
> He writes that crowds gathered to see this

---

[6] Bruening was appointed Chancellor by von Hindenburg in 1930; dismissed after only two years, one of a series appointed and dismissed by the then ailing 80+ year old.

man who had ten years before been a bitter enemy. He stepped off the train and with tears in his eyes saluted the people and they broke into tremendous ovations. Next day he went to church for two hours, then before Pierre Laval[7] to plea for help, saying that Germany was starving and that if some help didn't come, some strong leader would rise to lead them into a chaotic cycle of force again. Laval shook his head and ushered him out with cold cruelty. He would not even place Bruening's request for a loan, or a moratorium, before his colleagues in the cabinet. He refused to hold out the least strand of hope. Van Paassen wrote, "It was a sunny day in Paris when Pierre Laval signed the death warrant of the German Republic," and started Hitler on his way to world conquest.

Ah, young people, we live in a universe of laws, and unless we have imagination enough to learn the meaning of laws, it will be too bad for our civilization.

It seems terribly poor use of imagination to find so many young people leaving school to take defense jobs, because money happens to be a little easier to make now. Now is the time to be prepared for the brave new world that must be built out of the ashes of this one....

Creative imagination is faith—facts with wings.

---

[7] Laval was in and out of the French government several times, holding important positions. Initially he was a Socialist, but then a Conservative; increasingly supportive of Nazi Germany as the war progressed. Finally, a ruthless enforcer of their policies after France fell to Germany. After the war he was tried as a traitor, sentenced to death, and after an unsuccessful attempt at suicide, executed.

174. Justice, Peace & God

> In more than one sermon Frank posed the question: "*What would have happened if just a small portion of the same energy and power being leveled out now [against Hitler and Stalin] had been used in programs of construction and love before?*" Then he adds, "If we could once more get the zeal of those early Christians, there would be no worry about what would come to this old world....You see, these early Christians believed enough in Christianity to give their all for it..."

In yet another undated sermon, Frank again raises the question. He quotes two R.A.F. [Royal Air Force] boys as saying: "All our fellows know this war is a bloody wrong, that it came because we had everything, and the jerries had nothing. If it had been the other way around we would have started it."

Later, Frank told of the time when an officer ended his preparation of the men for battle by asking, "Is there anything you fellows would like to have?" Yes, said a large rawboned southerner, "We'd like to see Chappie, and have him say a prayer for us." Chappie was the Chaplain, and from then on an integral part of "briefing" was a last minute word of prayer and a hand clasp from Chappie. Questionnaires have revealed that such preparation is far more important to the fellows than all the heated pep talks possible.

> What might have happened had there been one quadrillionth of such preparation as we make for war were made for a peaceful world? Once and for all we must get clear that the formula for construction is as important as the formula for destruction. PREPARATION FOR L I F E

OUGHT TO BE AS HIGH AND NOBLE A JOB AS PREPARATION FOR DEATH. We have parades and dinners and medals to honor heroes of destruction. What is done for heroes of construction?

† † †

December 7, 1941, Japan attacked the U.S. at Pearl Harbor.

Soon after, Germany declared war on the U.S.

Despite its positive aspect, it pained Frank deeply to hear young men say that the war finally gave them a "a mission in life." In an undated sermon, "Happiness Hunting," he said:

> One of the exciting sights of this terrible hour is to see young men who probably got their first impression of a job or career from the local W.P.A. debacle, going off with their chins up and a spring in their steps because they have someplace to Go. Here's Lieut. Lee writing from Bataan [1942 after fall of Philippines]: "Here at last we have found a mission in life! Something bigger than we are that needs us!" That's wonderful in a way, but what a tragedy that it takes a total war to give young men SOMEPLACE TO GO! For shame on the Christian church! ...

During this sermon, Frank quotes a poem, "Opportunity:"

> Thee do me wrong who say I come no more
> When once I knock and fail to find you in

Each morn I stand beside your fast closed
door
To bid you rise, and fight and win!

Frank earnestly believed that God still lived, and that man's ways were not God's ways and that progress would only come when man learned "to make his ways God's ways....We will crush ourselves if we go on in our sinful ways, our indifference to the needs of man...."

† † †

Frank pasted a clipping in his scrapbook whose headline read: "Roosevelt's Youngest Son Was Conscientious Objector." The sub-headline read: "Story Told of How John Changed Stand for Sake of His Father, After Mother's Night-long Plea; Now He Wears Medal for Heroic Service." Though the clipping is undated and without naming the newspaper, the content states that the story can be told "now that the war is over." It was told by the secretary of the National Service Board for Religious Objectors.

Despite his youngest son's strongly held pacifist beliefs, President Roosevelt felt that for him to declare himself a conscientious objector would set an example that "might jeopardize the draft throughout the nation." His mother, reluctantly, and despite her own pacifist leanings, supported her husband's position as to how it would look if John chose to go to prison or a civilian public service camp rather than serve in the military. John finally gave in, becoming "the first conscientious-objector President's son in the nation's history who went into the armed services." He was drafted on March 13, 1941, commissioned an ensign, and became a lieutenant in

1943. "As supply officer on the carrier Wasp, he was in the thick of the bombing on Okinawa, Leyte and the general Philippines." In fact all four of Roosevelt's sons saw active duty during WWII.

Up to a point, Frank perhaps felt that he shared something with John. He initially refused to register for the draft but one of his parishioners, Lucille Spooner, recently told this writer that her uncle and other deacons talked to Frank and he finally agreed to register. The implication was that otherwise he might have been forced to resign as minister. Of course, unlike John, Frank never was drafted and never served. As a full-time minister he would have been classified "4E," above only "4F," those so classified rarely called. Whether or not Frank also claimed conscientious objector status is not known. In any case, we do know that he counseled eligible church young people about how to gain conscientious objector status and sought to dissuade them from joining the army.

† † †

Lucille tells of her own experience; how Frank influenced her entering the service; affected her life.

> I graduated from High School in 1940 and went to RI Hospital to be a nurse; at the time I wanted to be a missionary. Worked especially hard because 100 of the hospital's staff and doctors left to serve as a medical unit; resulting in our getting especially good training; had to work 7-day weeks. When Sara Sue was born in 1940 and Woody in 1942, we used hospital cotton to make stuffed animals for them.
>
> One Easter while I was still at RI Hospital, Mr. T had pneumonia, and was unable to preach (when typically he had three services). Loretta called

me and asked if I could take care of him, at their home, while she went to church, sang in choir. He was miserable [Lucille didn't say, but I assume the Assistant minister, Mr. Selby, must have done the sermons.]

After I graduated from RI Hospital in Feb., 1944, I wanted to join the Army, had no problem with going as a nurse since I wouldn't be shooting anybody, but Frank encouraged me to go on to school. He persuaded me to go to Columbia Teacher's College and I got a full federal scholarship; started September 1944. That's where I met my husband; at Riverside church. One day I was late to bible class and the only seat empty was next to Ferdinand Votta. We shared a book and sat together at worship service. When he asked me to go to the church bowling group, we discovered that we both came "from a place that only had small balls;" found out we both were from Cranston, that he was a member of Arlington Baptist, whose minister was friends with Mr. T. Also discovered that Ferdinand was a chemical engineer as was my brother. "Seemed the Lord had just put us together."

Then, near the end of my first semester at Columbia, before Xmas, I got a notice that I was 1-A. The Battle of Bulge had just happened and they were in desperate need of nurses, so in March 1945 I enlisted. When I went overseas, there were 5,000 soldiers and 120 nurses and we were headed for Japan to set up a front line hospital. I told everyone when the atomic bomb was dropped, just before we left, that Ferdinand had saved our lives. He had been working on the Manhattan Project (the atomic bomb). It was very secret, but he had told me that if Germans got it first, it would be a disaster.

Lucille did not go to Japan, but she was on Leyte in the Philippines, and wrote Frank of her experiences there. It's unfortunate that we only have a copy of his reply, dated October 24, 1945, but significant how supportive he was of service people, despite his own pacifism:[8]

> Your descriptions of the various peoples and programs with which you have been occupied certainly were interesting. I was fascinated by your description of your own personal work. I suppose you remember my particular interest in psychiatric therapy and the occupational therapy which you undoubtedly are using there. It must be one of the greatest blessings one can receive to see these young fellows who have been wrecked by this [war], being brought back to some manner of sanity and hope and health.
>
> We have been trying our best to measure up to the challenge that is ours, of meeting these men when they return and holding out some hope to them that the church can and will be their real friends, and their spiritual sustainer in the hours of readjustment that are ahead. I would give a good big piece of my own arm to have the new church now so that we could have adequate room to invite these men in for games and programs where we could be very informal and yet in the atmosphere of the church. But then, that doesn't seem possible, so we will press on toward the high mark of the calling of this unique opportunity we have here in good old

---

[8] We earlier noted how he immediately visited Virginia Droitcor when he'd read in the paper that her brother had been killed in action.

Eden Park.

Thanks so much for your splendid letter and we continue to pray you Godspeed as you minister to the needs of those many persons out there. If you come across some particularly interesting stone in an historic spot, would you pick it up and bring it back to put in our memorial fireplace. As you know, we are trying to include as many historic churches or places of interest as possible, in this memorial fireplace, that will be in the new church.

Lucille preserved another letter from Frank, dated December 28, 1945, while she was still away from him. After discussing gifts she and her family have made to his family and the church, Frank comments on one gift specifically.

We hadn't planned to go by your place, thinking that with your big family reunion it would be better not to barge in on them but planned to go there later in the week. However, Sara Sue [who then would have been five] would not let us go home until we had gone to see the people who gave her Gretchen's twin [a popular doll with children at the time]. Her mother had concentrated all our Christmas contribution to Sara Sue into one fine big life-sized doll and of course Sara Sue liked it, but her favorite Christmas present she maintains to any and all who ask her is the little doll which is Gretchen's twin. You can't convince us there isn't something deep and mystical to that kind of selection. She just recognized the spirit that covers over and beyond that tiny little peasant dolly. We constantly pray that your strength will increase and that your service will continue to spread by leaps and bounds as it has in the past....God's richest blessings upon you and your work of mercy.

In her recent conversation with this writer, Lucille told of her return to Columbia after the war:

When I returned from service I returned to Columbia; took a battery of tests and got maximum credit, so needed only a few credits to graduate. But Ferdinand wanted to get married and was already teaching at URI, so I transferred there. Frank met my husband, and was very nice to us.

The day our engagement was announced in 1946, we had Thanksgiving dinner with Mr. T. and Loretta and assistant minister, Mr. Selby. There were 16 of us at the well known Seekonk restaurant, the Gristmill. We were engaged in October but hadn't announced it. I had just gotten my ring that morning at church; so at the restaurant my father got up and announced our engagement.

Frank helped us with all the planning for the wedding; orchestrated the whole wedding that took place on June 10, 1947. I was especially pleased that my husband's Italian Catholic Grandmother,[9] who spoke no English and lived on Federal Hill, came. The church was crowded but Mr. T personally went out and ushered her in and took her up to the front to sit with the family. He'd made us learn our vows so we could say them without any notes. The wedding was just beautiful.

† † †

---

[9] For complicated reasons, Ferdinand had converted as a teenager.

In Frank's scrapbook, right next to the clipping about Roosevelt's son, was another titled "They Also Serve." Authored by Frank, it, too, lacks a date or name of the paper in which it appeared. It reads:

> If you want to see vital democracy at work, visit the State Institutions at Howard. Less than a year ago, a critical situation developed there due to the manpower shortage. In January, the government allowed 25 conscientious objectors to be stationed at Howard. Nurses and doctors were outspoken in their criticism. "Allow slackers and draft dodgers to work here while our loved ones are off fighting" was a characteristic objection made by those who didn't understand what C.O.'s really were.
>
> It wasn't long before everyone was praising the young men who had stepped into the breach. Twelve hours a day, six days a week, they carry on, fifty strong now, doing the difficult and menial jobs about such an institution. Their pay has been raised from $2.50 per month to $10 per month.
>
> These young men, along with 7,500 others, are serving their nation in the only constructive way they feel is consistent with their Christian understanding. They have dropped from planes to fight forest fires. Some are working as "guinea pigs" for dangerous medical experimentation. Others are working in war torn lands in hospitals and on farms. Yes, they are doing work which the Army claims is of national importance. They serve our state by relieving one of the most critical manpower shortages we have had. They serve broken people whose conditions are tragically needful. They serve their consciences by losing their popularity and place

> in society in order to make their testimony to God. And so, they are not asking exemption from the horrors of war, but rather for understanding that they, too, are determined that war is mankind's greatest enemy and must be overcome....

But Frank didn't just write about conscientious objectors, he brought representatives to the church, wanting us to understand–and it certainly impressed me to have the contrast with the pervasive patriotism that was thick as molasses–innumerable Hollywood movies were barely a step away from pure propaganda, the Japanese made out to be even greater monsters than the Nazi, portrayed as wily, bug-eyed beasts who looked like monkeys and worshipped an Emperor as God; Kate Smith seemed to be everywhere singing *God Bless America*, and signs saying, "Loose Lips Will Sink Ships" were all over the place.

I still remember the Sunday we entered church and found three women seated in a pew near the front wearing long dresses and quaint little bonnets. If we were told if they were related to those working at Howard, or were part of a traveling group on an education mission, I don't recall. I do recall that Rev. Thompson introduced them as Mennonites and said one of them was going to talk to us instead of his preaching a sermon.

Then, in her quiet, timid voice, our guest told us how the Mennonites didn't believe war could ever achieve peace. "*Had the First World War been the war to end all wars as it had been heralded? Did the Civil War bring peace and justice for black people?*" she asked.

She told us how some of the Mennonites, like the Quakers and a few others who reject all violence, were refusing to fight, and for this, were being mocked, ridiculed, looked upon as cowards, disloyal, a threat to our national security. Some were even being refused admission to churches. Just counseling them, she noted, could subject you to suspicion and lead to *your* questioning by authorities.

As she talked, I recalled that Mr. Thompson did such counseling. We'd heard him talk to young men during our youth group meetings. But, somehow, instinctively, we hadn't talked much about it.

This tiny, wisp of a lady added vehemently, in so many words,

> We love our country, even if we can't condone violence! There are many people of faith serving without pay, in mental hospitals, poor houses, and all sorts of other places needing help. But there are other conscientious objectors," she told us, "who have been declared insane and sent to mental hospitals, or to prison for their beliefs. They are often mistreated in these institutions because of their beliefs. Some have spent months in solitary confinement, with too little clothing to keep them from chills, too little food, no exercise. Some prisoners have bravely led hunger and work strikes, demanding better food and uncensored mail; opposing Jim Crow segregation.

Even then, I was asking myself, why we were doing this to people just because they believed differently from us. Wasn't ours a country that prided itself on freedom for all? I thought that was what we were fighting for. Regrettably, today, I am asking why people from certain countries are being asked to register, while others are being held in concentration camps or prison, without being charged, denied visitors, or even an attorney. What a ruckus we would be raising if it was our citizens being held in these circumstances in another country!

Lucille Spooner has a more complete memory of the Mennonites who, as conscientious objectors, were in fact working at the Adult Correctional Institution in Cranston, replacing the regular staff which had joined the services. Lucille recalls them as having done a wonderful job there; "turned things around," as she put it. Phillips Memorial had always had a special relationship with the ACI because, as noted previously, its namesake had been a "missionary" there before going to India. Members of Phillips had various of the Mennonites to their homes for meals, Lucille went out with one of the men, and Shirley Gallup went to her senior prom with another.

† † †

Having for many years been concerned about our despicable treatment of the Indians as we moved westward across the American continent, and having frequently during his services at Phillips Memorial said the Lord's Prayer in Indian Sign Language, it is not surprising that Mr. T should have been concerned about our treatment of Japanese-Americans after the attack on Pearl Harbor. Following President Roosevelt's Order #9066, issued on February 19, 1942 and affirmed by the U.S. Supreme Court, an estimated 120,000 persons of Japanese origin, most citizens, many born in this country, were unceremoniously rounded up and put in concentration camps. Approximately two months later, on March 21, 1942, another order was issued that allowed seventy-five college students to leave the confines of the camps. Most Americans now know of this unconscionable act by our government against its own citizens, but most claim to have known nothing of it at the time. Thanks to Mr. T, this writer, then in high school, claims no such thing.

We were curious that day in 1942 when we entered Phillips Memorial and saw a beautiful young Oriental girl sitting in the chair beside Mr. Thompson on the altar platform. When it was time for his sermon, Mr. T explained that she would talk to us instead, and introduced her as a student at the University of Chicago who was risking her freedom to speak to such groups as ours during her vacations. This young woman told us what had happened to her family and their friends [*told in first person even though not based on her own words but on my memory of what she said to us that day*]:

> One day my family was suddenly uprooted from its comfortable, beautifully decorated, meticulously cared for home in Los Angeles. Given only a few days notice, we were told to meet at the bus depot and to bring only bedding and such other belongs as we could carry, no pets and no cars. All our Japanese-American neighbors were told the same thing. Not long afterwards, we found ourselves in the middle of the Arizona desert--the sun blazing hot, a suffocating wind regularly covering everything with sand. There was no shade anywhere, nothing green, little water, poor food, nothing to do.
>
> My mother, Dad, two younger brothers and I shared a barren barracks with another mother and her two young daughters. A curtain was strung between us, but privacy was something no one any longer had. There was a shower building for communal use--one side for men, one side for women; an eating hall for communal meals; a latrine

> with rows of wooden seats covering holes in the ground, one side for men, one side for women. Surrounding it all was barbed wire fencing, dotted with guard towers, manned by armed, uniformed men.

You could *see* the sadness in her eyes as she continued:

> Our mother tried to maintain spirit and 'face' for the sake of us children, but at night when she thought we were asleep on our canvas cots, we could hear her gently sobbing. All day, our dad just sat in the corner, head bowed between his knees, ashamed. He no longer talked. He was no longer in charge of his family.
>
> I didn't understand why any of this was happening, nor why those in charge of interring us one day posted a notice that college students were being released to continue their education. I knew just how lucky I was. I knew that because I had been accepted at the University before the round-up, I would be released after only five months in that horrible place so I could start with my class in September.

Who could help but see the injustice as she closed by urging us to write the President, urging him to release *all* her people. Thanks to Mr. T, we had been privileged to learn of this attack on our civil rights in the name of wartime necessity even as it was going on.

† † †

Closer to home, on June 25, 1942, Frank officiated at the wedding of his half-sister, Mary Jo, to Ensign David

Partington. Mary Jo still laughs thinking about the double role Frank played that day. After walking her down the aisle, he'd slipped away to appear again a short time later in his minister's robe to hear their vows and pronounce them man and wife. The newspaper account read, "Minister performs dual ceremony." May Jo writes: "I often teased him and said that it was nice that someplace in the article Dave and I were mentioned."

Believing a newly married couple needed more privacy than afforded with her around, Mary Jo, by the time of her own wedding, had been living for some time with "very good church people," next door to the Thompsons on Tallman Avenue. Frank and Loretta had moved from Colonial Avenue, where Frank had been living prior to their marriage, to a larger house on Tallman Avenue that was more suitable as a parsonage. At the time of her move, Mary Jo was attending secretarial school and working part-time at "a very special tea room," as she described it.

Frank, Loretta, Woody & Sara Sue about 1943

189. A Lifelong Pacifist

The Thompsons' house on Tallman Avenue was just a few blocks from this writer's home on Myrtle Avenue. And she was just one of many young people in the church who were only too delighted to baby-sit for the Thompsons' young children when called upon. And this was often necessary as Loretta continued to direct the choirs, sing solos, and put on musical comedies and skits. She solved some of her problems, by having practices at her home, as well as holding a Sunday School class there; the church short of space in any case.

A little later, Loretta could send her children several days a week to the "Kinderkirk" (nursery school) run by Doris Stapleton and Ruth Miller in the church basement. Virginia Droitcor told this writer of an incident that happened there between her daughter, Judith, born in 1943, and Woody, a year older, which she found amusing. It was during their rest period, stretched out on their blankets on the floor, when Woody started kicking Judith. She retaliated by biting his ear. Judith was the youngest child there, but had been allowed to attend because she wanted to so badly (her sister, Priscilla, two years older, went). After Doris told Virginia about the incident, she suggested that maybe Judy shouldn't go. Doris, however, said, "Oh, let her stay. Don't keep her home. She makes my day!" Virginia didn't say what happened to Woody for instigating the incident.

† † †

Several of Frank's sermons reflect his concern for the rise in juvenile delinquency that he blames on the fact that so many parents are in the service and the mothers have joined the war-industry workforce. In his May 9, 1943 sermon, he approaches the subject through the story of "The Pied Piper of Hamlin." He first reviews the story of the "Pied Piper" who came along and said he could rid the city of rats by piping to them on his pipe. The City Council, which had been impotent in its efforts, agreed and committed to paying him, but reneged once the rats were all drowned in the River Wiser. And so the pied piper blew his pipe again and all the children followed him. "Alas, alas, for Hamlin, the piper and children were gone forever out of Hamlin Town in Brunswick Land and never seen again."...Frank then brought the story home:

> The parable of Hamlin is a parable of today. A scourge faced the world and our elders decided the only way to do away with that scourge was with total war, but total war demands sacrifices which must be paid. The Piped Piper is piping a dire tune. It is unrest which is manifesting itself in terrifying nervous reactions.
>
> We go on our way...but there is a terrible wave of juvenile delinquency in the young folks....In Detroit, Chicago and Los Angeles the young marauders are wild and the police can do nothing about them....Murders in great cities go unnoticed because the police are too busy fighting a great war to be concerned about the pranks of the junior demonstrators. Children are feeling the terrible conflict in the world...The mothers are off making money; how many are there who answer their patriotic duty and are working today? We see their children running wild with no one to care for them....
>
> More love is needed and love is the only thing that cures the conflict of the world....I think I have heard echoes of another tune, a consciousness of the plea to do something about the starving children of Europe. ...I think I hear this tune beginning to be played by the piper for missions in

many countries saying we will take care of these children whose parents have to work.

...The best tunes are from people who are worried about their own ways and are ready to take God's way at last.

In an undated sermon, probably in 1944, Frank brings his concern for the growth in juvenile delinquency even closer to home. He asks:

Have you been appalled at the juvenile delinquency lately—houses broken into, ladies attacked, property wantonly damaged?...A crime every 22 seconds over the nation as a whole, the majority committed by mere children—15 billion last year—110 for every man, woman and child in the U.S....Mrs. Thompson has had her purse rifled several times while she has been singing here. The last time they found no money but they found all our ration points for the next month!...J. E. Hoover throws light on the situation and on the way out: "The American home is still the basis of our social order, and the nation will never be any stronger than the home. The one thing that most juvenile criminals have in common is a lack of proper home training."

And again, in a later sermon, referring to his concern over "this juvenile crime wave," Frank asks:

Why is it that always in war time children start tearing down too?[10] We can condemn them,

---

[10] This writer, without any success, tried any number of resources to track down this wave of delinquency Frank has referred to in several sermons, and that I have reprinted. Statistics apparently were not collected then and until several decades later.

and imprison them, and curse them, but when we understand their driving motives, when we see that they want to keep up with their elders who have been having one glorious time tearing down too, then we are born of the spirit and we begin to find constructive substitutes to put in the place of negatives.[11]

So on in each realm of life. Nations must be born anew of water and spirit. Purified motives and spiritual understandings of neighboring nations' actions. And so Industry and Labor must be born anew!

† † †

The war and Americans' greediness is much on Frank's mind in another undated sermon. He asks us:

> Are we wanting to escape the limitations of rationing to return to the unlimited orgies of indulgence–to get back into the sin of superfluity? Are we wanting escape from the equalization that rationing at least attempts? Are we wanting to escape the horror of this cosmic convulsion called war to get back to the kind of peace we called peace before–The kind of peace that Berdyaev says "rots away into war." Why are we trying to get back into a life of easy complacency where each man's liberty is so inviolable that it becomes license? Such escapes are evil. They can be spelled with a small word with large meanings SIN, and our job as Christians is to face reality with frank fearlessness, saying with God's help this condition can

---

[11] Remember the previously recounted story of Frank's leading a group of youngsters on Halloween, enabling all to have fun and no destructive mischief occurring.

be surmounted.

In another sermon based on the story of Lot's wife who looked back and turned to salt, Frank is again concerned about our selfishness. He suggests that Lot's version of the anthem, "O beautiful for pilgrims feet,..." might go like this

> O beautiful for dividends
> Of twenty-five percent
> On oil and steel and real estate,
> *[what if Iraq didn't have oil?]*
> On money freely lent.
> America! America! May riches be our fate'
> Increase our wealth
> And guard our health
> America, the great!

Frank continues: "My concern is to get our good liberal-minded people to think, study, believe and act." Over and over in his sermons, Frank emphasizes action, concern for the poor, as integral to religion.

† † †

Germany surrendered on May 7, 1945; Japan on August 14, 1945, after we'd dropped atomic bombs on Hiroshima, August 6th and Nagasaki, August 9th.

In an undated sermon, Frank begins:

> No scene in all the glittering pageantry of either war or peace has equaled that which now is spread out along the shores of Asia. Hundreds of ships of war cover the ocean. Thousands of planes

thunder in the sky. The war lords of Japan, humbled for the first time, leave the dust and ashes of Tokyo and board the mighty battleship Missouri...These beaten statesmen sign the hard terms of surrender, surrounded by the victor powers, indicting their names in humility and affixing the great seal of Japan. History has been made, and dramatized, so it will never be forgotten....

Kipling might have written the recessional for this pageant. "Yea the shouting and the tumult dies, the captains and the kings depart, but still stand thine ancient sacrifices, an humble and a contrite heart. Lord God of Nations, be with us yet lest we forget, lest we forget."...

Time magazine wrote, "Military alliances, balances of power, League of Nations all in turn failed...We have had our last chance. If we do not now devise some greater and more equitable system, Armageddon will be at our door."... "War is the great enemy of mankind," said none other than General MacArthur. "This is our last chance to rid ourselves of it."...

The Christian Church has the medicine that can drive out this cancerous curse by driving out the causes of hatred, fear and fretful anxiety....We can go forward ...until this sad old world shall truly reap the promise that has been held before it since Isaiah, and John and Jesus and Augustine saw a new heaven and a new earth coming down out of heaven. [Again Frank asserts his faith in Christianity as the solution to the world's problems.]

† † †

195. A Lifelong Pacifist

In another undated sermon Frank asks: Is there any word more prayed for, more longed for, than the word Victory? He suggests ways the church can assert its influence.

> What a hollow sound it will make if it's just a military victory again! ...As individuals and as the church of Christ, we can set in motion tiny whirlpools of influence, small ripples of enlightened understandings and tide-changing attitudes that may forever have bearing on the course of history—for this cause let us shout, "Thanks be to God which giveth us the Victory."...
>
> Giving thanks to God makes us aware of the source of all true and meaningful victories. There is no lack so damming as the lack of gratitude, no attitude so absolutely helpless and hopeless as the attitude of taking everything for granted. Screwtape [of *Screwtape Letters* by C. S. Lewis], the senior Devil in Hell trying to win people to the nether regions, reminds Wormwood, the missionary to earth, that he doesn't need to sign people up; just get them to assume that the world owes them a living, that they are masters of all they survey. Then their entrance to Hell will be but a matter of little time...
>
> Let us give thanks to God for Victory over things, but listen to Jacques Maritain: "Hitler is not cause but effect; he is the effect of the errors and weaknesses of two centuries of materialism..."

Frank optimistically expresses his belief that the war has engendered the cooperation of men of different colors, classes and creeds to fight a holocaust, and so enabled man to recognize that they are all made in the image of God. No longer do we sing the old-time song: "We are the best selected few/ Let all the rest be damned,/ There's room in Heaven for me and you/ but we can't have heaven crammed." *This would rarely or never be sung today--too politically incorrect–but, for many, have the sentiments changed?*

In Frank's sermon on May 20, 1945, "The Rushing Wind of Pentecost," he reiterates his belief that all men are one under Christ, whatever their country or language. The war in Europe having just ended [May 7], he once more insists we need to heed that lesson. On this occasion, the message is tied to the lesson of Pentecost [Acts 2: 2].

> We don't understand too well the technical details of that day, but we know the rushing wind of God's spirit blew into the sultry atmosphere of man's smug little domain, and the church was born. Bethlehem was the birthplace of Christ, Pentecost was the birthplace of Christianity.
>
> "During the course of the day they were all together, when suddenly there came a sound from heaven like a violent blast of wind...and they began to talk in foreign tongues" There were sixteen different language groups listed and each heard the other in his own tongue. They were together! The Rushing Wind of God blew them together, and the spirit of God settled on them and they called it the Holy Spirit. Under its influence they were able to understand each other, even if they couldn't speak each others language.
>
> Where is the rushing wind of God today? Well, one thing we can be mighty sure of and that is that it is where there is a spirit of togetherness!...

197. A Lifelong Pacifist

You know who got together in those careless and selfish days before 1939. Those neglected in the careless 20s nurtured hate in the thoughtless 30s and became so cohesive that they almost captured the world in the fearful forties. They had a togetherness of spirit, but they failed as THEY will always fail when their goal is evil and their means corrupt. But they failed at what a terrific cost to the world, and their failure will be the world's failure unless those who have used their methods to destroy them now turn and put those methods to a just and righteous purpose....[12]

We need to read *Mein Kampf* again now that its author is dead and his party soon to be wiped from the face of the earth. Read it to see how it could be that such a diabolical creature, could come so near to doing what he set out to do. [He

---

[12] Cartoon found on page 36 in "World Federalist Association 1947-1997 Historical Survey"

> developed a spirit of togetherness] by having a cause–wrong cause, yes, but a cause, a world view, not just three squares a day and a movie a week. They had a purpose in life....Well, you know the fanatical kind of loyalty they had to one another....My god, such loyalty to a pagan, putrid and ghastly purpose, but can we match it? Just to destroy their system won't be enough unless we can replace that with a mighty, positive and purposeful plan of our own using this spirit of togetherness. [*A message for the conquering powers in Iraq*, 2003.]

Frank hammers on the dangers of victory once more in the undated sermon, "The Tempering Flame of Victory." [Malachi]

> The most dangerous hour in the life of an individual, an institution or nation is the hour following victory. To some that may sound strange. Surely, the hour of greatest danger is the hour of attack. But no, that is the hour that calls forth heroic actions from people, that unites them, that makes them forget selves in great deeds of self-giving devotion to causes beyond themselves. It's the hour after victory when conquerors go off quarreling among themselves....That's why so few nations have ever survived successful conquests.... [And] when self is at the center of our focus, the very forces of life begin to disintegrate and pull in all different directions.... What we're doing now is standing in the hour of greatest testing, watching to see how many survive the tempering flame of victory....[*Listen up, you who declared we won the war in Iraq*, 2003.]

199. A Lifelong Pacifist

In church doorway at end of sermon

Frank ends his sermon on June 11, 1944, "Life's Crusades," with something of a challenge to his parishioners:

> No one of us can find [the gleam of truth] alone, but all together we shall find a torch that shall light the darkness of this age and show the shape of the design of the future, signs I believe to be great and beautiful and with its great power it shall purge the earth of all its diseases and heartaches and poverty and war and disaster. Each new age has had its own dreams. Leave then the dreams of the past, take up the light and press toward the new tomorrow. Take up the torch, leave behind yesterday's dreams, take up a new dream and light the way toward the plateau of tomorrow. Let's have a crusade for truth, for discipline, for positive values in life.

† † †

There were two post-war groups of people that troubled Frank sufficiently to make each, separately, the focus of a sermon. The first group is discussed in a lengthy undated sermon, befittingly titled, "G. I. Joe." The second group is the subject of a sermon, "Re-conversion" [John 3], delivered on January 30, 1945.

He begins the first by telling us about the young man, Pat Gilmore, who wrote a "gay and lilting song" near the end of the Civil War, but it collected dust for many years, unused at the time because the "internecine war which matched brother against brother and father against son," caused just too much sorrow. But then near the end of WWI it became the hit song of the world. "That song, as many have guessed, was "When Johnny comes Marching Home."

> We felt at that time that the War to end all Wars was a success. The world had been made safe for democracy. When Johnny comes marching home, Utopia would be ours! But in this tragic WWII, there has been no [such] hit song, because we know when G. I. Joe comes marching home, the job will only begin. As Lincoln said, "After you have fought the war, you still must decide the issues that caused the war." So when G. I. Joe comes marching home, the job will be upon us....

Frank then reminds us that too many G. I. Joes won't come marching home, and asks, "Have you thought with pain in your heart of the number of composers, artists, great statesmen and leaders that are lying under some white cross on a foreign field?" He continues, reminding us of the problems they and we face as "fifty thousand per month are being turned loose in a society they probably won't understand." Some will be riddled with anxiety that has never found an outlet [*what came to be called "post-traumatic stress syndrome" after Vietnam*].

> They may have gone through the heat of the toughest battles of the war and come home to explode over such minor issues as the color of their

wife's hat. We must be aware of the need for an outlet for their anxiety.

Further, Frank suggests

> Probably every single fellow has dreamed of home and home conditions and has glorified them in his dreams. But when they do get home, they more than likely will be disillusioned. We have not been running fast enough to keep up with them.

Frank believes that many developed a new sense of values.

> Lying in some foxhole, G. I. Joe has wondered how a God great enough to keep those stars from bumping into each other could not be great enough to help man work out his problems too. And out there he has discovered man's most precious gift which is the freedom to think for himself and to act for himself after the manner of his own creator, and he has come back asking the powerful question, "Why must this ever go on?" "Why must old men cause the wars that young men must die to fight?" You see, our civilization has been built on a false standard: that things are the important thing in life. But G. I. Joe is beginning to wonder if they are....After all, it doesn't matter how many things he has at home if he can't be at home to enjoy them.

Frank then reviews at some length a Lillian Helman play, "The Searching Wind," then playing in New York. The play ends leaving the audience wondering "how we ever could have been so dumb as to have caused [our young men] to pay such a price." Frank closes this sermon with a poem by an anonymous boy:

Look, God/ I have never spoken to you,
But now I want to say/ How do you do.
You see, God
They told me you didn't exist
And I like a fool believed all this.
Last night from a foxhole I saw your sky
And then I knew they had told me a lie
If I had taken time to see the things you made,
I would have known that you weren't calling
a spade a spade.

† † †

In the second sermon, "Re-conversion," Frank is concerned with what will happen to a labor force that was needed during wartime, but may find itself unemployed after the re-conversion of industry for peace time. [*Frank's remarks reflect the culture of the time in that he ignores the impact on women, who were in fact the most affected.*]

> Just think of men who have lived all their lives under the subsistence level, never knowing what a full dinner pail or a full stomach meant until the war came. And rightly or wrongly, they had everything for that period [of the war]....Re-conversion brings the dread spectre of bread lines and bent shovel handles before their eyes, and, [determined to keep the advantages which the war gave them], they react in ways which seem to some barbaric. Of course, they think that industry acts barbaric because it is not willing to share more of the 10 billion dollar profits they made in 1944; more than 2½ times the profits of 1939.
>
> Yes, the problems of re-conversion are terrific, but of course we of the church have little or

no say in the solution of these problems. But we have the majority say in the moral conceptions and the ethical backgrounds and the spiritual conditions which surround this problem. Society is our concern. Society must be on our conscience. We are society. The great war of aggression has been won, but the civil war goes on....Our crying need is for re-conversion within [ourselves].

We do not call it re-conversion today. This being born anew, this ceasing of a new set of values, losing life on a lower level in order to find it on a higher one. It's today called re-adaptation, re-integration re-alignment, transmutation and re-orientation. But whatever they're called, they all mean being born anew, and being born anew means born with the water and the spirit. Water, the symbol of purification....Spirit, the symbol of inspiration.

† † †

A Thanksgiving sermon, "Swinging Toward the Light," delivered on November 18, 1945, has a more optimistic tone than do most of his sermons.

The world seems to me to be swinging toward the light because it has probed the very blackest spots of existence and just can't get any farther into blackness. ...I believe the world is swinging toward the light because for the first time it has discovered the full meaning of the 139th Psalm:

Where could I go from thy spirit? Where could I flee from thy face? I climb to heaven, but thou art there; I nestle in the netherworld and there thou art. If I darted swift to the dawn, to the verge of ocean afar, thy hand even there would fall on me, thy right hand would reach me. If I say, The dark will screen me, night will hide me in its curtains, yet darkness is not dark to thee, the night is clear as daylight.

...Heads of aggressor nations are discovering in the criminal trials [at Nuremberg] that they can no longer hide their identity behind the skirt of a state party. Nations are discovering that they can no longer pronounce beautiful doctrines like the Atlantic Charter without being held responsible for the fulfillment of such statements. Native peoples aren't satisfied to merely change taskmasters. They want freedom, individual freedom. It's in their very skins....

Think how new a word is "international" itself. Think what a short time men have been trying to work out a world government, compared with the length of time spent trying to work out state governments and social structures....

[Creating] the World Council of Churches is another in the plus column of light. ...Another sign of the social swing toward the light is the fact that the churches have adopted AFRICA for their study course this year. Many of us believe that Africa will be a test case for the United Nations Organization....The world owes Africa a great debt. Her people were carried away to make white nations wealthy. Now that a world conscience has awakened, what will we do? [*We and the UN failed, I'm afraid!*]

...I am grateful that man is discovering he can't hide in the darkness of his own inner self....When he discovers that he can't hide in himself, that his soul is really God's parade ground

> where time and eternity meet, where history is formed, then man, enlightened man, comes swinging into the light.

†††

This writer well remembers the early hopes for the new United Nations Organization, and Mr. T's enthusiasm when arranging to take a group of young people to see it in action. Not only did the trip offer us that experience but it was the first time for many of us, including this writer, to visit New York. To recount the experience on a personal note:

> I believe it was in the late-Spring of 1947 when the United Nations was meeting in the New York City Building in Flushing Meadows, awaiting the completion of its final home. The United Nations wasn't exactly the world government we would have preferred, but it was a start and we were duly impressed and hopeful as the guide took us around. I was especially intrigued by the headphones the delegates wore that almost instantaneously translated what was being said into a choice of English, Russian, French and Chinese.[13]
>
> Afterwards, we went into Manhattan for lunch, ate in a cafeteria, a first for me, and later was impressed by the Automat where sandwiches were displayed in

---

[13] The UN charter was signed by "the big three" in San Francisco in June 1945, ratified in October that year. The first meeting of the General Assembly and Security Council was in London in January 1946, at which time they decided to locate in New York. The first U.S. meeting was at Lake Success in Long Island, then in Flushing Meadows. In December 1946, John D. Rockefeller had given the organization $8,500,000 for purchase of a piece of land for a permanent site. At the time of our visit, the permanent headquarters was still under construction.

little glass boxes; purchased by dropping in a quarter and seeing them drop down for retrieval.[14]

But perhaps it was the drive back that ended up making the most lasting impression on me. As we listened to the end of a Dodgers' game on the car radio, we talked about the controversy swirling around Jackie Robinson's being allowed to play on a white major league baseball team, the first black ever. We all asked, "*Why had it taken so long? Why did so many whites hate blacks?*" Mr. Thompson tried to explain about custom, fear of what's different and ignorance, but it was hard to understand. For me, it still is.

† † †

About this same time, Frank preached a sermon based on the story of Cain and Abel. Recently, his son, Scott, called it "the leit motif of his ministry." Since Scott was only five in 1947 and his sister, Sara Sue , only seven, Frank must have preached it often, or at least alluded to its theme often, in order for it to have elicited the comment from Scott that "my sis and I used to joke that we'd pay him anything not to subject us to it yet again."

The Bible story tells us that in a fit of jealousy, Cain, the older brother and struggling farmer, killed his younger brother, Abel, the pastoralist--provoked by the praise Abel received for the "fat lambs and choice calves" he brought to the sacrificial altar, while his [Cain's] "scrawny offerings" were declared unacceptable. This story is the source of two questions that have passed down through succeeding generations: God asks, "Cain, where is thy brother Abel?" and his rhetorical answer, seeking to excuse himself, "Am I my brother's keeper?" They were

---

[14] I was recently told that the automat still operates in NYC but the sandwiches now cost four dollars.

questions receiving tremendous consideration by those discussing the formation of the United Nations.

Frank's concern is that asking the second question, *after* the crime, is too late! He asks us to consider, rather, what the outcome might have been if Abel had responded to the question, "Abel, where is thy brother, Cain," and thence shared his surplus with Cain? That, Frank says, "would have been preventative morality, and preventative morality is religion. [Our self-proclaimed religious president, President Bush, might do well to heed this before declaring, in the name of security, a policy of preventive war.] True religion is not concerned with crime and punishment, but with prevention." And Frank looks to the United Nations as our best hope for preventing future wars.

Frank then begins to bring his theme of religion's preventative role home, and so it becomes another example of what his half-sister, Mary Jo, described as his gift for preaching "the most wonderful 'day to day' sermons." Reflecting his consistently anti-war stance, Frank says:

> Our main contention is that there are some modern Cains that we can be fairly certain could have been controlled had we, who call ourselves Abel, been more aware of a higher morality–a preventative religion. I'm thinking of some Cains in the Rhineland. Terrible their crime against civilization, and right that they should suffer, every Cain among them. It's the popular thing to do now, dream up horrible punishment for the beasts of Berlin! But hadn't we who call ourselves Christians better ask some more penetrating questions?
>
> What brought on the crime of these German Cains? Where was Abel, their brother, when the spokesmen of the Weimar Republic were appealing to

> the world for help before some strong man arose to regiment them? Where was Abel when Cain was trying out his vindictive power on his despised brother, the Jew, or down in Spain where he really got his weapons sharpened? Where was Abel when the financiers of other countries were saying, "This man Hitler needs financial backing, he will provide a safe barrier against Bolshevism." Now is the time to ask ourselves these questions—we who like to think we are as virtuous as Abel.

Frank reminds us of a quote, one of his favorites, made by General Eisenhower in the midst of a tumultuous tribute from hero-worshiping New York. "Typical of a farm boy poignancy," Eisenhower said:

> Our task is still unfinished, that task is peace. Remember, prosperous nations don't need to fight but hungry nations have to fight. While there are hungry nations there will always be war. Our task is peace.

Frank then alludes to the Cains right here in our own society. He asks if our national leaders who are calling us to prepare to live better, are including "those 40 million that perpetually live under the subsistence level."

> Do you suppose they were including those 14 million Negroes that we are being told must be "put back into their places" now that the duration is about over! I wonder just where their places are? ...Do you suppose that leader included the hundreds of thousands of children who can't have the support and protection of a Child Labor Amendment because the newspapers—our most powerful force for preventative morality, if they wanted to be—depend upon child labor to get their papers sold?

What might be done if we harnessed our power to the great tasks of Preventative Morality. Think of it, with the interest on ONE month's war costs, I am told, we could clear every slum in America, those great open sores on the face of humanity. But will we? [*We never view this as preventative security so never are willing to commit the same resources to it as we do to war.*]

Frank closes on a theme he expanded on in another sermon, by asking "What would happen if [at the end of our worship service], we each went out to make everything right between us and our brothers?"

† † †

It was late 1947 or early 1948 that Frank preached a sermon, "The Gathering of His Enemies," that gives us an unusual look at aspects of post-war America not generally found in accounts by American, or even Allied, writers. It begins with a concern that some of "our liberal churches" have developed attitudes that have become "crystallized into a shell," then goes on to say:

The whole Christian church must rethink its mission, its raison d'être, in the light of a ONE WORLD strategy! Paul Hutchinson in *Life* [magazine] fairly shouts that never before have so many peoples and so many lands been hungry for the Christian message, and people in powerful positions are more interested in the principles of Christianity than ever. BUT ALSO THIS IS TERRIBLY IMPORTANT: NEVER HAS THE ORGANIZED CHURCH, THE FORMALIZED INSTITUTION OF CHRISTIANITY BEEN LESS INTERESTING, had less chance of influence, unless

> there is a change.
>
> So let's get our gospel straight. We're not interested in carrying our customs or preserving cold and crystallized doctrines. We're here to carry a light–a light made from fire–fire that will burn anything that is not pure and powerfully important for this new hour. Ah, Christ come back and give us a chance to live with Thee, to make our truth become courageous and our faith creative! Come back and weigh us and see wherein we are wanting–don't count us to see our numerical strength, but weigh us to see our eternal significance.

Frank goes on to express his concern that we not allow the military, which "standardizes" all life, to lead us.

> That's why, if we are interested in preserving democracy and the Christianity that gave birth to democracy, we work to oppose this with every effort....If our Christianity really meant anything to us, we would take up the cry of Speaker Joe Martin and demand universal disarmament, or would back Senator Tydings on his proposal to have the President call a great disarmament conference of all nations.[15] But no, instead we must administer the coup de grâce to the UN and take the whole world in our hands. While the Russians go on gaining the following of the little people because she proposed disarmament of all arms, we turn a deaf ear.

---

[15] Joe Martin, a Republican from Massachusetts, was a member of the House of Representatives from 1925-1967; Speaker of the House from January 1947 to January 1949 and again form 1953-1955. Millard Tydings, a Democrat from Maryland, was a Senator from 1927-1951.

211. A Lifelong Pacifist

This statement by Frank, made at the time, is significant since it gives credence to a claim made by Andrei Gromyko in his book, *Memories*, published in 1989.[16] In it, Gromyko states:

> In April 1946 I was made permanent Soviet representative to the United Nations, and not long afterwards I became Deputy Foreign Minister...From 1946 onwards, in the UN alone, the USSR has introduced more than a hundred initiatives towards ending the arms race and achieving disarmament. The USSR made the first proposal on universal and total disarmament combined with universal supervision, and there have been countless Soviet proposals to limit or stop the arms race.
>
> Back in 1946, when the memory of war was still fresh, the UN established a special commission which met in London with the participation of the USSR, the USA, Britain, France and Canada. It soon emerged that only the USSR was in favour of disarmament, while all others blocked every proposal aimed at disarmament and ending the arms race.
>
> The American representative was Adlai Stevenson....At the commission Stevenson stubbornly repeated that it was impossible for the US administration to accept any resolution on disarmament.

Gromyko then tells of a confession Stevenson made to him when he was his invited dinner guest.

> He [Stevenson] admitted for the first time: "Big business in America cannot conceive of existing

---

[16] Pp. 174-175, *Memories: From Stalin to Gorbachev*, Andrei Gromyko, translated by Harold Shukman, Arrow Books, London, 1989.

without arms manufacture. Nobody in Washington takes the idea of disarmament seriously. But I can't say that openly at the commission."

I could not have asked any representative of the administration to be more frank than that.

"But in that case," I replied, "what do you think is the proper course for countries to take on this issue?"

"Controlled rearmament," came the reply.

So it was to be rearmament.

In his sermon, Frank continued:

> It's the ghastly fact that physical violence immobilizes all our spiritual forces that appalls us.[This immobilization] is even more appalling than the physical destruction of war, for upon it the maintenance and extension of spiritual powers and the permanence of the race ultimately rests. The progress of the race has never depended upon violence, for violence always destroys the principle of consent by which progress alone is possible. The more violence, the less consent; the less consent, the more violence. Just now we are in a phase of human history in which trust in violence as the only adequate force is all but universal; and yet the more we trust it, the more we imperil the civilization that was built without it, and that can endure only if this madness is purged from our breasts. It is war that creates and sustains the things that make war inevitable. War to end war is like starvation to end hunger....

Regrettably, a message as valid in 2003 as it was in 1947- 48.

11. Moving On

I am trying the difficult task of giving a picture of the Bible–not as a relic to be dusted from the shelf occasionally, but as a guide to each day's activities, business and pleasure. There is so much that we miss in the Bible by trying to find a "religious" lesson in every chapter, instead of finding the everyday instructions and practical applications in it...

†††

Because Frank both opposed the war, and in his sermons often seemed to praise Communism as more responsive to the needs of the poor than was America, many may have thought he was a "Red" or at best a "Commie sympathizer." [McCarthy's witch hunt was yet to come in the 50s.] But as Frank made clear in a very long speech titled, "The Church's Answer to Communism," given at Brown University on March 9, 1946, it was Christianity's lack of a counter-message that was his concern. The speech was part of something called the "Brown Embassy" when students, for three days, turned their attention to religious answers to secular problems. For his part, Frank told them:

> The generation that came back from WWI thought they had made the world safe for democracy and they had a feeling of having been on a great crusade, but this generation is finding out all too soon what a disillusioning mess it all was and they're beginning to question everything. And they wonder where there is an answer. What hope remains, if any?

Frank agrees with Theodore Ferris, from the Old Trinity Church in Boston, who said in his keynote address, "All the problems of the world could be solved if we treated each member of society as though he were a member of our own family. But, Frank asserts, since that's what the Communists try to do—"win the world into one big family or community"—we need to define the difference between our goals and the Communists' goals. But name-calling, labeling people "RED," threatening anyone who says or does something we don't agree with, will not help.

> We in the Christian Church must not fall heir to this fatal disease of name calling or witch hunting. Let's establish a simple test for our minds so that we won't be caught engaging in Fascistic activities, for that's exactly what is being threatened now. Communism is wrong for us, no doubt about it, but if we remember anything about history at all, Fascism is even more dangerous than Communism. Only now it's more popular to exonerate the Fascists and to anesthetize the Communists. The simple test is this. Is this individual or group or nation doing what it's doing for the good of mankind and the glory of something greater than itself?—Call it God, if you will....We need to remind ourselves that no one ever overcomes a false idea with another false idea....We're not going to destroy Russia's influence by barking at her or criticizing her or arming ourselves to the teeth against her.

Frank quotes a reporter, Paul Hutchinson, who has just returned from Russia. Hutchinson said:

> While the Russian policy at present is an adventure in power politics, it is not solely that. The Communist revolution is still a reality. The world still teems with hundreds of millions of wretched, desperate poor to whom the Communists' promise is

as dazzling as any Christian apocalypse....

I am returning from this journey of exploration more than ever afraid of the threat to human freedom implicit in the totalitarianism of the Communist state. But I am by no means persuaded that freedom can be defended against that danger by war....Neither do I believe that guns or atom bombs or germ-scattering rockets can long suppress the desperate longing of the exploited poor for an easing of their lot and an opening of the door of opportunity to their children. And so, as far as the Christian church is concerned, if it ever allows itself to bless a holy war against Communist advances, it is going to find itself speedily entangled with a deplorable crew of allies who will stigmatize it indelibly as a tool of reaction and complacent partner in exploitation. [With a few substituted words, we could utter those same words in 2003.]

Frank continued:

If we will but keep constantly clear in our minds what Communism essentially is, we should be able to chart a constructive course of our own. Communism is a dynamic revolutionary force promising heaven on earth to the masses. As such, it is a beacon of hope to the hordes of exploited....We must prepare to prove that our social and political system can provide more comfort, more security, more opportunity, more liberty and more satisfaction than any other. Christianity may sound like Communism in seeking to build the brotherhood of man on earth, but one is a decree from an authoritarian rule by and of men, the other

> is a development from within the individual outward to other individuals and on and on until like the mustard seed it becomes a tree that shades the whole earth.

Frank goes on to implore the students to "hold our Christian ground immovable" against Communism, Fascism, Ku Klux Klan and Vigilante groups, Nationalism and Secularism. "Start with the home, make of it what it was intended to be, a little society of heaven where there is true Christian concern for each member...Expand the walls of this fellowship, this work for the Lord outward to take in the community, the nation and the world....

† † †

Wes Hall, active in the Youth Fellowship at Phillips Memorial, relates an experience that reveals, surprisingly, Frank's lack of self-confidence. He states:

> I was extremely nervous prior to the Youth Sunday service and when I told Mr. T, he said that he felt exactly the same way every Sunday. I recall that whispered conversation very vividly, and it is still very hard for me to believe that he actually was nervous as he stepped into the pulpit ANY Sunday.

Loretta, indeed, shared with the Spooners, the families being close and frequently exchanging dinner invitations, how Frank regularly came home from Sunday services depressed, convinced he had failed to get his message across. Lucille states that Loretta, to get around this, made Sunday evenings the time for company, frequently inviting folks in for one of her tasty suppers.

217. Moving On

Given his final years, one must conclude that underlying Frank's warm, charismatic, appealing personality was another, haunted by a sense of inadequacy and failure. Whether this was an inherited trait, as suggested by some who

knew him, or the result of growing up with a step-father whom he, at least on occasion, felt didn't accept him as completely as he did his own children, we cannot know. What we do know is that Loretta, thoughtful here, with her own pleasant person-ality, rich singing voice, and work with the girls' choir, was a great asset to Frank in his ministry.

† † †

Frank had had an experience that prompted him on November 3, 1946 to comment on Catholics in a sermon he called, "A 400 Year Testimony." It began this way:

> A business friend burst into my office this week fairly beaming. "I have just witnessed something I never expected to see." Naturally I prepared for a thrilling account of some remarkable phenomena. "I have just seen a Protestant out argue a Roman Catholic." Now

> forgetting for the moment that no one ever wins an argument, I want you to see with me the problem pointed up here in this incident. For it is true that the Protestant member of a discussion usually gives in or gives up. Not necessarily, however, because his position is any weaker, or his convictions less deep, or truth foreign to his side, but due to the very nature of liberal Protestantism. For you see, the more truly Protestant one is the more one comes to know that there is no corner on Truth. And the further one delves into truth the more one discovers the many-faceted multi-natured, extremely complicated character of truth. As a very natural result, therefore, too many of us are too prone to inertia to exert sufficient effort to even begin to understand the nature of truth.

Frank discusses this at length, making it clear that Catholics don't need to search. It is all spelled out for its members. Then, acknowledging that Protestants are a minority in the world, he concedes we must get along even if the two faiths are, he believes, irreconcilable.

> By the very nature of the two doctrines there can be no amicable solution to the conflict. The Roman Catholics recognize no other church; they will give lip service to some programs building toward better understanding, but such programs are always rendered ineffective by the constant awareness that two utterly opposite ideologies confront each other. We on the other hand, recognize most other groups as having truth, but we don't recognize why it is so terribly important that we have our own grasp of truth so firmly implanted that it can afford to be tolerant but

still hold with stubborn faith to the essentials of our belief. We can't overcome false ideas with other false ideas, nor can one maintain true ideas held loosely against false ideas held firmly.

Frank suggests it's time we were able to win arguments with Catholics. This rather intolerant opinion of Catholics reminds this writer of Roger Williams whom Frank greatly admired—both known for their belief in religious freedom. In Frank's case, he shared the fear of Catholicism with its allegiance to a Pope, common in the 40s; in Roger Williams' case, he feared the Quakers would disrupt a non-religious based civil government of laws. The sentiments of Frank's expressed here perhaps forewarn us of the open opposition he will manifest later while a pastor in Arlington, Massachusetts.

† † †

It was propitious that Frank would have another "encounter" with Catholic doctrine less than a year later. In 1947 Louise Anthony and Jack Green came to Frank to talk about their getting married. Louise recently talked to this writer about it:

> My husband, Jack Green, was Catholic so we went down to see the priest. But he told us, when I wouldn't sign something promising to raise my children Catholic, that the best thing we could do was just to cut it right off and not get married. I was crying when we left and lamenting, "Oh, what are we going to do?" Jack said, "We're going up to see your minister."
>
> Mr. Thompson was wonderful to Jack. He was just great; told Jack how he'd known me and how all the boys had wanted me but I hadn't picked any of

them; had gone elsewhere and found you. So we were married by him on August 2, 1947; Loretta sang at our wedding. I believe Sara Sue was there, too. That was a wonderful thing.

I'd been impressed by the beautiful ice sculpture I'd seen at another wedding recently, and wanted one too, so had hired an ice company to do one for our reception. But it melted, and Mr. T just picked the darn thing up, brought it out to kitchen, and dumped it in the sink. It was just a big flop. I think it was in the punch.

† † †

Less than three months earlier, on May 10, 1947, a newspaper (unnamed) reported that "construction of a new $130,000 edifice for the Phillips Memorial Baptist Church was unanimously approved by the church body at a meeting held last night at the church." The plans introduced at the members' meeting, drawn up Howe & Proutt, call for it to adjoin the present wooden building on Pontiac Avenue; the basement to be built first, covered with a temporary roof for use for services until the main church is constructed later. Also planned for the initial phase is a two-story brick wing that will house the pastor's office, a chapel and meeting rooms.

Soon after, on May 18, 1947, "A service for Breaking Ground for the New Church" was held. The service opened, appropriately with the hymn, "The Church's One Foundation and closed with the hymn, "Lead on, O King Eternal." The Litany preceded the actual ground-breaking.

Minister: For the faith and sacrifice of thy children that have made this hour possible.

People: We thank Thee O God.

Minister: For a land of freedom and prosperity which Thou hast blest with golden opportunity.

People: We thank Thee O God.

Minister: Make us conscious of our responsibility to this community and to the world because of these Thy blessings,

People: We pray Thee O God.

Minister: Prosper us in this building program. Let not our zeal wax cold. Keep us from being weary in well doing but inspire us to press ever onward until we reach our goal,

People: We pray Thee O God.

Minister: Solemnly do we dedicate this church we build and all the gifts and labor and effort with which we build and most of all we dedicate ourselves to the great goal of Thy kingdom's work in this community.

People: In the name of Jesus Christ our Lord. Amen.

The newspaper covered the event on May 20th, reporting that over 250 attended the service, including the Cranston Mayor and the first vice-president of the Rhode Island Baptist Convention. The Rev. Earl Tomlin, executive secretary of the Rhode Island Council of Churches, also present, "commended the members for their loyalty and devotion to Christ. He said, 'The vigorous growth of the local church indicates that the Protestant people will stand together for the things in which they believe.'" Four life deaconesses, the oldest being Mrs. Franklin Spooner who joined the church in 1900, and four children broke the ground. The building program had actually been launched five years earlier with a projected cost for the completed Church given as $300,000.

The Pastor's Annual Report for 1947-48 begins with a reference to the groundbreaking, and, for the most part, concerns itself with the church's growth:

> It's been a wet year. That ought to make it a good Baptist year....Never will we forget the precipitation of May 18. The ground breaking was like mud-pie making: the weeping sky seemed to reflect the un-dry eyes of those who had worked and dreamed and planned so long and hard for that event only to have it sabotaged by Jupiter Pluvious and avoided by so many who were needed! [Strange this wasn't mentioned in the newspaper article.]
>
> It's been a year of change. The old asparagus patch is almost filled with new houses now and the barren patches of the parish are few and far between. [*In 1940 when this writer was in Junior High, there was still much open land in the Eden Park section of Cranston that offered us shortcuts when en route to school.*]

Though replaced by new members, Frank laments the loss of a number of old members, suggesting that church growth planning somehow played a part:

> Growth always costs, but the price of our growth here seems inordinately high. We'll pray that the final results will be so rich and plentiful that the costs will be well compensated in the coin of another realm.
>
> It's been a year of maturing too. Perhaps maturity comes harder and slower to those who have

> grown too fast physically. The failures, and frustrations, the internal aches and pains of a growing boy, the awkward and often stupid responses he makes to challenges all presage a better grasp of the process of living later on if his heart is right.
>
> Phillips Memorial has crossed the threshold from the limited area of a small community church into the expansive region of an institution known throughout the denomination and rapidly assuming a place of leadership in city and state affairs....A fine "crop" of young adults has begun to assume more and more leadership. Quiet confidence is beginning to come to those who have undergone violent changes and still can see God's flag flying from that mighty fortress!
>
> The next few years should be GREAT YEARS at Phillips Memorial. The splendid new structure will provide facilities to integrate the new and the old. The people who have felt their hearts and powers expanded by these deeds of faith and courage and some self sacrifice will not rest content with a job half done....
>
> The four "T's" join in thanking you one and all for the privilege of being with you and of you for another year of growth together!

The Thompsons had always been loved by the vast majority of the congregation and the feeling was mutual. Both the men and the young people had always readily volunteered their services to do repairs around the church and to paint rooms and such.

Now it was hoped that the first phase of construction of their new church would be completed by Easter 1948, and, believing it would help, Frank introduced a program he proclaimed would "warm the stomachs and the souls of the workmen." It began in the summer when Girl Scouts were "selling lemonade for the building fund." Frank bought up and gave the workers the unsold portion. As the weather got colder, he recruited volunteers, who made and served hot coffee with cookies or donuts every morning.

The news article reported:[1]

> Sometimes the church workers join with the men in consuming the refreshments. The men sit on folding chairs at long serving tables. Usually there are 17 or 18 of them and they enjoy their treat for 15 or 20 minutes (between 10 and 10:30).
>
> Olaf Ahlberg, the contractor, is so pleased with this practice that he has made a contribution of $500 to the church, Mr. Thompson said. The workmen themselves also are making a financial contribution. "The men go back to the job in better spirits after their repast," the pastor said, "and they work with a zest that more than makes up for the time lost. They are more than willing to work overtime when necessary."...
>
> Since the contract was awarded last May prices have soared on building costs as well as most other things, Mr. Thompson said. [*Prices he enumerates that then seemed staggering, seem only a pittance compared to what costs would be today for the same work.*]

The article and picture must have appeared in October, because on the 21st of that month, Frank enclosed a copy of the

---

[1] Article with picture is not dated nor paper noted; probably the *Providence Evening Bulletin*..

picture and article in a letter to his old friend, Beulah, whose financial assistance had enabled him to attend Redlands. The letter also had something of a surprise announcement. He wrote:

> As you can probably see from the sights there, it is only started but moving along so fast now that each day brings the fulfillment of our ancient dream nearer into reality. The tragic thing about it is that the spiral of inflation has cut our whole program in half or else necessitated the raising of twice as much as we had originally contemplated...In the midst of our preparation here for another campaign to raise more money has come a rather thrilling invitation to go to Bacone College as president.
>
> I know that I do not have quite the equipment for such a high calling and would not feel justified in tackling it, but nevertheless it is a rather stupendous opportunity and something to feel very humble about even having been considered for it. No definite decision has been made yet but we feel fairly certain that this is our God-given task here until they have reached a stage where no more growth or building possibility will present itself for the time [*foreshadowing, perhaps, why ultimately he did leave*]. We wondered when this opportunity came if it might not be the hand of God, because it is so true that the builder is not often the continuing administrator, and yet there seemed to be so many reasons why it would be wrong for us to leave in the midst of a program that we worked for for nearly a decade that I suspect we will be led to turn down that rather thrilling opportunity at great old Bacone.
>
> I knew you'd want to share the thought with

me and perhaps help me make a decision so am just sending this note along with request for your prayer and happy counsel. Ever devotedly yours, Frank.[2]

Sara Sue, Woody, Frank & Loretta about 1948; about the time Frank announced that he was leaving Phillips Memorial.

Nearly four months after his letter to Beulah, on Sunday, February 8, 1948, as Frank told the congregation he had accepted a position as President of Bacone, an Indian College in Muskogee, Oklahoma, effective July 1, tears could be seen running down many a cheek. It was the Home Missionary Society of the Northern Baptist Convention that had nominated Frank for the position. A newspaper article on February 9th, among other things, stated that the

[2] Though this writer seldom mentions Beulah in this biography, Beulah remained sufficiently close to the family that Loretta, at times felt jealous, and the Thompson children and grandchildren all called her Aunt Beulah.

membership at Phillips had tripled since Frank became the minister:[3] It continued:

> He was responsible for establishing two morning worship services, being one of a few Protestant churches in this area to offer this service. His interest in forming young people's groups has created many new youth organizations in the church.
>
> It was under Mr. Thompson's leadership that the church obtained a gift of $25,000 from the Northern Baptist Convention to aid in the building program.
>
> When part of the new building is occupied in a few weeks, only a small mortgage will remain. The church, Mr. Thompson said, has arranged the loan on a long term, non-interest basis.

Less than a week later, on February 13th, the newspaper reported that the day before, at a special meeting called to consider his resignation, "a resolution was passed expressing the wish that the pastor would remain but leaving the ultimate decision to him." Yet another article reported that Frank had told church members in a letter that he would give his final answer at the annual meeting on April 15, giving him time to "meditate and weigh again this great decision."

† † †

---

[3] Though the actual figures are impressive, if those in the official local Baptist annals are correct, this is something of an exaggeration. According to these records, there were 356 member in 1938 and 750 in 1948. Of the 102 members added that year, 34 were baptized at one time, the largest number at once in the history of the church. After Rev. Frank Snell's first year (1949), there was a net loss of 72 members. Phillips Memorial was part of the Roger Williams Association, a grouping by the state Baptist Convention of churches within a similar region.

228. Justice, Peace & God

Meanwhile, on March 21, 1948, Frank preached what would be his last Palm Sunday sermon, "Victory Missing—Victim of Amnesia" [Luke 19: 36-44]. His message was, basically, the same as that given for the Brown students almost exactly two years earlier—one, regrettably, still not heeded—even now.

> The triumphal entry! One brief flashing moment of Victory and sweet peace! The shouts, waving palms, a pathway of garments, joyous faces of those he'd touched lining the eager crowd! Those eyes of his—reflected in the new-opened eyes of Bartimaeus-Zacchaeus...! I wonder what he thought as he rode along that wall of wretched humanity made glad for a moment at least! Well, we know something of what he thought. He knew it was only a momentary victory. Unless something more were done, it would vanish with the fresh strewn palms!
>
> From the noisy beginning of the parade to the brow of the mountain, Christ must have wondered, and then, pausing on the peak, he looked out over the sprawling mass of human need and cried out words that really climax the parade, "Oh, Jerusalem, Jerusalem, IF ONLY YOU HAD KNOWN THE THINGS THAT MAKE FOR PEACE! Just an instant of heart-rendering yearning for that fair victim of amnesia we call PEACE. Then on—even though it was late; only a few more years remained for Jerusalem, only a few more days for Jesus—but on, "seeing the end from the beginning!" He plunged right into the midst of reforming that city—building for eternity, the things which time cannot destroy.
>
> Jesus felt the thrill of VICTORY. The parade

must have been as exhilarating to him as to any parade lover, but he saw the end from the beginning. Surface level loyalty wasn't sufficient for THAT kind of era!...

Note how this Palm Sunday experience has implications for every realm of life today—personal, organizational, international....In my opinion, Christian citizens have been challenged this week as only in the days of our greatest crises of history. There is tremendous danger from abroad, ghastly danger. The reason it's so ghastly is that we apparently have no fitting answer to it. The Communists are not going to make the foolish mistake the Nazis made of waging open conflict. Theirs is the conquest of ideas—false ideas, yes! But to try to displace ideas with mere force alone makes the chaos greater, eventually.

We deplore the fall of little countries into the grasp of pagan dictator-controlled giants of force. But what did we do to support these little countries when they were starving?? We refused to vote enough funds to keep UNRRA going another year, so now we are being called on to vote enough funds to have supplied UNRRA for fifty years, but now it's not for food, it's for war materiel!...[*Why do we always have money for the one and not for the other?*]

The head of this government is asking its citizens to embark upon one of the most undemocratic campaign in our history I urge you to ask your government these questions:

1. Why was the news of Russian's recent attempt to meet in a neutral spot for peace talks kept from the public? And why was our answer to

that request a flat, "NO"? Why were we surprised then that the next step was a new aggressiveness by Russia?

2. Why are we persisting in the "eye for an eye" philosophy of the Old Testament when the New Testament teaches a method far beyond that? Hasn't the time come since our "eye for an eye" policy has so abysmally failed, to try some new approach?

Frank quotes Charles Wells as saying, "We rudely closed the door on what may be our last hope for reconciliation....America is strong enough, but we are not Christian enough." He then continues:

> The great atheistic country we fear...is certain we are going to war against them....They see great quantities of arms and soldiers being sent to Greece, Turkey, China. Our fleet crowds their shore. We grab oil off the Near East which is at their doorstep,...we establish American air bases among our oil fields, within 30 minutes by bomber of their cities....Is our leadership so spiritually impoverished that no gestures or approach can be designed except on the age-old level of failure?...
>
> This is not surrender—or appeasement talk. THIS IS A CALL FOR US TO WAGE ACTIVE PEACE WITH THE SAME COURAGE AND FORTITUDE AS OUR BELOVED FELLOWS WAGED ACTIVE WAR.

Frank suggests we aggressively clean our own house of thieves and robbers, of fascist groups like the KKK, and of those who are "selling our democratic way down the river with plans for imperialistic empires, great cartels, pagan philosophies, and Church controlled institutions of state and nation. And, above all, of those who are seeking a way of shaping the minds and wills of youth to a military philosophy of life." Finally, Frank says, "Drive out those trying to communize us, yes, not using *their* weapons...but by a campaign to out-run them, out-think them, out-live them and out-love them...."

He closes with a quote by Norman Cousins, whom he calls a brilliant editor: [4]

> "The only question today that counts is this: is some supreme moral effort to build a meeting-ground between East and West still worth the effort—even at this late date? And if we decided that it is, let the proposal for the idea reflect some sense of magnificent destiny, some throb of vital purpose, some capacity for communicating and sharing the ideal of world citizenship. IT IS NOT TOO LATE, BUT IT HAS SELDOM BEEN LATER!"

† † †

It might have been that same Sunday, while Frank was preaching upstairs, that his son, "Woody" (Scott) and a friend, "Hammie" (Hamilton Hanson), were busy elsewhere in the church. As was common at Phillips Memorial, as it is in most Protestant churches, the younger children remained in the main sanctuary for the opening part of the service, and then were escorted to the Sunday School classrooms in the church's basement. Somehow, on this day, Woody and Hammie, only six and five years old respectively, managed to

---

[4] Cousins would later be elected President of the World Association for World Federalism, at a time when Frank was West Coast Director of the United World Federalists.

get separated from the group, and found themselves on their own in the basement's large West room. Just recently Hamilton described for this writer what happened next:

> The large double doors were easily closed, and so long as we were quiet, it was probable that no one would look in to see what was happening. So, as boys will do, we set about finding something fun and exciting to do!!
>
> By the time church had let out and our parents came looking for us, we had stacked every single chair in the room in a pyramid around one of the supporting poles! So, when my mother opened the doors seeking the whereabouts of her son, the look of astonishment on her face was precious as she loudly exclaimed, "What did you do!!" Everyone who now walked through that hallway saw that two boys–children of two of the church's most prominent members–Scott's father, the minister, and my mother, Sunday School Superintendent–had done a most improbable deed–right there during the time of Sunday morning worship services and Sunday School!

"Hammie" doesn't recall what the repercussions might have been, but wouldn't be surprised if he had a lecture and sound spanking when they got home, since that kind of punishment was so common in their household that he tended not to remember any specific time. It's more likely that Woody's family just thought it funny, which it was. Some have called the Thompsons' children spoiled.

†††

Frank's office was atop a winding staircase, so Sara

Sue, with her friend, Nancy Olson, liked to sneak up and surprise him there. They also liked to play hide-and-seek in the many intriguing corners offered by the old church. In recalling it, Nancy states, "Our reasoning went that since it was Sara Sue's dad's church, that made it her church; and since we were best friends, it was also my church. So we thought of the church as a sort of play-area too."

In September 1947, at the beginning of 2nd grade, Nancy, the same age as Sara Sue, had moved to Cranston from Virginia. So, Nancy tells this writer, "I knew Sara Sue only that year, but we quickly became fast friends; lived only a few blocks from each other, and had frequent sleep-overs at each other's houses." When asked, she confided, "Both of us were serious students but learning came to us easily."

Nancy also recalled the Spring that Sara Sue and she had a discussion about whether they could get poison ivy; they thought they couldn't.

> So we went to a nearby field and managed to rub poison ivy all over ourselves. We came down with a really horrible case, eyes swollen shut, had to stay home from school while in terrible agony. We were taken to the doctor, but the only treatment was dousing with Calamine Lotion. We learned the hard way that "yes, indeed, we could get poison ivy."

A final story Nancy recounts is the time she had walked over from her nearby house on Fairfield Road, and the family was eating supper.

> So I was asked to wait in the adjoining room where they had a piano. Sara Sue, at the time, was taking lessons from Lucille Spooner's mother, so I started plinking on the piano and once I figured out where "middle-C" was, could play some from her

beginner's books. This got me interested in Music and I started taking from Edna Spooner too. I remember the terror of recitals but am not sure if we were ever both in one.

Lucille says of her mother, Edna:

> She was a marvelous pianist who taught hundreds of children; she didn't make much money but loved children. She graduated from normal school in 1912 but got married to LeRoy Arnold Spooner so never was able to teach kindergarten as planned; married teachers weren't allowed to teach. Edna died in 1981.

After the Thompsons moved to Oklahoma, Nancy says she missed Sara Sue terribly.

> We wrote each other and they sent me a doll dressed up like an Indian, but I didn't see her again until the summer before my 7th grade; that would have been 1952, when the family came back. After that we didn't keep in touch any more. Sara Sue had changed and I didn't feel close anymore.
>
> I was at Phillips Memorial when Frank came back again with the Bacone College choir [when he was President of Bacone]. I forgot about the choir, because it was him that was important to me, not the choir. The church, the new basement then serving as the sanctuary, was jam-packed because so many people had loved him, and people who couldn't fit in were outside looking in the windows listening to the choir and to him speak.[5]

---

[5] We'll hear more of this choir and this event later.

235. Moving On

By April 15th Frank had not changed his mind about leaving Phillips Memorial. Much as he was loved by most of the congregation, he had been in conflict with others over fund-raising for the new church. Dickson Kenney recently said to this writer:

> My dad, George, was in charge of the building committee and didn't think much of Frank's business ability, which kept them apart: part of the tension that led to Frank's leaving. [*An odd opinion since he'd been primarily responsible for raising the money for stage one of the new church building, and would go on to be a success as chief fundraiser for both Bacone College and Redlands University.*]

As another member recently put it: "It was a big disappointment to him that the church was not ready to commit to building the whole church; would settle for the basement—that was a tremendous blow for him that people were not ready to be challenged to build the whole church. He had been outvoted by people who were more conservative; it caused a rift." [*At the time, still in my teens, this writer also remembers this controversy; there were times at church you could feel the tension.*] It's hard to say whether this was a factor, perhaps the deciding factor, in Frank's decision to reaffirm his resignation.

On the positive side, however, Frank clearly had a biding concern for the Indians and must have felt it a real honor to be asked to be Bacone College's President. Virginia Droitcor recently conveyed to this writer her own believable explanation: "Frank went to Bacone because he wanted to help people and thought he would be doing more of a service there than at the church where people didn't really need him as much."

† † †

Almost exactly a year after the Breaking Ground ceremony, on the Wednesday afternoon of May 19, 1948, Phillips Memorial held a cornerstone service, attended by many of the same congregants and community leaders. The *Providence Journal* next morning reported that "a large crowd overflowed the lawn....The strong box which was placed in the cornerstone was filled with [a list of the charter and present members of the church] coins, stamps and newspapers....The first trowel of mortar was placed by Mrs. B. Franklin Spooner, church historian and one of the first deaconesses of the Church. She used the same trowel used on the cornerstone of the original church." This marked the end of phase one of the church's building program.

† † †

On June 22nd, Frank wrote his last letter to the congregation, beginning: "THIS IS IT!" evoking a double meaning. "The new Church Opening, an Operetta, its first Worship Services, first Baptism, last Communion, farewell to Phillips Memorial–ten years all rolled up in one week."

The letter continues:

> Since no message from me would be complete–not even the last one–without a request or two, let me "give with them!" Will you pray for us Thompsons? We have a tremendous task before us. Phillips Memorial has provided the opportunity to prepare for this magnum opus, but whether we can meet the challenge depends on power far beyond our own. Help us get some of that power, will you?
>
> Next, will you support our musical extravaganza, Friday and Saturday evening? Six

months of grueling efforts will be climaxed with the help of Von Flotow, sixty youth et al, and that grand new stage and hall.

And next Sunday? Two worship services in the new church with brand new chairs, a good choir, an old sermon and YOU!

Last, but not least, will you help the interim pastor who comes to bridge the gap between ministers? He will be your guest for a few short months, give him the finest hearing and [be the most gracious hosts possible]. Above all, LOOK FORWARD to that fine new man that God will send to lead you into the next area of achievement.

"Expect great things from God,
Attempt great things for God."

William Carey started one of history's most significant movements with that dual demand upon his soul!

In a P.S. Frank notes that his inauguration as the new President of Bacone will be on October 1st and that a special train will be provided for those going to Oklahoma for the event!

† † †

The Operetta, *Martha*, mentioned in the above-quoted letter, was a roaring success, lots of fun for those in it [this writer one of those in beautiful long dresses with parasols, who, in one scene, strolled along in the park with many others, part of a chorus for the talented few who sang], and greatly appreciated by the audience which filled the new church hall for both Friday and Saturday night's performances, June 25 and 26, 1948. Loretta, who'd been practicing with us for months, was there to conduct this final farewell to her own incredible vocal and directing talents she'd offered Phillips.

On July 8th, newspaper columnist Madeline Chaffee congratulates Loretta and her assistants on their fine collective efforts. She goes on to say:

> Amateur musical offerings often suffer from the fact that the leading characters cannot really sing. Such was happily not the case in "Martha." All four principals were possessed of excellent singing voices and used them to good effect throughout.

Chaffee also notes the quality performances by the more comic characters, and those of the singing chorus of approximately 50 voices. She also comments on the "extremely pleasant," "well proportioned hall seating 500," which someday will be the basement "as the steepled sanctuary rises above it." The article also reminded its readers that Loretta would be missed as well as her "publicly spirited husband. A gifted musician herself, Mrs. Thompson has been generous in sharing her talents and has directed more than one successful musical presentation during her years in Cranston."

On the Sunday evening following the *Martha* productions, "an overflow crowd filled the new auditorium ...as parishioners and friends gathered to tender a farewell reception" for the Thompsons who would be leaving the week following for Bacone. "The congregation gave the Minster and his wife a large console radio phonograph, luggage, and gifts of money." The Junior High group gave them a croquet set. There was an hour's program of mixed musical numbers and short tributes by community leaders, clergy and parishioners to the work of both Frank and Loretta during their ten years at Phillips [which would prove to be his longest stay at any one place]. Music included harp solos, piano selections, and a surprise group of songs by the girls' septet that had been formed and directed by Loretta. One of its members, Eleanor Boudreau (Goodge), recalls with affection for Loretta, the many times she had them to her home to learn songs and to practice.

†††

Frank returned from Bacone to Cranston to give the dedicatory sermon at the service held on September 19, 1948 for the partially completed new church. A newspaper account reported:

> State and national Baptist ministers, church officials and Mayor Hoyt W. Lark attended the dedication ceremonies which were held in the new building at four o'clock...Special music for the occasion was presented by the church choir and a quartet....The building committee chairman, George M. Kenney,...told [the congregation] that 47 years ago a small group of people founded the church and dedicated the old edifice which now has become a part of the new building....

Frank was not present at the annual meeting when the 20-year mortgage of $150,000, paid off in seven years, was ceremoniously burned.[6] By then the Rev. Frank H. Snell was pastor. Also present was Mrs. Charles Anthony, whose father was the contractor for the original white wooden church building.

Eight years passed before the church was completed in its entirety. To celebrate, a series of dedication services were held from March 11-18, 1956: Frank had by then resigned as President of Bacone College and returned to the ministry in near-by Arlington, Massachusetts. Lucille Spooner recently had this to say: "Mr. Snell was then pastor and Mr. T couldn't come back and divide the church. Personally or as a Christian he wouldn't. He was more or less forgotten very quickly–surprisingly, given how much he'd contributed in building both the membership and the new physical church."

You might well say Frank was slighted given his contribution, as Lucille pointed out, but she was wrong about

---

[6] Probably in 1955, but church historian could find no information regarding this event.

his being totally absent from the celebration. The program notes that there was a "Home Coming Service" on Friday, March 16th, when several previous pastors were scheduled to participate; Frank to give the main address. There is a newspaper clipping indicating that Frank is also giving the address at a 4 p.m. service on the 18th, but there is no mention of this service in the formal program, and no indication that he either attended or participated in the closing and final service at 8 p.m. on the 18th to which invitations were sent urging "all Baptist Churches in the State to participate."

Rev. Rasmussen, who followed Rev. Snell as pastor, probably was accurate when he recently said, "Instead of opposing Frank, the trustees should have listened to him and finished the church as he wanted. When they finally did finish it, the cost was twice what it would have been then."

†††

One newspaper article on March 5, 1956, reported an interesting "side event" to the new church–the story of a 118-year-old, 870 pound church bell that would ring again after having been silenced for six years (after the tenure of Frank), as a result of its weakening the old church tower. As the paper noted:

> As the tower weakened and the bell remained strong and loud, its booming vibrations began causing cracks on the tower ceiling, and the bell was sentenced to silence. But with the completion of the new church and tower, the historic bell was given its new lease on life....

"The bell had been cast in Medway, Mass., in 1838 by one G. H. Golbrook, an apprentice of none other than Paul Revere." It's first home was at the Pine Street Baptist church, then the Richmond Street Fire Station. In 1911 it was purchased by the Eden Park Volunteer Fire Company and hung in the Eden Park Grammar School for use as an alarm signal. It was not until 1929 that volunteers donated it to Phillips Memorial in memory of Robert P. Scott who had been killed in WWI.

12. Bacone: A Challenge He Couldn't Resist

> *A full-blooded Creek Indian student wandered through the rambling structure of the Third Baptist Church in St. Louis. He was looking for dressing rooms for the Singing Redmen of Bacone Indian College to change into buckskin and feathers so the choir would look Indian during their performance. Our Indian "scout" found a boy dashing wildly about and asked, "Can I help you buddy?" "Naw, I'm looking for some Injuns," the boy panted. "Maybe I can help you; I'm Indian." The youngster put his hands on his hips and with all the scorn of a twelve year old replied, "Aw go on, you're human."*
>
> *To dispel the myth that Indians are less than human beings, implied in the boy's declaration, was the main purpose of our whole public relations effort at the unique little college in Muskogee, Oklahoma. We like to boast of being the only college for Indian Americans.*[1]

† † †

It's this writer's opinion that, even though Frank did many things in his life and preached in many places, his heart and soul belonged to the Indians. As late as 1968, over a dozen years after he'd left the Presidency of Bacone College in Oklahoma, he had this to say in one of his very first sermons to the congregants at the Congregational Church in Alameda, California:

> We were in the process of dedicating a great new church (debt free, of course, because it was in New England) when the "Call" came to try to make

---

[1] From a piece Frank wrote about an appearance of the Bacone Choir in 1955. More will be said of this later.

right some wrongs that had been done to our Brother, the Indian American. And what wrongs they were: one of the saddest stories of our American epic is our misunderstanding and mistreatment of these people who met our ancestors with an open palm—who kept the Pilgrims alive, who could so easily have destroyed all.

> We found when we arrived at Bacone College in Muskogee, able students who came to the college with resentments and apprehension—wondering what was to be taken from them next. Our task was to build confidence in them, and to interpret what they really were to the people of this nation. To those ends we launched a public relations program that sent groups of students out to all areas of the land. The lack of rapport between students and citizens was terrifying at first, but gradually they began to see that people were eager to know them and show concern for their needs.

He ends by saying he hopes the long and dramatic story of the Indians will pique their interest enough so they will attend discussions on the subject he plans to arrange soon.

† † †

It was not until 1943, when Frank was still at Phillips Memorial, that Bacone had its first Native American President, the Rev. Earl L. Riley, who had degrees from both Bacone College and Redlands University. After Riley resigned in 1947, Rev. Charles Detweiler, anxious to retire to his home in Colorado, reluctantly agreed to become Acting President until Frank arrived.

245. Bacone: A Challenge He Couldn't Resist

On January 20, 1948, at a meeting in New York City, the Board of Directors of the American Baptist Home Missions Society, which controlled Bacone, elected Francis Willard Thompson to the presidency of the school. It seems possible that his selection was influenced by their belief that he was 1/16 Sioux Indian, and one could imagine some of his features reflecting an Indian heritage, but, as indicated previously, this writer has not been able to establish either the accuracy of this belief or the Baptists' rationale for choosing Frank.

Be that as it may, at Frank's request, a public announcement of his selection was withheld until he could personally inform his congregation at Phillips Memorial. As we know, he did that on February 8th and on July 1st assumed his new duties as Bacone Junior College's tenth President, and, simultaneously, as Superintendent of the Murrow Orphans Home and Minister of the Bacone Baptist Chapel.

† † †

In early April, prior to his self-stated deadline for a final answer to the trustees at Phillips Memorial about his decision to leave, Frank made a trip to Bacone, with a stopover in St Louis, Missouri, from whence he wrote Loretta a postcard. "Your sweet notes in my clothes make me very lovesick for you. This travelling without you is forbidding." And from Bacone he wrote another card to his "Sweethearts":

> I want you to know how much I am thinking and feeling for you and wishing you were each here! So many have expressed regrets you couldn't be with me, but soon you will be! The campus is beautiful and the prospects brilliant IF God's man comes as new president. Tell the children there is a fireplace in the ten-room plus President's house! Will see you soon with love galore for each and all.

Several years later, Frank wrote about his intentions when he made that early trip to Bacone.

> I had visited Bacone with the intent of rejecting the offer of the New York Board to assume the presidency. I found the campus, which had been a delightful gem ten years previously while I served as librarian and coach, grown high with weeds and cluttered with unsightly trash.
>
> I hurried into Muskogee to talk with Paul Bruner of the Chamber of Commerce, for whom I had worked when he was editor of the city's newspapers. I asked him frankly what the future was for Bacone. He declared strongly that there was no future as far as he could see. The school could not get one week's credit for bread, so indebted and overdrawn was Bacone. *I told him I had come to reject the offer to become its tenth president, but that I found the need so great I was tempted to accept the challenge.* He assured me that if I was foolish enough to accept, he would suggest what he thought might help us get back some of the rapport which had all but vanished.

> Being assured that I respected his judgement and would relish any help, he advised us to stage some dramatic events, and promote a top grade athletic program that would give visibility, assuring locals that Bacone was not just a stepchild of the far off New York board, with little interest in public relations.
>
> The distance between New York and Muskogee had been difficult to breach. Bacone could not have survived a month without the generous contributions from Missionary-minded churches, but local people had never been informed of the true concern and sacrifice on the part of far away people.

Nothing could illustrate better how deeply Frank felt about Bacone and the Indian cause than to have accepted the challenge of the Presidency under these conditions.

Meanwhile, even before Frank had given his final answer to Phillips Memorial's trustees, letters of congratulations, best wishes, and "sorrow," letters that would fill a scrapbook, began to pour in—from members of his congregation and from others all over the U.S., including one from Beirut, Lebanon. Typical was the one from Rev. John Clark, First Baptist Church, Knoxville, Tennessee:

> It was good news to learn recently of your decision to go to Bacone College as President, a difficult decision to make I'm sure, in light of the building program.
>
> How often is it true that one man builds, and another inherits the building. But that is true all through life and each of us is always coming into the

> inheritance from some spiritual forebear.
>
> Because of your love of Indians, your knowledge of them, and your ability, I'm sure the experience there will be fruitful for them and for you....

After extending his congratulations, Rev. Raymond Smith, Middle Street Baptist, Portsmouth, New Hampshire, wrote:

> While it will be a tug on your heart to leave New England, I know you will be very happy to be back at Bacone. Certainly when you leave little Rhody, you will leave a splendid record behind you. You have done a marvelous job there at Eden Park and have hung up a record that will last a good many years. I know your people must feel heartbroken to have you leave....

In a brief extract from his long letter, Mark Rich, Town and Country Work, American Baptist Home Mission Society, stated:

> I am sorry to know that some of your people still feel that you are running out on them. I should feel very happy for having had you for ten years.

Soon after Frank had announced to the congregation in February his intent to leave, Alice Brown, Dean of Women, who had been at Bacone through 30 years of its ups and downs, wrote him:

> I write to tell you how very much we are hoping and praying for your coming for we need you so very much! Someone has said that God does not change his mind. If he calls us to a task once, that is His task for us. But you are right in being sure...

249. Bacone: A Challenge He Couldn't Resist

You are not looking for fame, I know, but might I suggest that right now, in your decision, you practically hold in your hands the future of the great part of the on-coming generations of our Indians in all tribes. Thousands of these young people, especially the boys, have seen the far places of the world [returning from WWII], have been with other peoples and on an equal with them. They are not going to settle back on the reservations and be hedged about with restrictions like little children as their forefathers have, unless we fail to give them an opportunity for a Christian education, whereby they may walk like men in a world of men. They are eager for it, for they see the great need for it, for both themselves and for their people.

If we might have your leadership, with your interest both in the intellectual, as represented by your library work; in the physical, as proven by your boxing especially; and in the religious, above all and through all, as could constantly be shown as pastor of our church. God alone can measure what it would be possible to do for these next student generations.

At the time of Frank's arrival in July 1948, the campus, located on an elevation that overlooked the surrounding country, occupied about 50 of its 290 acres; most of the rest was in farm and grazing land used by Bacone for instructional purposes and to provide most of its own food. But there was also woodland, which, after gifts to Frank of four horses, offered him a golden opportunity again to indulge in what had been one of his loves when growing up in Arizona—horseback riding. When the family left Bacone and it was not feasible to take the horses with them, the College kept them in recognition of the fact that so many of their Indian students had always known horseback riding as their primary means of transportation. Meanwhile, for Frank, saddling up one of his favorite horses, Pal or Mino (Buck and Whirley were the other two), and rushing against the wind was a relaxing change from the rigors of travel and fundraising that occupied so much of his time.

Frank's horses Pal & Mino

There were a dozen plus modern buildings on campus, a faculty of seventeen, and a student body that numbered about 200 each year —60% boys, 40% girls—approximately half enrolled in the Junior College, the rest in the High School located on campus, which began with ninth grade. (The elementary school that was once on campus had been phased out in 1946, and the high school would begin its phase-out in 1955, the last year Frank was at Bacone.) Represented on campus were Creeks, Cherokees, Choctaws, Chickasaws,

Seminoles, Delawares, Apaches, Navajos, Hopis and a scattering of other tribes.

Bacone's budget for 1947-48, ending May 31, just prior to Frank's arrival, totaled $138,550. Of this, $55,000 came from tuition, $40,000 from dormitory and dining hall income, $13,595 from the American Home Mission Society, $9,500 from churches and individuals, and $41,117 from endowments and royalties. Most of the rest came from "dribbles and drabbles."[2] Maybe, after all, it was Frank's manifest fundraising ability in Eden Park (despite the comment by George Kenney) that had been the Home Mission's main incentive in selecting him as Bacone's tenth president. Certainly during his seven years at Bacone, he would spend many days off campus seeking money, perhaps expending more time and effort in this role than he had bargained for (but one at which he was amazingly successful).

It was on October 1st in a special convocation in the Bacone Chapel that Frank was inaugurated; the service culminating a two-day gathering of friends, distinguished guests and members of the advisory boards of Bacone College and the Murrow Orphanage. The weather was sunny throughout, and the campus, newly groomed for the events, sparkled. The inaugural address was given by Rev. Dr. George Pitt Beers, Executive Secretary of the American Baptist Home Mission Society, and Dr. Charles Detweiler, the out-going Acting President, offered the inaugural prayer. Frank responded to the prayer, accepting the post and

---

[2] From an article by Harold Johnson, in the *Daily Oklahoman*, Sunday, April 25, 1948 and another by Charles Detweiler, that appeared in the *Daughters of the American Revolution Magazine*, date unknown.

setting out his policies and plans. An important part of the service was the music provided by the Singing Redmen.

Writing of the inauguration, Madeline Chaffee, in her column [undated] in the Cranston, Rhode Island paper, described "the masculine members [of the Thompson family], father and six-year-old son, looking quite serious and the feminine side, mother and eight-year-old daughter, sparkling with animation." She went on to say:

> Some almost forgotten lines by Robert Louis Stevenson came to mind: "A happy man or woman is a radiant focus of good will, and their entrance into a room is as though another candle had been lighted."
>
> We have an idea that candles are being lighted at Bacone, even as they were lighted in Cranston.
>
> "Bacone," the new president stated, "is not just another school on a hill...It is, or should be, a way of life...Bacone is not concerned merely with stretching some IQ's and turning out perfected robots to take their places on the belt line of modern mechanistic existence...
>
> "The whole goal of education might be summed up in Jesus's words, 'Seek and ye shall find.' The person or institution that is humble enough, and energetic enough, to seek the way usually finds the path."

Just how much Loretta contributed to Frank's mission at Bacone is beautifully summed up in a citation she received from the members of the Muskogee Ministerial Alliance on December 8, 1952:

> For your ministry of music in our community

and as director of choirs in one of our churches;

For the generous use of your talents in community programs, as the president of the Muskogee Music Arts Society and on the World Day of Prayer; For your influence upon the young life of the Bacone Indian College, who have seen our community and the Kingdom of God through your eyes, and who are taking a larger place in the life of our nation;

Sara Sue & Scott with their mother, dresssed for one of the many musical events in which Loretta sang.

For your fine home and the impact you are making for a Christian tomorrow, and for your assistance to Dr. Thompson as he seeks support for Bacone College.

In a recent conversation with this writer, Linea Harman, who arrived at Bacone along with her husband the same year as the Thompsons, had this to say:

> It was a good community on campus when they were here; a wonderful place to raise children because all the parents who lived in the different faculty houses sort of kept an eye out for all the children, and they all played together. The Thompson children were very popular and Sara Sue, as the oldest, was sort of looked up to by the other children.
>
> I used to bake cookies every Saturday morning and Sara Sue, when about ten, used to come down to eat cookies with us. She loved to play with my younger children–Diana, four or five and Dan, two or three (I had a third born in December 1950). My children all thought Sara Sue was sort of an ideal person to copy after. After she outgrew a bicycle given to her by Burt Lancaster [more later] she gave it to Diana.

As noted, Linea and her husband, Leo (now deceased), had come to Bacone in 1948, as had the Thompsons, she as a part-time Chemistry teacher, he as the Math and Physics instructor. Linea had nothing but praise for Frank, whom she described as "very personable," and Loretta, from whom she said she learned a lot.

> The Thompsons were the center of social life on campus at a time when most of the faculty and staff lived in campus housing, so we were really a community: Bacone only came inside the city-limits

of Muskogee much later, after the city had grown and spread out.

Frank was impressed by Leo and helped him become Dean in 1950, a position he held until his death 25 years later. As Dean he ran the academic side, dealing with the courses, their development, publications, bulletins and things like that. He and Frank had a very good relationship and our families became very close.

We were both very young when Leo became Dean and so I feel very grateful to Loretta who helped me learn social skills, entertaining and all that. Loretta, as the President's wife was campus hostess, and as the Dean's wife, I often helped her when she had big things like receptions, teas and that sort of thing. During that time, they were frequent.

In the Fall they always had a welcoming reception for new faculty members–all the faculty and staff invited so we could meet them.

Both Frank and Loretta were very gracious people and these affairs were always very nice, usually taking place in their home, most often when Frank was not traveling. Loretta would, however, during times he was away, have meetings of the wives.

† † †

A postcard from Chicago to Loretta just five months after Frank's inauguration suggests the family's frustrations at Bacone; especially the need imposed on Frank for prolonged fundraising trips–the "prolonged" suggested in the card by the fact he'd sent dirty laundry home; the "frustration" suggested by his comment: "Don't despair of

Bacone. I found Franklin College much worse off in many ways." Frank closes: "Tell the kiddies I sure miss them and double for your own gracious self."

At least he could know that his way with words and charismatic presence were effective. After a visit to the Exchange Club of Cleveland, Ohio in November 1949, they had this to say in their newsletter:

> Recommended as an unusual speaker, [he] really exceeded all expectations in one of the most interesting and informative addresses of the current season. ...To champion a cause [the plight of the American Indian] and to attempt a job simply for the reason that it is a job which should be done, takes great courage and an uncommon amount of personal ability. The record shows that we have apparently taken the easy way in our handling of important and serious Indian problems, and much to the disadvantage of the Indian. Dr. Thompson has accomplished wonders in organizing an adequate procedure to meet the special needs of the college and is now touring the country for the purpose of securing support which will eventually place the American Indian in a position to participate on an equal footing in our modern life. Our sincere appreciation to Dr. Frank Thompson for an inspiring message which it is hoped may benefit in more ways than one.

Appreciated or not, it must have been wearing. Four postcards postmarked at various times in 1950 from Kansas City, Missouri; Pasadena, California; Syracuse, New York and Washington, DC suggest just how often and how extensive his travels were. The California card, addressed to his daughter, Sara Sue, expresses poignantly his pain in being away, at least partially alleviated by the chance to see relatives:

> Don't tell anyone but I miss you and Mother and Scotty so much I could sit right down and put my feet out and cry for you!
>
> I am going to see Uncle Lewis [his brother] and his family in a few minutes...Uncle Ford [his half-brother] next day.

Growing tensions can be deduced, at least in retrospect, by his son Scott's account of the interaction between father and children on his return from these trips bearing gifts. Usually, he says, "we were overwhelming in our thanks cuz it meant recognition" [which, presumably, they craved]. But Scott recalls one occasion that included a criticism:

> We pointed out that the cowboy hats he'd brought were the wrong sizes, or something like that. He blew up and said there'd never be any other presents. On this occasion as on many others, we calmed him down, assuring him, over and over, how grateful we were. What we didn't realize was that these were his insecurities flaring up—an actual term I didn't grasp until near the end when he confessed to thin skin and terrible insecurities.

† † †

Always a big supporter of the United Nations and all it stood for, it's not surprising that in October 1949, Frank took the lead in seeing that Bacone should actively participate in Muskogee's celebration of the United Nations' fourth anniversary. Unfortunately it was a miserable, rain-soaked day that kept the participating bands and such confined to their buses as they traversed the parade route. And the weather also resulted in a lesser number in attendance that evening at the concluding celebration scheduled at the City Hall Auditorium.[3]

[3] Years later, in 1967, while briefly a pastor at the First Congregational Church of San Francisco, he would again talk of the U in UN at another Town Hall, in Valley Plaza. And then again, on the occasion of the UN's 26th anniversary, while pastor at Alameda's First Congregational Church, he talked on "The UN–Good for Children and Other Living Things."

As part of that program, Frank spoke of the "U" in U.N., stressing the need for everyone to get behind the organization if the world's young people are to mature into men and women. "There are too many of us who have branded the United Nations as unsuccessful." He urged them to "give it a chance," not to "sell it short," insisting that our very tomorrow depended on the support of Christian churches, synagogues, PTAs and such other organizations.

Among the outstanding singing groups which performed that evening was Bacone's Singing Maidens, directed by Loretta. They sang the Indian's Lord's Prayer as Thelma Whirlwindhorse translated it into sign language (see above). After the benediction, as a finale, the audience sang

Father of every race, Giver of every grace
Hear us we pray!
Let every land be free; may all men brothers be,
All nations honor Thee now and for aye.

† † †

In an interview by James Rogers that appeared in the *Muskogee Times-Democrat* sometime in 1950, Frank emphasized his belief that "there can be no education without religion, because religion is that from which all facts take their meaning, and is the center of reference for all reality." Later he tells the reporter that he believes the purpose of the minister is to aid people in "integrating life."

> The modern world, in the words of Arnold Toynbee, has a schism in its soul, and this schism is caused by the gross materialism which has been rampant as the alternative to a spiritual conception. The minister's job is to help heal the schism and

integrate the individual around a healthy, wholesome approach to life. [The principal message] the world needs is the message that it is a sick world.

That Frank had time to preach at all, with his multiple other responsibilities, is surprising: that he recycled some of his earlier better sermons on the occasions when he did preach is not at all surprising. In fact, twice-a-week assembly was required for all the students, college and high school, one a religious assembly at which Frank preached whenever in town. Sunday mornings (Frank often a guest preacher), they all attended church in Muskogee, but there was an evening vesper service on campus where Frank was also expected to preach. Guest speakers filled in for Frank at these services when he was away from campus.

One recycled sermon, "The Judgement Bar of History," first used on Palm Sunday in 1946, Frank delivered again at Bacone in March 1950. In it he calls Judas "a mistaken blundering zealot." Pilate he describes as "a cruel, rough and ignorant peasant soldier, risen from the ranks to a vaunted governorship" who, when faced with what to do with Jesus, was "a frightened pawn in the hands of terrorizing superiors." He says Pilate became even more conflicted when his "lovely, capable, artistic, esthetic and gracious" wife, warned him of her foreboding dream that very morning.

Frank goes on to say that after several failed attempts to cast the burden of decision off to someone else, Pilate "threw the haunting question over the stone parapet to the crowds below."

> "What then shall I do with Jesus who is called the Christ?" And the answer to that question rises up to haunt each individual of each age forever

> more! Remember Pilate was only a poor, rough, frightened, blustering soldier, whose gods were Jupiter, Mercury, and Mars, so we are not to blame him overmuch in his terrible dilemma; for Jesus was to him a revolutionary, a poor Jewish teacher of no significance, yet with something so lovable that, after all, Pilate paid him a great tribute by saying, "Behold, the man!" He is in your hands.
>
> Poor Pilate, he tried to escape passing judgement on Jesus, but the very evasion of judgment was history's most drastic judgment on Pilate himself. For in reality, he stood that day before the judgement bar of history—in very fact, History itself stood before the Judgement Bar of LIFE.

Near the end of the sermon, Frank asks each of us to ask ourselves: "Where do I stand?" He concludes with these thoughts:

> If we'll just allow ourselves to be exposed to Him, if we'll not shut our mind, or busy ourselves so much we can't see or hear Him, I don't think we'll make Pilate's mistake!...
>
> You and I stand before the Judgement Bar. How will you answer? What will you do with Jesus who is called the Christ?

The same month Frank preached that sermon was also the month of "wild onions." Linea described the occasion this way:

> In spring, usually in March, wild onions came up everywhere. They bloom if left alone, but it is an Indian custom to have a wild onion dinner. The student Indian Club gathered the onions,

> cooked them with scrambled eggs, and served them along with other Indian foods. I remember once when they had purple dumplings. The faculty and students were all invited; the Murrow Hall dining room used to accommodate us all.

† † †

As these events were taking place in March 1950, it is unlikely that Frank was yet fully aware of two major events that were about to envelope Bacone. The first had its origins that same Spring when he read in the paper that Warner Brothers Studios was searching for a small campus that could be the location for a film on the life of the storied Sac and Fox Indian, Jim Thorpe. A substitute locale was needed since Carlisle Indian College in Pennsylvania, from which Thorpe had graduated, was now used as an army barracks. Frank writes: [4]

> My two years as President had convinced me that Bacone needed national exposure if it was to survive. The clouds of the Korean War were gathering and most of our men were in that struggle. Faculty salaries were so low that only dedicated missionary-minded instructors could be recruited. Scarcity of funds precluded an adequate public relations program. If we were to maintain even a semblance of college life, more funds and new friends were imperative.

---

[4] Frank wrote a lengthy account on "Jim Thorpe: All American" as experienced by Bacone. Quotes are from this paper unless otherwise noted: Frank's account supplemented by those found in Fishgall, pp. 92-101, Buford, pp. 109-113, and several newspaper articles from Muskogee papers.

263. Bacone: A Challenge He Couldn't Resist

Contacts with Warner Brothers finally resulted in a visit in July by the proposed film's director, Michael Curtiz, who had directed *Casablanca, Yankee Doodle Dandy, The Adventures of Robin Hood* and a number of other noted films, along with three others from the studio. They met with members of Muskogee's Chamber of Commerce and toured the campus. Frank writes:

> [Curtiz] was pleased with Bacone's spacious grounds, fine buildings, and, especially, the prospect of having Indians to provide the proper setting and personnel. He told us later that he was impressed with the general tenor and warmth of the people he met and later worked with.

It took another month before the contract could be signed.

> It was necessary to secure the approval of the Home Mission Society in New York. Several members looked with jaundiced eyes at a gang from Hollywood invading a church-related campus. When all had been finally cleared with our authorities, preparation began for the big event.
>
> The campus was manicured to ship-shape condition. Students, faculty and maintenance workers volunteered to make a good impression on the celebrities soon to appear.

As for the students, when Frank told them the film could be one of the greatest experiences of their lives and would rebound to their benefit, "they were typically unresponsive, as is the wont with Indians." Frank might have been equally unresponsive, himself, to Warner Brothers' warning that absolute security was necessary–that curious crowds were not to be allowed entrance except on pre-arranged visitors' days.

> Such precaution seemed unnecessary, for in our two years [at Bacone] there hadn't been a baker's dozen visitors, even for the colorful ceremonies and exciting contests we had invited the public to attend. Nonetheless, we hired guards for each gate and published ads assuring our neighbors that there would be open house days to see Hollywood in action.

After a 1950 Associated Press poll had chosen Thorpe as the greatest football player and athlete of the first half of the twentieth century, Warner Brothers had decided the time was right to film his story. Now 62, Thorpe himself was far past his prime, had drifted through a variety of odd jobs after his sports' days had ended, and was known in Hollywood primarily for the stereotyped Indian he had been reduced to playing in a number of cheap movie productions. But he was still a hero to many, having been an All-American football player while at Carlisle, having won two Olympic gold medals for pentathlon and decathlon in the 1912 games in Stockholm, and, later, had had careers both in major league baseball and as player-coach in the newly established professional football league.

Though not an Indian, Burt Lancaster, under contract with Warner Brothers, was chosen to play Thorpe—he was much the same size and physique, and with a little makeup-darkened skin and black-dyed hair, could reasonably look the part—*prior to the days when "political correctness" might have made this an issue*. His main task was the need to learn to play football, and Thorpe was hired to help with this.

265. Bacone: A Challenge He Couldn't Resist

Frank continues his account of the movie-making this way:

> Our introduction to the movie personnel was a surprise. During an evening chapel service, I was exhorting the students to be on their fittest behavior during the Hollywood invasion....During my message, a group of strangers walked in to occupy the rear pews. The stoical and phlegmatic students paid not the slightest attention, but those of us non-Indians could not contain our excited reaction [to having with us] guests from the fabled land of moviedom.

Frank quickly ended the service, but the visitors vanished before he had a chance to greet them.

> As I walked disconsolately across the campus musing on the problems that might be lurking before us, a tall and striking-looking young man tapped me on the shoulder. "I'm Burt Lancaster," he said. "We appreciate what you were saying to the students and are eager to get to know you and your students better. There seems to be a wonderful spirit here and you have a magnificent campus. I want to get the true Indian feeling and spirit because there is only one Jim Thorpe." Thus began a thrilling relationship.

Frank then recounts that Jim Thorpe's story became Burt Lancaster's passion.

> He urged that we help him interpret not only the fabulous athlete, but the Indians of today and their needs for tomorrow. So involved had Burt become that he ran around our athletic field every

morning to be in good shape. He had only a fruit drink for breakfast, a cup of soup for lunch, another fruit drink in mid-afternoon when he would stop in at our home to listen to great records which he invariably could identify. Then, at night, he would put away two or three normal meals.

Given his credentials it is not surprising that Frank was equally impressed by the Hungarian-born director, Michael Curtiz; calling him "as scholarly and erudite a person as one could conjure."

> Aside from his ability to give depth and tone to a scene, he had a sense of humility and reverence that added a new dimension to our respect and surprise. He constantly urged his actors and crew to remember that they were doing more than depicting the life of a famous person, they were trying to portray a people who had been wronged and in need of a new image. He placed signs around the campus reminding his people that Bacone was a religious institution and thus no smoking, drinking or swearing on campus. [*Frank doesn't reveal, what others who knew him have affirmed, that he himself was a heavy smoker who kept it hidden from the students since no smoking was allowed on campus.*]

Burt was unquestionably the movie's star, but he had a "lovely and beautiful" leading lady in Phyllis Thaxter, who played Thorpe's lover and first wife (Thorpe was married three times), a most demanding role. And it was she with whom Sara Sue became quite enamored.

As a Caucasian, she needed to understand the complex nature of her famous Indian husband. As the mother of his children, she must prepare them for the

changing world into which they would emerge. We found her spending more time with our students and with the faculty children than any of the other stars. Though none of the actors, including Burt, quite caught the quiet dignity of the Indian, Miss Thaxter came as near as anyone to understanding what it meant to be an Indian in a white man's world. Only crusty old Charles Bickford, the fabled "Pop" Warner, [who coached Thorpe at Carlisle] remained aloof from the campus life and sought escape when shots were completed.

Frank tells about the making of a climatic scene in the film that was brought to his attention one day by his son, Scott, who was so omnipresent that Curtis gave him a "Director's chair" and told him to sit in it and keep it afterwards.

> The scene Scott urged me to watch will never be forgotten. Young Jim Thorpe was making his entrance to college and several of the players asked him if he was going out for football. He shook his head, "Me not know football."
>
> "Here, we'll show you," one of the men grunted in disgust as he rolled a sweater into the approximation of a ball. "You run with ball and get

by us."

Burt plunged forward and was tackled with a resounding thud on his head. Mike Curtis shouted "Again," and Scott whispered to me, "Count the times," for he had been trying to tell me the number of repeats they made of each scene. Knowing how easy it is for a preacher to lose count, I marked on my diary the gruesome record. After five head bashings, Jess Hill, the famous USC coach who was on the set asked Burt if he didn't want his stand-in to take the beating. But Burt said, "No, this is a key scene. I'll do it myself." My diary shows thirty-two repeats.

I later told the students, and have repeated it to anyone who would listen, that such a display of discipline is a lesson to us in religious or educational work. If a group of entertainers can go through that meticulous and torturous a drill to show two minutes of a film, what would happen if we copied them in adherence to the dictates of our professions?

Altogether there were about 100 actors, technicians and production workers on campus during the film's making. Frank tells us that to reinforce their expressed enjoyment of their time at Bacone and their belief in its mission, before they left, they had a meeting that raised enough money to provide four scholarships for worthy students. Those on campus had learned something about movie stars, too. They had gained a new understanding and appreciation of their dedication, discipline, hard work and attention to detail.

When Burt did a number of selections from Shakespeare at a banquet given for the cast during their final days in Muskogee, those who already believed him a better actor than given credit for, felt he'd just confirmed it. Ray Evans (of whom we'll hear more soon) says, "He held the crowd, which included many local VIPs, spell-bound." Frank, as was his usual forte, had seen to it that Hollywood's presence was felt in the town as well as on campus. Frank writes:

> I took as many of the stars as I could corral to every civic club and community organization as possible to talk and answer questions. One could feel the mounting enthusiasm of the area, and in fact across the nation. Our mail increased so unbelievably that we had to put on extra secretarial workers to keep up with the correspondence and to record the increased contributions. Our income from "Churches and Individuals" more than doubled, invitations for speakers and performers from Bacone tripled, and applications for enrollment by students from across the nation quadrupled. It is almost unbelievable the magic of Hollywood on the average public.

Frank notes that the bank clerk who previously had "never bothered to give me the time of day," now "almost catapulted over the brass rail" to serve me. And Governor Roy Turner phoned to say he'd like to host a dinner at the Skirvin Hotel for the cast and officials of the college, and, especially, Jim Thorpe himself.

> The event lasted past midnight with Jim and the governor recalling the historic events that had made the Sac and Fox tribesman a legend in his time. I will never forget the unIndian-like show of emotion that came to the old Indian when the subject came up of his medals that had been taken from him following his triumph in Stockholm in 1912 [for having played one summer in 1909, for $2

a day, with a minor league baseball team considered professional unbeknownst to him]. The governor was prophetic as he swearingly proclaimed that those medals would be returned to him [but, unfortunately, not until the 1980s: Jim had died in 1953].

The Indian students took the filming in their usual noncommittal stride, but the faculty children, most of them Caucasian, were agog from morning till evening. Truancy was rife as the school bus that transported grade school children to Muskogee went half empty day after day. Each of the movie stars "adopted" one or more of the eager children who crowded near on every set. Sara Sue, Frank's then-ten-year-old daughter, became a favorite of Burt and when she leaked the news that she was having a birthday, he gave her the first bicycle she had ever owned. He would have preferred giving her jewelry costing much more, but tomboy that she was, she preferred action to sparkle.

The benefits accruing to Bacone as a result of the filming lasted even after the crew's departure.

Two years later, Ed Sulllivan granted our request to appear on his popular "Toast of the Town" in New York City. Grouchy Ed assured me that he would never have accepted our offer for singers and dancers to perform on his show had he not seen the Jim Thorpe picture and wanted his 50 million viewers to know more about our American Natives. [We'll hear more of this later; their treatment certainly not reflecting the sentiments expressed here.]

> Also, two years later, the Junior Chamber of Commerce of Pasadena invited Bacone to represent the east in the Junior Rose Bowl [in December 1952]. They told us they had learned about Bacone from viewing the Jim Thorpe picture. That game attracted nearly 50,000 to the famous Rose Bowl and gave us media coverage across the nation.

In his February 1953 "Echoes from the President's Office," Frank wrote of the game that ended in a 20-20 tie as the result of an incorrect call by an official, but nonetheless one that drew praise for the Bacone team's magnificent game, their fine attitude and their behavior. "In that sudden moment of testing it was still THE WAY THEY PLAYED THE GAME OF LIFE that counted and the demeanor of the players was not lost on the crowds." Frank, who had accompanied the team along with Loretta, preached at the First Baptist Church of Pasadena on the Sunday morning following the game, and the team, pep squad and Indian Club, all attended as a group.

> It's not often such enterprises as modern sport redound to the honor and glory of the mission enterprise. We feel this may be an exception. The outstanding impression made by our team and pep squad and the ceremonial performers who went along to California will be felt for a long time to come.
>
> Over a thousand townspeople saw the team off at the railroad station when they left. Fifteen hundred waited nearly two hours on a blustery afternoon for the late train that would bring them home. There was a band and city dignitaries to welcome the team; also, a television set was presented to the boys for their

dormitory. The team's fares were paid by the Pasadena Chamber of Commerce, as was their stay at the Huntington Hotel.

As for the movie-making experience, Frank expresses his belief that it marked the turning point for the school. It provided the "major event" that his friend, Paul Bruner at the Chamber of Commerce, had advised as necessary when he first visited Bacone in 1948. Frank, however, in retrospect "confesses" to what he calls "my blatant mistake in accepting Warner Brothers' first offer for use of the campus."

> Later, I inadvertently learned that they had budgeted much more for rental purposes, but I was so sure "Jim Thorpe: All American" would provide a Phoenix Bird miracle that I was loathe to bargain. When one weighs the effects of the filming, only partially outlined above, its fairly easy to call in the old saw about birds-in-hand.
>
> After the hue and cry subsided, the dust of the last van settled and students could return to the business of uninterrupted classes, we gathered with the Muskogee Chamber of Commerce to evaluate the foregoing experience. Several businessmen spoke glowingly of the lasting value the filming would provide. [To their financial benefit, the entire group from Hollywood had stayed and eaten in Muskogee, as well as having attracted tourists.] Paul Bruner winked at me and claimed credit for having prompted the big event.
>
> We secured the aid of the Chamber in providing a gala night for the premier of the movie in Muskogee [August 23, 1951]. Burt was not able to attend [in Italy making another picture], but Phyllis

> Thaxter and several lesser stars came to the buffalo feast we had prepared. Our hall was overflowing as Alumni, state VIPs and dignitaries from near and far enjoyed an authentic Indian meal. Cherokees from the hills near Tahlequah provided dishes few non-Indians had ever savored. Mrs. Thaxter spoke warmly of the "Bacone Extras" that had made her fall in love with the entire school.
>
> It would be almost impossible to overstress the importance to Bacone financially, promotionally and personnel-wise of "Jim Thorpe: All American."

Despite Frank's praise of the film, and its unquestionably positive impact on Bacone, it was not a big hit with critics or the public. In her biography of Lancaster, Gary Fishgall has this to say:[5]

> Most of the critics correctly labeled [the film] standard Hollywood fare. Even though the filmmakers had tried not to sugar coat the athlete's personality or troubles [in his personal life—alcoholism and failed marriages], they set the story within the framework of a testimonial dinner, which muted its dramatic potential. Moreover, except for Thorpe, the characters were largely one-dimensional. The biopic ended up a disappointing seventy-sixth among the year's most popular films.

† † †

Before Hollywood had descended on Bacone in the summer of 1950, another important event, with national repercussions for the college, had also had its origin in the

---

[5] p. 101, Fishgall.

Spring that year. It began when Ray Evans, in his second year as Minister of Music at Muskogee's First Baptist Church, was seated next to Frank at a banquet held at the Severs Hotel in downtown Muskogee. Ray was to sing a number of selections (which he can't remember) and Frank was to speak (a stirring speech Ray still remembers).[6]

> He kindled the fires of patriotism in the hearts of every person in attendance, and closed his talk by quoting the words from "The Ballad for Americans," a majestic and challenging piece of choral literature....One readily sensed that here was a man of intense patriotism, a leader with unusual vision and a strong dedication to fulfill a task for which he felt called....
>
> Our conversation covered a variety of subjects and eventually settled on that which was nearest and dearest to his heart–the American Indian and the cause of Bacone College....Dr. Thompson talked about his desire of combining [Bacone's two singing] groups into a mixed choir and have one choral group represent the school.

Replacing Bacone's male and female choirs, The Singing Redmen and The Singing Maidens, which had always been popular in Muskogee and other nearby locales (they had even performed on local radio and TV stations), was a rather bold idea–a way consciously intended to promote fraternization at a time when Bacone still had the men sit separately from the females at Chapel and in the cafeteria. Ray says: "Dr. Thompson wished to see this

---

[6] Ray Evans wrote a lengthy account of his time with the Bacone College Choir, 1950-1954, and offered it to this writer to use freely. Quotes are from it unless otherwise credited.

disappear and allow the usual boy-girl relationships to blossom on this campus just as it existed on other co-ed campuses."

Loretta, who'd been directing the Singing Maidens, approved of the idea, since recruitment for this group had proved difficult. If Ray took over direction of a mixed choir, she'd have more time both for her own solo performances, and for working with the soloists in the choir. Ray, too, rather liked the mixed-choir idea, and accepted Frank's invitation to visit the campus sometime soon. When he did so less than two weeks later, he was duly impressed with the dedication of the faculty and the serious approach of the students. A bit hesitantly, Ray's church gave him the permission he needed to spend part of his time organizing and directing a mixed-sex choir at Bacone.

On the first day of the school year, at Chapel, Frank told the students of the plan and the time of the first rehearsal—twelve girls and eight boys showed up.[7] Despite the one-on-one recruitment efforts that followed, a number of students from Bacone's Junior High and High School classes had to be included in order to achieve the needed forty-voice choir, with a good balance of parts. Their budget was so small that the first music was borrowed from Ray's church's library and the choir's robes were hand-me-downs from another of Muskogee's churches that was just then purchasing new robes for their adult choir. Ray writes:

> Though faded and tattered, they were repaired and made presentable through the loving care of Mrs. Roy Spinks, wife of our bus driver and

---

[7] Though Ray doesn't mention it, this could well have been the same chapel service referred to previously, in which Frank told the students about the film-making that would be going on at their school.

> maintenance supervisor. Mr. and Mrs. Spinks were graduates of the college and stayed on to serve on the faculty and staff throughout their lives. These robes served us faithfully for two years on our limited tours and at home for the Chapel services. ...[These early programs were] enhanced by a performance of Indian ceremonial dances by the members of the Indian Club under the direction of Dick West, the art instructor.

Almost immediately after its formation, Ray writes, "the choir began to take one-day trips away from the college to sing for Indian gatherings around the state; or for civic club luncheons in some of the larger cities. He describes one before an Indian gathering in Anadorko, Oklahoma that made a deep impression on him:

> Several of our singers were from that area and their parents and family members were in attendance. I shall never forget how gracious these people were as they expressed their deep appreciation for the opportunity their young people had in attending Bacone College. Before the concert, we were treated to a feast of Indian cooking and the choir members found unusual delight in watching me sample the various offerings! We sang a full concert for the people, and while I'm not sure all the selections were to their liking, they applauded as if we were the greatest thing that ever happened. They were proud of their young people and we were grateful to have shared this time with them [*It was, undoubtedly, occasions like this that made Ray "fall in love" with the Indians, as he has said he did.*]

The first big challenge for the newly organized choir,

which now numbered fifty, would come at the end of May 1952 when Frank had accepted an invitation for them to represent the state of Oklahoma at the national convention of the Musical Arts Societies of the United States being held in Salt Lake City. With this to be the highlight, a fourteen day tour was planned that included a two-day stay in Salt Lake City, and eighteen other concerts in Oklahoma, Kansas, Colorado, and Utah on their way there and back. As with all their tours, expenses would be kept as low as possible with churches requesting the choir's presence providing room and meals, and, hopefully, "love donations" that would at least cover the rest.

With this challenge ahead of them, intense rehearsals began in January 1951, even before the college reconvened to start its second semester. As became a general practice, Frank "arranged to have the dining room and dorms open early for the choir members and the football team, and an anonymous donor paid the expenses for the group." Ray writes: "As director, I could not have asked for any more than these young people were giving in preparation." The one year they'd have been together by the time the tour started was hardly adequate to meld them into a quality group, and yet they knew it was crucial to the college that they perform well. Ray goes on to say:

> The people of the various congregations welcomed us into their homes, their churches and their hearts. The Indian young people were most pleased to find such honest, heartfelt acceptance, and I was elated by the response of these people who had long been supporters of Bacone but had never met the young people before this time. The hard work of the young people was beginning to reap rewards.

They arrived in Salt Lake City on a Sunday afternoon, scheduled to give two concerts at the First Baptist Church and one at the Musical Arts Societies Convention, with a tour of the city fitted in on the Tuesday, before they left for Ogden, Utah on Wednesday morning. An unpleasant encounter with the church's senior minister altered their plans.

> It was evident that he really didn't want us there, but would go through the formalities of making it look good to the public. We were certain [of his prejudice against Indians] when, at the Sunday evening service, we found his own church choir in the loft to lead the service, and we were asked to stand on one level on the rostrum and sing three numbers. We crowded over forty singers into a space that would barely hold twenty-five. Fortunately, all our music was memorized, but we were working at a disadvantage. Following the evening service, the Indian Club presented their ceremonial dances in the Fellowship Hall directly below the sanctuary. The members of the church were cordial and appreciative.

However, Ray asked representatives from the convention who were present if they could be moved up a day for their appearance at the convention. After being accommodated, he decided they should leave Salt Lake City a day earlier than planned and skip their second appearance at the church. When told that evening, the chairman of the Board of Deacons was "distressed to hear of our problem with the minister" and Frank, when phoned, "was not too happy to hear about it either." However, he told us "to go ahead if we really felt it wise." The students had not yet been told of the decision as they readied, next morning, for their performance at the Convention.

> [Backstage] we sat there stunned, my knees knocking, as choirs of 80-110 members [from fine colleges all over the country], in fall evening dress, took their places on the stage and sang difficult, complex compositions of the Masters. [These choirs] had been established many years ago. We had only existed for one year! [And my voice asked], "Why in the world did you get yourself in a spot like this?" [As we got ready to be No. 8], I certainly was tempted to walk out the door, but I had a deep loyalty to these young American Indians, and together we had to go on stage and prove that we, too, were human beings created in God's own image and trying our best to use the talents He had given us to sing His praises.
>
> In their old discarded choir robes, the singers gave the performance of their lives. We sang four anthems, good music of the Masters, and added sign language to one of them. I have no idea how it sounded, but I do remember that the audience gave the young people a standing ovation....An important value which evolved from this experience was an intense unity of purpose among the singers and an acceptance of their director as their true friend and champion.

The next morning they bid farewell to those in the First Baptist Church who had housed them, and, after a brief tour of Salt Lake City in their old red bus, headed for Ogden, Utah, where they were greeted with such enthusiastic audiences at their two concerts there that they felt "rescued" from the unpleasant experience they'd encountered with the minister in Salt Lake City. After a final stop in Moab, Utah, they headed home.

Frank was elated by the many letters of thanks that followed from people along the route they'd traveled. It was obviously a success as a mission of goodwill, and some of the churches even pledged to increase their financial support. The choir's appearances having produced the results Frank had hoped for, he immediately began to put together another two week tour for the Spring of 1952, securing bookings in Kansas, Iowa, Indiana, Ohio, Michigan and Oklahoma. But about this same time, another important event was taking place on Campus.

†††

On Easter Sunday 1952, the lovely mural of "The Indian Christ in Gethsemane," done in the Indian motif by Richard West, head of Bacone's art department, was hung over the baptistery at the center of its beautiful Chapel.

"The Indian Christ in Gethsemane"
Original Painting by Dick West in the Bacone College Chapel, Muskogee, Oklahoma.

In the future this painting often is seen as a backdrop in pictures of the choir. Frank wrote in his April 1952 issue of "Echoes from the President's Office":

When a group of friends were brought in to view the painting before it was presented to the student body as a whole, without exception they gasped and then sank in reverent silence upon the pews to remain in the most powerful kind of meditation for several moments before anyone made a sound.

Dick had come to Bacone the year before Frank and left a distinct impact on the College before his retirement in 1970. He stated his philosophy thus: "My own thinking is that you are successful as a teacher only as you are successful as a practicing artist in the field."[8] Accordingly, both he and his students won a number of national prizes for their work. A flyer dedicated to West, who died in 1996, calls the "Indian Christ in Gethsemane" a blend of old and new American Indian art.

> [It] depicts the universality of the Christ figure. Kneeling in the traditional prayer stance, the figure bears the face of an American Indian alone. Painted as an expression of thanksgiving for the

---

[8] Pp. 93-98, Williams & Meredith. West had a son, Richard, Jr., who was about the same age as Frank Thompson's son, Scott, and they were playmates during Frank's tenure as President of Bacone— and have remained friends over the years. Presently Richard, Jr., a Stanford-educated lawyer, is director of the new National Museum of the American Indian in Washington, D.C. (open September 2004) which sought a collaborative relationship with Native Americans at each stage of its development. West is quoted as saying, "The National Museum can be a point of departure for a cultural reconciliation between those who were here and those who came." (Parade, September 5, 2004, p. 10) His father would be enormously proud!

> spared life of his wife [who was suffering from a potentially deadly malady at the time], the work was finished in about 20 hours...

In an account of the painting by Minter Uzzell in the President's Echoes, he tells us that West shut out the world while painting it, except for a student briefly admitted to pose for the face in the painting. In conclusion, Uzzell states:

> The Indian Christ in Gethsemane is a painting that tells the story of devotion to the Father's will. It is an expression of the artist's gratitude to the God who heard and answered his wordless prayer. As you look upon the face of the Indian Christ, ask yourself: Can I come to God with the same kind of commitment and faith?

For a painting so beloved for so long by so many, it is indeed sad to note that in 1990 a fire destroyed most of the Bacone Chapel and with it this priceless work of art. This writer is told that another famous painting is also no longer there, that of Roger Williams, who was a frequent subject in Frank's sermons.

At the time of her visit with the Thompsons in May 1954, Louise Green, an old friend of the Thompsons from Phillips Memorial, described the Williams' painting this way: [There was] "a beautiful picture window of Roger Williams standing with a book in his hand on which are the words, 'Soul Liberty 1636.'" She also noted a plaque in his memory that proclaims him as "Apostle of Religious Liberty, First Missionary to the Indians, their protector, defender and friend." Louise also was impressed by the inscription on the outside of the chapel that reads: "There are two freedoms; the false, where a man is free to do what he likes, and the true, where a man is free to do what he ought.

† † †

May 1952, immediately following commencement, the choir took off on its second two-week tour, filling its old red school bus, a station wagon and a car. Again they stayed in church members' homes and depended a lot on "love offerings" at their performances, but they were also fortunate that Thomas Gilcrease an oil man from Tulsa, Oklahoma, allowed them to use his credit card for gas, oil and maintenance of three vehicles.[9] They also had $200 to $500 given them by Bacone to cover expenses such as the lunches they had to purchase while on the road.

Prior to the start of school in the Fall of 1952, they accepted an invitation to come to the Detroit area for eight days of appearances in its various churches, to be climaxed with a full concert at Covenant Baptist.

Ray writes: "I had often heard people in Oklahoma, particularly church folks, say that people did not attend church well in the North." Given Frank's experience in Rhode Island, he should have been able to put that belief to rest. However, they found out its untruth for themselves, for there was good attendance at every church, and some loved hearing the choir and seeing the Indian dancers in their costumes so much that they attended a second concert at churches other than their own. For their final performance at the regular Sunday evening service at Covenant Baptist, "more that 1,600 people crowded the sanctuary....[Ray said] I discovered that people will attend church in the North or the South if they are spiritually fed and appreciated by the

---

[9] Bacone was fortunate to have someone with his money and prestige s o involved with Bacone. In 1949 Tulsa opened its beautiful Gilcrease Museum with one of the best collections of early American art provided by him.

leader—"under the shepherd of the flock—the pastor!"

Despite the singers' efforts to keep up with their schoolwork by doing assignments on the bus, this was an almost impossible task. So, on their return from these tours they were always faced with trying to make up for the time they'd lost from classes. Catching up "meant a lot of extra hours in some of the classes so they could keep up the grade average required to continue being a travelling member of the choir." Simultaneously, they also had to work on new numbers for an important eleven-day tour of the Western States that would start soon after they resumed classes in January, following their Christmas break. The Bacone Choir was making a fabulous public relations contribution to the college but certainly not without a lot of commitment and hard work on their part.

After one month of intense rehearsals during January, the choir and their entourage was on its way to Chicago with performances scheduled en route in several Kansas, Iowa and Illinois locales. And they were excited to be wearing their new Indian costumes for the first time, rather than the hand-me-down choir robes they'd been wearing for the last two years. Ray described their new outfits:

NATIONALLY FAMOUS BACONE CHOIR

> The boys wore beautifully colored tunics and white pants with conch and silver belts, made at Bacone under the supervision of Russ Titus. The elk tooth, sequin and rawhide-trimmed white dresses of the girls were the handiwork of the First Methodist and First Presbyterian Churches of Muskogee, working under the direction of Mrs. Zoma "Ma" Perry and Mrs. Roy Spinks.

This combining of college and town working together might never have happened prior to Frank's presidency, for he, from the beginning, unlike his predecessors, had sought to make the town feel that the college was part of Muskogee. Ray continues:

> How grateful and proud we were to appear in these new outfits at the Folk Festival [which was] an annual event at the Oak Park Church in Chicago. Each year a different race was featured. We were indeed fortunate to be thrust in the spotlight for this event in 1953.

Frank, as he sometimes did, had come with the choir on this tour, and had reason, like the others, to return home with "happy memories of some wonderful people and their generous response to our musical offerings." As Ray put it, "We truly felt that we were making a worthy contribution to Bacone and the American Indian." But now the choir members felt the pressure of preparing for final exams, just two and one-half months away, while continuing rehearsals in preparation for another big tour in May 1953.

This tour would take them to Wichita, Kansas and to Lamar, Spring, Pueblo, and Grand Junction, Colorado, ending with a three-day stay in Denver, Colorado where they'd sing several times for the American Baptist

Convention and on the 7 a.m. national broadcast of the Church of the Air. They also sang at the Red Rocks Amphitheater, a few miles into the mountains west of Denver, a site of beauty that this writer can attest to from personal experience. Ray quotes from a newspaper reporter's description:

> There, by the art which is man's nature, legions of seats have been fashioned between colossal cliffs of red, striated sandstone glacier–carved by nature, which is God's art. It is a favorite resort of Denver people, especially on cool summer nights to listen under the stars to the symphony orchestra that plays from a platform in the cleft.

The reporter didn't say, however, that a wind blowing across the platform interfered with the acoustics and made the choirs' performance a special challenge.

In general, it was an especially exhausting trip with more performances scheduled en route home–at Trinidad, Colorado; Albuquerque, New Mexico; and Clovis, New Mexico. But tired as they were, Ray reports that the young people "rose to the challenge" and the "soloists, in particular, performed their repertoire in the finest fashion and gave no hint of how tired they really were. Great troupers!" Finally, back in Muskogee, the singers would go their separate ways to different parts of the country for the remaining Summer months before school resumed. It was not a time without regrets, as Ray writes:

> The bonds of friendship, which grow strong from such an experience [traveling and singing together], was felt deeply by all of us and we bid each other goodbye with a note of sadness. We looked forward to the Fall of 1953, when we would renew

> our friendships and continue our choir work as ambassadors of Bacone.

On their return in the Fall of 1953, they were greeted by Frank who told them that on May 30, 1954, they were scheduled to appear in New York on Ed Sullivan's popular TV Show "Toast of the Town." It was to be the highlight of an 18-day tour that would see them singing every day from May 24 through June 9 in churches and civic centers in Missouri, Indiana, Ohio, Pennsylvania New Jersey, Rhode Island, Massachusetts, and Connecticut in one directions, and then New York, Ohio, and Indiana before again returning to Bacone.

During that school year 1953-1954, singing engagements were kept to a minimum so the choir could concentrate on preparations for this big tour, but some were intentionally arranged to "test out" the selections they'd take on tour. They were embarrassed on one occasion when blacks in Muskogee were turned away from a performance of "Elijah." As a consequence, Ray arranged to give a second performance to which the blacks would be specifically invited.

> Phone calls were made to all the Negro pastors in the city to inform them of the presentation and to assure them that their people would be most welcome. ...About seven hundred people attended this service and approximately 450 were from the black community.
>
> Needless to say, this was a great experience for the Bacone choir, not just musically, but spiritually and interracially as well....The Indian young people could identify with this problem because many of them had encountered similar

rejection in their own local communities. However, they were able to learn from this situation that not all people embraced such prejudices.

Immediately following the college's commencement exercises on May 23, the Bacone Choir set off on their extensive 18-day tour. Louise Green, the Thompson's friend from Phillips Memorial, had been there for the commencement and saw Frank off in his private car as the others left by bus. Afterwards, she spent the evening with Loretta, Willard and Sara Sue "where each played excellent selections on the piano." Before Louise left Bacone later on Monday, she states that she gave Loretta a permanent [reminding this writer of the time she too had given Loretta a perm].

The choir's stop at Phillips Memorial on June 1st was, without doubt, the closest to Frank's heart, especially since it would include an opportunity for him to preach there one more time. And he must have been thrilled with the attendance and article by Ruth Tripp in the local paper:

> A capacity audience overflowed the auditorium into the vestibule. Many listeners were grouped outside the windows on the lawn of the church in an effort to hear the singing. Others were standing near the door in the few remaining square feet of floor space. The mixed choir of 45 voices was colorfully dressed in the costumes of the various Indian tribes of which they are members.
>
> ...The choir included Cherokee, Kiowa, Choctaw, Navajo, Chicksaw, Creek, Chickahominy, Pawnee, Apache-Klamath, Nez Perce and Sac and Fox Indians. Their singing in the sacred numbers showed fine training. Mrs. Francis Thompson is

> teacher of voice at the college and her artistic singing is well remembered here....
>
> It is impossible to report on the last portion of the program because I gave up my standing space in an effort to find a better vantage point outside. It was impossible to recover my position and I left, feeling sure that the young people of Bacone College Choir would not miss my applause. I regretted extremely missing the sign language interpretations listed to be demonstrated.

For the choir itself, the highpoint of the tour was to be their appearance on Sunday, May 30th on the Ed Sullivan show with its TV audience of forty million plus a live audience in the theater. They arrived at the theater at the designated time of 4:00 p.m. only to have to wait one and 3/4 hours before being called to the stage. Then they discovered they would not have the three-step risers that had been agreed upon in advance, but instead were expected to be positioned in a way that prevented the girls from singing their highest notes– seated on the floor in front, squaw-fashion with their legs crossed. The second row was kneeling on one knee, and the third and fourth rows were standing. The young man and young lady who were to do the Indian sign language on the singing of Newman's "Twenty-third Psalm" were placed in the center of the back row, side by side (see following photo of two signers). We had always had them stand at each end of the front row so that it would not be obvious if they were ever out of synchronization.

When Ray complained, the producer said, "You are just god-damned temperamental musicians!" To add to their mistreatment, their original appearance of eight minutes had been cut to six," which necessitated leaving out a stanza, somewhat ironically, of "This is My Country." Further, the piano was inconveniently located on a ramp about twenty-five feet away to the front and left of the choir. They were the last act of a show that night that had included Liberace and Red Buttons, "a most difficult spot under trying circumstances, but the power of prayer [said before starting]

electrified us and the Lord allowed the young people to sing beyond their greatest hopes and the audience responded with a standing ovation!...We could not help but feel that God's hand had guided us through this achievement and we would be forever grateful to Him for divine help.

Their stop at the First Baptist Church of Worcester, Massachusetts perhaps did the most to wipe away the unpleasantness they'd encountered with the producers of the Ed Sulllivan show. Two different local papers covered the event. Ray quotes from the one by Raymond Morin of the *Worcester Daily Telegram:*

> In appearance, attitude and cultural musical talent, the Bacone College Choir from Muskogee, Oklahoma completely annihilated all the tommyrot we've been fed from Hollywood and other unreliable sources about the American Indian–in fact, last night's concert in the First Baptist Church was a mighty inspiring and educational event...

This tour would be the finale of Ray's involvement with the Bacone Choir for he was leaving Muskogee to accept a position at the Park Cities Baptist Church in Dallas, Texas. Of his four years with the Indian young people of Bacone, he said it would always be "most significant."

> All of us wish to be needed and wanted; and I felt these desires amply fulfilled at Bacone. I know that I was a better person for having been permitted this opportunity to know, to love, to appreciate and to work with these wonderful young Indian men and women. My sincere hope is that through this opportunity, I was able to help in enriching the lives of these young people in some small way.

† † †

Meanwhile, in the month preceding this last tour of the Bacone Choir under Ray's direction, Frank, accompanied by Loretta, had gone to California at the invitation of the University of Redlands for its Founders' Day celebration on April 20, 1954. Frank was to give the main address, "The Grand Inquisitor Confronts Us Again," followed by President George H. Armacost presenting him with an honorary Doctor of Divinity degree.

The occasion had been preceded by at least one exchange of correspondence when, on March 23rd, Frank had written George to discuss a number of Bacone students he was recommending as prospects for Redlands [Bacone being a junior college, Frank tried to place his better students in a university to continue their education]. Then, in concluding paragraphs, Frank wrote:

> Sorry you feel my Founders' Day topic is foreboding, I thought it was a safer topic to use than

the Columbia University theme. That is so utterly controversial in the minds of our fear-ridden folks today. [He doesn't tell us to what he refers but amongst other things, early in 1954, McCarthyism had not yet been squashed, and the constitutionality of school segregation was before the Supreme Court.] I'll do my dead level best not to be unnecessarily controversial and will certainly try to help the cause and not hurt it, Maybe I'm wrong, but it seems to me that some of these folks we fear to offend are most flattered by being challenged to think on both sides of subjects occasionally.

Thanks, again, for your confidence in my judgement on this matter. I will wrestle with the "Grand Inquisitor" according to the rules that I think are implied in Columbia's great theme: "Man's Right to Knowledge and the Free Use Thereof."

In the reply letter from George, he states, among other things: "I am sure I can trust your judgement concerning the development of your theme for Founder's Day." In a P.S. he writes: The University of Redlands will provide your hood for the doctorate. We assume you have your own cap and gown and will bring them with you. If such is not the case, let us know your hat size, coat size, and height so that we can order a cap and gown from Los Angeles for you.

The diploma Frank received from President Armacost that day reads:

Your leadership in providing the possibilities of education to our Indian young people has opened opportunity to hundreds who otherwise would have found higher education impossible. You have carried the burden of a great institution through crucial years and have given of your energies and talents without stint or reservation to advance the welfare of Bacone College and through it the achievement of the American Indian. You have by unremitting effort found means to house, feed, clothe, and educate Indian orphans and have been active in promoting their complete welfare. You have laid far-seeing plans for Indian education in general and Bacone College in particular. You have preached by word and deed the moral and spiritual undergirding of our society and have not failed to bring the water of life.

They have given a surprisingly complete overview of Frank's work at Bacone, and, at the same time, an insight into why Frank was beginning to suffer from both physical and emotional exhaustion. This recognition must have given him, at least temporarily, a new burst of energy.

In an undated letter from California, perhaps written during this trip, Frank writes his son, whom he addresses as Bud. In it he comments on the early-blooming flowers and suggests they plan to go out in the hills, when he gets home, and find as many wildflowers there as possible. "It's always a good education to know the flora and fauna in one's own state." The letter continues:

> A boy I met at Redlands about your age had a whole box of wonderful stones that he had found and identified. He knew just what the name of each piece was. Did you know that different stones have different names? Some stone comes from places where water has been, those are called sedimentary stone—most of those on the walks and buildings at Bacone are of that type. If you look at them real carefully, you will see places where shell fish and other sea life have been deposited. The study of stones is called geology—it's one of the most interesting studies a fellow can make. It will tell you many things about the history of our earth....

The concluding paragraph states:

> Yesterday morning I had breakfast with Burt Lancaster at his lovely home in Bel Air, which is a rich part of Hollywood, But I will tell Sara Sue about that part of my experience....

† † †

In November that year, Bacone undertook a major fund-raising campaign in anticipation of their Diamond Jubilee celebration coming in 1955. In his February 1955 issue of "Echoes from the President's Office," Frank not only discusses that campaign but also the plans for Founder's Day on February 9. They included a Buffalo Barbecue [the buffalo donated by O. C. Cargill, owner of one of the largest buffalo ranches in the world]; an open house and tour of the campus; and, finally, a convocation service when awards would be presented to "outstanding Baconians" and "Distinguished Indian Leaders" following a program by the now nationally-famous Bacone Choir. One of those to be honored, Patrick J. Hurley, is described in a long article that appeared in the *Muskogee Sunday Phoenix & Times-Democrat* on February 6th, as Bacone's most famous graduate:

> Patrick J. Hurley, lawyer, soldier, statesman and diplomat, was a veteran of two World Wars, becoming a major general in the Army. He also served as ambassador to China, and was a member of the President's Cabinet as Secretary of War to President Herbert Hoover.

Frank, in his "Echoes..." took special pride in describing a symbol their art instructor, Dick West, had designed for the occasion.

296. Justice, Peace & God

In honor of our seventy-fifth anniversary, Dick West has presented a symbol that contains the story of this unique college. In the background one may see evidences of the symbolism and ritual of the old Indian culture. Overshadowing and rising high above is the stately cross on a steeple. Within the scope of the diamond, the conflict of cultures has gone on. Today the best of two cultures is preserved. That best symbolizes the up-reach to and from God and the outreach to all who need the guiding and girding influence of God's love of man as exemplified in the Cross of Christ.

The national Baptist paper, *The Watchman Examiner*, headlined its article about the 75th anniversary, "Lighting New Fires at Bacone." To quote from its opening paragraph:

> On February 9, on a day that saw a typically Indian blending of dignity and relaxation, Bacone College for Indians, celebrated its diamond jubilee anniversary with feasts, historic pantomimes, award presentations and religious services.... "The Purposes of a Christian College" was the topic of an address by Dr. Edwin T. Dahlberg, a former president of the American Baptist Convention. [He] depicted Bacone's work as a four-fold program designed to teach the skills and "know-how" for a modern age and an understanding of the culture of our day, and to develop Christian character and Christian beliefs in its students.

Frank made a point of encouraging all Muskogeeans to take part in Bacone's Jubilee Founders Day, and stressed that there would be plenty of barbecue for all.

297. Bacone: A Challenge He Couldn't Resist

† † †

The same "Echoes..." just referred to, announced Ray Evans's departure as director of the by-now famed Bacone Choir, stating: "His loss was a great one to our musical causes. Several important singing programs have had to be cancelled in the readjustment period." Frank goes on to say that Loretta "has been secured on a temporary basis." He continues:

> She has been in the background preparing solo voices for the past seven years. Aside from caring for the many activities that take place in the President's home and directing a church choir in town, as well as performing a full teaching load at the college, the new director has plenty of time to carry on this important program (on a temporary basis, we hope!)
>
> The new director's first great challenge will come the first of June, when the Bacone Choir will be the featured musical organization at the International Rotary Convention in Chicago....Pull for our temporary director, that she may live thru it all and return to the normality of being the wife of the President of Bacone.

Perhaps as a warm-up for this big tour, the Choir, under Loretta's direction, first made a shorter one to several cities in Texas, a state where they'd never before performed. It included attendance at a Metropolitan Opera production of "The Barber of Seville" (something Loretta undoubtedly wanted for herself as well as wanting her choir members to be exposed to this kind of music), and a concert at the First Methodist Church of Dallas that saw Ray Evans in attendance to see "his own" choir once more.

What must have been the last big event for the Thompsons before they left Bacone was the tour he'd mentioned previously that would end on June 1, 1955 with the concert before the Rotary International Convention. Some years later Frank wrote a lengthy piece about the event:

> President Eisenhower was scheduled to address the 22,000 delegates from Rotary clubs from over sixty nations. We had been granted top billing, immediately following the President's address. ...As President of Bacone, I saw it as an occasion to get at the very fountainhead of influence.

Not surprisingly, Frank's account is concerned less with the musical aspects, as had been the case in Ray Evan's story of the Bacone Choir, and more with U.S. policies toward the Indians, and their feelings about "the American Concentration Camps, euphemistically called Reservations" that most of Bacone's students came from. Frank's hope was that the Choir's appearance would "lead to a shift in the government's shortsighted Indian policies, as well as a chance to secure immediate backing, through scholarships, by Rotarians." Frank writes:

> The students hated exploitation, and couldn't have cared less that they were to perform before the Great White Father....During the long and tedious rehearsals of glee club, ceremonial dancers and sign language performers, we constantly held the carrot of improved conditions for their people before them as an objective justifying every sacrifice.

Frank cites an example that illustrated the depth of resentment inherent in most Indians–something Ray never mentioned if it occurred on his tours.

> The leading soloist and dancer, a colorful Apache, failed to show. When I accosted him in the furnace room of his dormitory where he thought he was safe, he almost snarled, "You didn't tell us we had to sleep in white man's house." [He must never have been on tour with Ray's group.] Obviously, the dual purpose of billeting students along the route was to show people that Indians are human beings and not drug store statues, and, of course, to save lodging expenses. After an hour of cajoling and threatening, I convinced Ray Taneb that he couldn't let his people down. Without him, the whole show would have fallen flat. In fact, success beyond our fondest dreams accompanied our every stop.

Oddly, Frank never reveals who is directing the choir on this tour. They were certainly prepared by Loretta, but was she with Frank on this trip? If she was, it's very unlike Frank not to mention her. But if she wasn't, then who was? The Choir could not give a big concert without a director. Perhaps her role was uncharacteristically neglected in this account as Frank's focus, as noted, was not on the music. He tells us:

> ...During each program, a question and answer period provided white people the opportunity to expose the abysmal ignorance that exists about this least known of all minority groups. The questions were always the same and inevitably in the same order. "Indians are rich, aren't they, with all that oil and uranium?" "There aren't many of your people left, since you're the vanishing Redskin?" "Isn't it true that Indians aren't capable of

absorbing white man's knowledge?" Occasionally, a questioner would reflect a pseudo-sophisticated knowledge of anthropology: "Isn't it true that your people are not immoral but amoral?" "Do your people have no tolerance for alcohol because they are still immersed in a primitive culture?"

To prevent a complete turn-off by the students and their sullen refusal to talk, Frank began to deal with some of these flagrant misconceptions of the Indians in a preliminary statement, and to change the thrust of the questions more to the campus life of the students.

On arrival at the convention, they discovered that Eisenhower was not coming after-all, but that Vice President Nixon would be speaking instead. You may remember that Frank had previously known Nixon; they had debated more than once while Nixon was a student at Whittier and Frank a student at Redlands in California. Hence the substitution of speakers may have given Frank an access to "power" that he might not otherwise have had. He writes:

> Presuming on our former acquaintanceship, I needled Nixon about his administration's unwise Indian policy. Just two years previous, his administration had set its policy in House Concurrent Resolution 108, which declares that the object of Congress is to terminate, when Congress chooses to do so, and without regard for the wishes of the Indians, the trustee relationship which the government assumed over Indian affairs at various times in the past [known as the "termination policy"]. This had been a contractual relationship, but one party to the contract, i.e. the U.S. Government, had failed to keep its part of the

> bargain. In return for millions of acres of land relinquished by the Indians, the government promised to educate the Indians and to rehabilitate them economically and socially. The land had long since been received, but the Indians had never received more than tokens of what they bargained for. Most demoralizing was the part of HCR 108 which granted the government the right to abrogate its side of the agreement whenever it chose.
>
> I made my case as strong as possible and urged the Vice-President to remain on the platform after his speech to see "some Indians that are worthy of more consideration than your administration is offering, and who would someday be leaders of their people as well as wielders of their recently won franchise rights." ...Mr. Nixon most graciously heard me out, and even agreed to reverse the agenda so the convention would not be disrupted by his departure.
>
> After posing in war bonnets and tom toms with the students, he sat spellbound as they danced and interpreted patriotic ballads in graceful sign language. Following the dramatic portrayal of the Statue of Liberty with its plea to the poor abroad and the raising of the Flag on Iwo Jima, he signaled the assembled crowd to stand in an ovation. When J. B. Dreadfulwater climaxed the program with the sentimental, "This is MY Country," he sprang forward to embrace the singer.

Afterwards, Nixon posed for more pictures with the students, and told them he was glad he'd been persuaded to stay "for your thrilling program."

Fifteen years later, in 1970, in an address to

Congress Nixon repudiated the termination policy and asked it to redress the many injustices being inflicted on "the most deprived and isolated minority group in our Nation: namely, the first Americans, the Indians," Frank heard then-President Nixon using the same words he had spoken to him that day. Frank continues to quote "*his* words" that the President spoke: "On virtually every scale of measurement—employment, income, education, health—the condition of the Indian people ranks at the bottom of the Totem Pole."

In 1970 Frank was full of hope that things were looking up for the Indians. What might have been the result had we followed Frank's advice when he urged America to launch a Marshall Plan for the original Americans, proclaiming:

> We can do more to replace the luster of our image abroad by erasing this blot on the escutcheon of our national conscience than by nearly anything else we might attempt. The restoring process will not be easy or quick, [but] can be attained by providing training such as has been offered at Bacone College for ninety years....

Frank might have added to his point by quoting an inscription on the outside of the Bacone chapel by Pleasant Porter, Chief of the Creeks:

> The vitality of our race still persists. We have not lived for naught. We are the original discoverers of this continent, and the conquerors of it from the animal kingdom, and on it first taught the arts of peace and war, and first planted the institutions of virtue, truth and liberty. The European nations found us here and were made aware that it was possible for men to exist and subsist here. We have

given to the European people on this continent our thought forces—the best blood of our ancestors having been intermingled with their best statesmen and leading citizens. We have made ourselves an indestructible element in their national history. We have led the vanguards of civilization in our conflicts with them for tribal existence from ocean to ocean. The race that has rendered this service to other nations of mankind cannot perish utterly.

The Thompson family in 1955, about the time of Frank's resignation

It must have been shortly after the completion of this tour that Frank informed the Board of Trustees and Baptist Mission Society that he was resigning. It's unclear whether it was before or after this tour that he'd had a mini-stroke on the golf course, and even though it hadn't proved serious, it had undoubtedly been scary enough to want him to stop the grinding travel-fundraising schedule he'd been keeping. Perhaps he thought it impossible to "put the college on autopilot while he recharged, and then continued with its expansion," as his son, Scott, recently suggested would have been the prudent thing to do. Scott added: "His awesomely hard work for Bacone was just beginning to pay off, even a new President's house was funded. And he had a base in Muskogee and Tulsa that gratified him; a position of influence."

In Williams and Meredith's history of Bacone, they have this to say:[10]

> In 1955 Bacone College celebrated its seventy-fifth year of operation. Under President Thompson's leadership, the Diamond Jubilee Fund Campaign was initiated with the goal of obtaining funds for restoration of existing campus structures and the building of a number of new cottages for the faculty and administration living on the campus. Thompson worked so hard at this that in 1955 his health began to fail noticeably, and he offered his resignation to the Board of Trustees and the Mission Society.

On August 14th the family is "feted" by the faculty and staff at a tea held in their home. The article in the *Muskogee Daily Phoenix*, explains that they will be "leaving the city the latter part of this month for Arlington, Massachusetts where...Dr. Thompson will assume the pastorate of the First Baptist Church of Arlington." As reported, Frank told them:

---

[10] p. 103

305. Bacone: A Challenge He Couldn't Resist

> Even though I will no longer be associated with Bacone College, I will continue to actively support several promotional efforts which were planned before my resignation became urgent.

Maybe if they'd *heard* him in his "Echoes of Bacone College" written in May 1954, Frank's health wouldn't have made his resignation urgent. He sounded discouraged when he wrote:

> Surely such an institution as Bacone doesn't deserve to barely eke out an existence! So much is being done [at Bacone] for a people that have been so neglected and are so needy. I have traveled the length and breadth of this nation this year, neglecting important duties at home and on the campus, to try to find ways to keep Bacone's ever increasing financial needs met. We have been hard pressed because of the many financial drives our denomination is engaged in and due to the death of three of our largest contributors....There are great days ahead both for the Indians and for Bacone, but the agonizing months of deficit financing and unpaid bills are hard to reconcile with the tremendous service that this mission-minded college is rendering.

Despite Frank's ending optimistic note regarding the future, this writer doubts it ever really got any better, or required any less effort on his part.

There is no doubt that Frank's efforts were appreciated. No greater tribute to *all* the Thompsons could possibly be written than that passed as a resolution by Bacone's Advisory Board on December 1, 1955. (Reproduced following)

RESOLUTION

A resolution of appreciation to Dr. and Mrs. Thompson was presented to the Board and was adopted. The resolution follows:

As members of the Advisory Board of Bacone College, duly assembled in regular meeting at Bacone, Oklahoma, December 1, 1955, we record our gratitude for the seven years of dedicated service that Dr. Francis W. Thompson has contributed as President of the College. Coming to Bacone in 1948 at a time of great crisis in the life of the school, he has through great personal sacrifice and an extraordinary ability brought Bacone to the highest level of achievement in its history. Particularly has he been successful in developing a fine relationship between the College and the surrounding area, as well as in placing the name of Bacone in the conscience of the American Baptist Convention and of the nation as a whole. Always concerned with a high academic standard in the life of the faculty and the student body, he has none the less consistently recognized also the public relations value of Bacone's nationally famous student chorus and football team. During his regime, the Chorus appeared in many of the greatest churches of the country, as well as, before the International Rotary Convention and on the Ed Sullivan Television program. The Bacone football team likewise brought distinction to the school, tieing for the Junior Rose Bowl championship in 1952. The accomplishments of Dr. Thompson during the years of his presidency were notably dramatized on the occasion of the Diamond Jubilee in February, 1955, when awards were given to seventy-five of the most distinguished alumni of the school in every type of vocation and profession. A Diamond Jubilee Fund raising campaign for $250,000 was a feature of the Seventy Fifth Anniversary year. While at the present time only $212,000 of this amount has been secured in cash and pledges, a host of new friends to the College has been discovered all over the country. His interest in Bacone will undoubtedly bring continuing support and gifts for many years to come. The affectionate regard in which Dr. and Mrs. Thompson and their children were held by the entire student body and community has made the sorrow of their friends correspondingly great at their leaving. As they now begin their new work in the pastorate of the First Baptist Church of Arlington, Massachusetts, we pray for them God's richest blessing in their new field of labor. Dr. Thompson's gifts as a preacher, a pastor, educator, and friend to all God's children assure him an unparalleled experience of success in his ministry at Arlington. We cannot conclude this statement without tribute to Mrs. Thompson whose talents as a hostess, homemaker, and director on occasion of the Bacone Choir, proved invaluable to the life of the whole community besides endearing her to the faculty and student body. We are grateful to God for the association of this Board with the entire Thompson family, whose services to the Kingdom will be enshrined in the history of Bacone forever. We take affectionate leave of them with the words of the Indian benediction, "May your moccasins make tracks in many snows, is our prayer."

The foregoing resolution was adopted by the Advisory Board of Bacone College on December 1, 1955.

Julian B. Fite

SECRETARY

One article commenting on Frank's resignation noted that gifts to Bacone had increased from $16,000 a year in 1948 to $100,000 in 1954, "principally as a result of Dr. Thompson's winning friends for the institution across the nation."

And certainly the ream of letters to Loretta from coast to coast, from Washington to New Hampshire, and from many places in between attest to the extent of his travels, and, more importantly, the impact they had on him. Aside from glowing descriptions of the beauty of many of the sites, and requests of Loretta "to act as greeter of visitors to the Muskogee Orphanage in his absence," "to be sure she mails their Income Tax return in time," "to tell his secretary...", the letters always include an expression of appreciation of Loretta's letters to him, and how much he misses her and the children:

> Darling let me say again what I ought to say to you each day, but it's the Yankee in me keeps me mum. I never believed even God able to provide the kind of deep and ecstatic love I feel for you and you radiate to me. Certainly my failures in life can always be conquered by the glorious and seldom realized fact of having a true and precious lover and growing love myself that makes the future so radiant with expectation that I never for one fleeting moment ever turn back to anything or anyone in the past.

In another letter:

> This has been a strange period. The stormy weather has kept me from much running around, and I really haven't had enough speaking to justify this long a trip, but maybe the change of pace—

reading, extra sleeping—will pay off in the more hectic days ahead!

And in a letter to "Suzie" [Sara Sue]:

> You should have seen your clumsy dad yesterday. I climbed up a snow bank to get a better view of Lake Winnipesauke and stepped on a slab of ice only to get a view of the lake from a horizontal position with every bone in my body broken—almost! If I were as graceful and coordinated as you or your mother, I wouldn't make such unorthodox landings.

And again to "Sweetheart" [Loretta], reflecting just how important she was to the well-being of Frank, who always seemed to be full of self-doubt despite his obvious abilities, his oozing of charisma.

> Thank you for the rewards of faith and restorer of hope that you had ready for me here....If you only knew how much your letters mean to the "traveling salesman" when he needs that extra boost, you would never leave me dangling on the precipice of uncertainly and loneliness again.

One other quote:

> It seems now that it will take a week of sleep and rest to catch up, but then a few days of your good cooking and loving care and all will be in readiness for the big campaign to start June 14th.

† † †

After the announcement that he was leaving, John Lewis Stone in his column in the *Muskogee Times-Democrat* praised Frank in a rather lengthy, somewhat light-hearted way, referring to him as a "bushy-browed gentleman" who would be missed in Muskogee. In part, he wrote:

> Frank has left his mark on Muskogee–a mark which time will never be able to erase. We can say honestly that he was one of our favorite religious men. He faced life with pretty much the same broad-mindedness we try to use. We worshipped together many times on Sunday mornings–and evenings. And, we played golf together a good many times on Sunday afternoons–something which too many religious men seem to think is sacrilegious.
>
> Frank made himself felt in the city's civic life. He did not live apart from the City of Muskogee. He tried to make himself, and Bacone, a constant part of Muskogee. And that's the way it should be....
>
> We have known for the past several years that Frank was literally working himself to death. He was on the run almost constantly, making speeches, campaigning for money... but he was never too busy to do anything he could for Muskogee....
>
> [Bacone] is a school of which Muskogee should be proud–something no other city in the United States can boast of to its visitors.
>
> We're not too happy about telling Frank and his fine family goodbye. We hate to see Muskogee lose men of his caliber. But we wish him all the success possible in his hew position...He's done his share in the past few years and is entitled to a bit of a rest.

Frank's last sermon before he left Bacone was preached on August 28, 1955 at Grace Episcopal Church in Muskogee. An earlier bulletin stated: "All of us will want to be there–to worship with Bacone's great president on his last Sunday in Muskogee and to hear a great citizen preach.

His sermon, which we do not have a copy of, was titled "Yoke makes for LIFE."

In Frank's September 1955 farewell edition of "Echoes from the President's Office," under a picture of the whole family, he writes:

> This is the beginning of a new era at Bacone. It is the end of another. A change is often stimulating for men or institutions. The change for me is most difficult. Bacone has been in the very marrow of the Thompson bones for seven years as president and for a score of years as faculty member and follower of its needs and deeds.
>
> Wear and tear on health and family life makes the change imperative. The change will not remove us from Bacone except in miles....Opportunities to publicize the school will continuously be presented. A steady stream of prayer will be offered for its well being. No, it is not the end. It is the beginning of another phase of service for Him Whom to serve is life itself!
>
> From that morning seven years ago when Loretta sleepily asked, "What will our Yankee friends think of us out here among the Indians before the arrival of the Mayflower? Until the day we reverse Horace Greeley's words we have tried to Bacone-ize the nation. [He then runs down all the "Highlights Along the Trail" during his tenure as President.]

Rightly or wrongly, Frank's son, Scott, in retrospect, assesses Frank's decision to leave Bacone when only 46 years old as the "biggest mistake of his life." He adds, not quite accurately, "The terrible thing is that when he left he had almost twenty-five years to live and they were filled with frustration."

311. Bacone: A Challenge He Couldn't Resist

†††

In September, following Frank's departure, a very young-looking William Connor was named Interim Pastor of the Bacone College Church. He had studied at the Julliard School of Music in New York and served as a chaplain in the Army in 1943. He received his B. D. from Andover Newton in 1953.

In January 1956, Roger William Getz, who had been made Acting Administrator at the time of Frank's departure, was selected as the new president of Bacone. Frank's "Echoes..." states that he was a former Missionary to Burma and had been Agricultural Instructor and Business Manager at Bacone for the past four years.

13. A Return to New England

We acknowledge our oneness each with all from every clime and culture, and in the challenge of Thy spirits guiding, we seek to tear down all barriers that do so unnaturally separate us from another–brother from brother.

Lord God we know thou has blessed this church with full measures of heavenly rewards, Thou hast given it a vision of high and holy plans beyond the mere purpose of existence.

Strengthen and lengthen the ministry of all who lead–and all who follow. Hasten the day when shadows shall disappear and Thine everlasting sunlight shall put an end to all earthly sorrows, and Thine eternal glory shall be our delight.

† † †

Not only had the constant travel worn Frank out physically, but, as devoted as he was to the Indians, he clearly felt the burden that the college's future rested squarely on his shoulders, and also felt tormented that constant begging for funds was necessary just to keep the college alive. Additionally, even though he was also chaplain of the college, and preached at the Bacone Chapel twice weekly when on campus, at other Muskogee churches (where he was an enormously popular guest preacher), and at churches he visited on his fund-raising trips, Frank still undoubtedly missed the pulpit and a congregation

as his regular venue. Thus he must have felt both pleasure and relief when he was called to the First Baptist Church in Arlington; his family having accompanied him for the initial interview held over lunch at the Fitchburg Old Mill restaurant.

Arlington's First Baptist Church

On September 11, 1955, after Judge Harold Magnuson introduced him to the congregation, Frank preached for the first time at Arlington's First Baptist. For his formal installation service in November, he could take pleasure in the fact that a number from his old church, Phillips Memorial, came for the occasion: among them, Wes Hall and Joan Stapleton (members of the youth group when he was there and who had married in 1953), along with their respective parents. This writer, too, just back from four years in England and living in Stoneham, Massachusetts, would certainly also have been there (perhaps on a regular basis) had she known Frank had left Bacone and was at nearby Arlington.

In Frank's first pastoral letter to the congregation soon after he arrived, he wrote:

> It's great to be here in Arlington with you. More and more, it has seemed to the Thompsons like a homecoming; a change from the glamour, glory and adrenaline pumping pressure of unique Bacone College has given us a chance to gain perspective. The Church of our Lord Jesus Christ is the matrix for so much that is regnant to American life.

> We hope the Lord can use us to aid all in driving stakes deeper into the fundamentals of Life, or to cut ties from unsafe moorings.

He continues with an account of his visits, and continuing visits, to the homes of his parishioners, and mentions the "multitudinous activities of this large parish."

He then refers to a poem (as had been his habit at Phillips Memorial) by Herman Hegadon, "The Bomb That Fell On America," and the momentous happenings it recounts of the atomic age that forces us to consider the future of civilization. The poem pictures America as people of "all shades, varieties, and qualities, people bewildered and boastful, cowardly and courageous, grasping and generous, an America which must grow up overnight if mankind is to be saved from destruction."

Frank then quotes from the poem: the Lord's response, when told we need a miracle:

> The Lord, He looked at me as a mountain might look at a molecule.
>
> "So you want a miracle," said the Lord, "My, my, you want a miracle."
>
> "I suppose you mean you want me to come sliding down a sunbeam
>
> and make one-hundred and thirty-five million self-willed
>
> egotists overnight into one-hundred and thirty-five million
>
> cooperative angels."
>
> "Brother," said the Lord, in a voice that shook the windows,

> "That isn't the sort of universe you're living in and that
> isn't the sort of God I am"...

Frank goes on to say:

> Then the poet traces Man's flight from the challenge that confronts him, and, finally, exultantly, against the dazzling pinnacles of heaven, the voice of the Lord speaks so that light and sound blended and came back singing fire; "There is power in the human soul," said the Lord, "when you break through and set it free like the power of the atom, more powerful than the atom. It can control the atom. The only thing in the world that can. I told you that the atom is the greatest force in the world, save one. That one is the human soul."

Frank closes his letter with these words: "Our business, yours and mine, is to direct our souls toward control of the atom and release of the new Adam!"

† † †

Frank, soon after his arrival, became involved in Arlington's civic affairs, drawn into the already existing Catholic-Protestant controversy that revolved around the granting to the Catholics of a piece of city property (referred to as parkland in one account, a dumping area in another). They had offered $4,000 for 154,650 square feet, taken by the city by eminent domain in the early 1930s at a cost of $12, 014.24.

Frank quickly became identified as the leader of the opposition, but was outmaneuvered when a petition favoring the granting of the land to the Catholics, signed by 6,000, was given to the Town Meeting in December. This resulted in a Special Town Meeting on January 9, 1956, where, by unanimous vote, approval was given for the Selectmen to offer them the land for $12,014.24 (less than 8 ¢/sq. ft.), to be used exclusively as the site for a new Catholic high school. This was certainly better than their original offer, but many still regarded it as a give-away.

Approval by the legislature was required, but this generally amounted to no more than a rubber stamp. Thus it was that on January 10, 1957, the land at Summer and Mystic Street was formally accepted by Msgr. Oscar R. O'Gorman, pastor of St. Agnes Church. The *Arlington Advocate* on January 17th noted, "the church did not have to accept the offer for one more year but accepted it quickly. The Town Council has been authorized to draw up the necessary documents for the sale."[1]

The writer was not able to document the timing and extent of the opposition, but it may be that it was behind the church's "quickly accepting the offer."

† † †

It's rather ironic that Frank's ecumenism at this stage of his life did not extend to Catholicism. But it's doubtful he thought about that when he quoted one of his loved poems at the end of a sermon March 3, 1957:

What care I for caste or creed?

---

[1] Later, at another Town Meeting, the Catholics were granted permission to change the condition of sale from "exclusive use to build a new school" to "for high school purposes," so they could use the land for an athletic field. Writer pieced this account together from information she obtained from the Planning Office, and articles in the *Arlington Advocate* dated 12/1/1955, 1/5/1956, 1/12/1956; also a page from a 100th anniversary publication of Saint Agnes Church provided the writer by the Robbins Library in Arlington.

It is the deed, it is the deed.
What for class, or what for clan?
It is the man, it is the man.
Hours of love, and joy and woe
Who is high and who is low?
Mountain, valley, sky and sea
Are for all humanity!

What care I for robe or stole?
It is the soul, it is the soul.
What for crown, or what for crest?
It is the heart within the breast,
It is the faith, it is the hope,
It is the struggle up the slope.
It is the brain and yee to see,
One God, and one humanity.

† † †

Frank's feelings about Catholics were about to move from civic opposition to personal. In Scott's words in an e-mail to the writer, he tells of the repercussions they had in the Thompson household:

> [Dad] decreed that Sue and I were not to date Catholics. Remember at that time Catholics and Protestants separated in school by how they said the Lord's prayer, so Dad wasn't exactly acting in isolation. The decree only had relevance to Sue who was 14 when we moved there [actually she would have just turned 15]. She promptly fell in love with Larry Cutter, a tall and striking 16 year old Catholic guy who had quite a following in the high school. They started having sex. It was probably six months before our parents found out. War ensued between

> Dad and Sue: chains on the doors, check-in times, etc. Of course, Sue found ways around everything. Finally, in despair, when Sue's will had pretty much caved in, Aunt Mary Jo [Frank's half-sister] agreed that she could come to Long Island and live with them in the middle of the school year. Sue agreed. Things had gone sour with Larry by then anyway.

In his autobiography, Scott's account of this time is rather more graphic as well as indicating the effect it had on him, thirteen at the time.[2] Describing his father as "strong-willed," Scott says he was "locked in battle against my only sibling, a stunningly beautiful sister." He goes on to say:

> Many young men wanted her and Father was determined to screen them, indeed to exclude whole categories; of course those screened out were precisely the ones my sister preferred. With one she fell hopelessly in love: tall, blond, gorgeous and immensely self-confident at only sixteen, Larry Cutter was bent on having her whenever he wished and did so.

Scott then describes how frightened he was when Larry came over to him in the school's gym shower, and "towering over me... making it clear that I'd regret it if I got in his way."...

> Life was ugly for awhile around the household, and I too was left with many psychological scars, enough to be greatly relieved in due course to get a scholarship to round out my high school days at Phillips Academy, Andover; my sister

---

[2] See p. 31, Thompson, W. Scott, for source of quotes that follow and for additional related statements.

went off to live with a favorite aunt in New York. Our family spirit was wounded from the crisis.

It seems possible that sibling rivalry and hindsight have caused Scott to exaggerate the extent of Sue's misbehavior and of Frank's response. However, it did lead to her leaving home for a period. Oddly we hear nothing of Loretta's input during this what must have been a tumultuous time in their household.

Sara Sue was in her Junior year of high school when things had come to a head and she went to stay with Aunt Mary Jo [Frank's half sister]. That she did so seems almost accidental. Mary Jo [Partington] recently told this writer that she had just made one of her frequent calls to the family and casually asked how everyone was. Not even knowing that Loretta objected, Mary Jo had agreed, when Frank, without going into a lot of detail, had responded by suggesting Sara Sue go stay with her for awhile. In the six months or so she was with them, Mary Jo had nothing but praise for her:

> She was a beautiful, delightful, talented girl; we all loved her; our four children loved her to baby-sit for them; she was popular at school, no problems, entered a talent contest–had a lovely voice she was self-conscious about using because her mother was so talented.

Whatever the truth of the blow-up, at the end of her Junior year, Sara Sue returned home and finished her senior year in Arlington and then, not only going to California with her parents, but becoming a student at the University of Redlands during the same years her father would be there as Vice President of Development.

† † †

We have no information as to whether or not Loretta also made herself heard during the controversy that shook their home, but we do know she was beginning to make her presence felt in their own and other churches in the area. In April 1956 there is an announcement in the church bulletin that she would quickly sing at a "city-wide tea for women from all our churches." She also soon organized and was directing four choirs at First Baptist: Alpha (Primary), Temple (Junior), Chancel (Junior High) and Antiphonal (Teen). All four of these combined with the Adult Choir for the Christmas services.

† † †

As for Frank, if the household turmoil had begun prior to January 1956, he must have been especially grateful for the chance to get away when the First Baptist Church of Bangor Maine invited him to talk about his beloved Indians on the 18th. An article in the *Bangor Daily News* notes that "some 60 Baptist churches have been personally invited to share in this evening program by the minister, the Rev. W. Stanley Pratt." It also notes:

> At the supper, Indians from Old Town [a nearby section of Bangor] will be represented by the Leo Shay family. Leo Shay, Mrs. Florence Shay, and son, Thomas Shay, who is a graduate of Bacone College, will be the guests of the church as a gesture of friendship to the nearest Indian neighbors.
>
> After the address by Dr. Thompson, there will be shown the challenging and moving story of the Christian Message working in the life of a young Indian. The movie is "The Rivers Still Flow," showing in an inspiring way the Christian answer for life-service with an answer from God by the solitude

of the flowing river.[3]

In his talk on the plight of the Indians, Frank emphasized a number of points that had become a regular theme with him: (1) the Indians' distrust of the white man, with good reason; (2) the need for education of the Indian to compete in an increasingly technological society; and (3) his belief that Indians needed a Christian education to learn forgiveness and to produce their own Indian leaders—emphasizing, of course, Bacone College's unique role in giving them just this. Also, apparently himself still having faith in U.S. government programs, Frank presented, in a favorable light, the government's five-year plan to transport Indians from the reservations to the cities with promises of education, housing and jobs—a program that proved all too soon to be sadly lacking in fulfilling its promises. He urged the congregation to get involved.[4]

† † †

Frank saved a copy of a letter to his parishioners written after "the honeymoon between church and new pastor" was over:

> One of the items we shall never take for

---

[3] The writer traced down two members of this family, one living in Austria, but neither knew of this event so could not elaborate.

[4] In a review of the Public Television Documentary, "Alcatraz Is Not An Island" (premiered 11/7/02), Diane Burns calls the government's Relocation Program in the 1950s and 1960s, here referred to by Frank, as one of its more "insidious, invidious" programs "designed to destroy the tribes completely. Indian families were promised a free trip to the city, a place to live when they got there, jobs and vocational training, and better educational opportunities. In practice, it often meant a bus ticket to an alien metropolis with no follow-up and no way to return home." No wonder Frank wanted his congregation to become involved.

> granted is the thoughtfulness and consideration people of First Baptist Church have for their Pastor. Your thoughtfulness in not expecting the impossible. Your healthy concern for our physical well-being, etc., all give us the warmest feelings of appreciation.
>
> Our introductory year has given us a glimpse of the immensity of the task before us if First Church is to fulfill its destiny. We are grateful that you have provided a home that will give us a center from which to serve....
>
> Our denominational effort for the next four years will be in the realm of creative evangelism. After all, that is the preeminent purpose of any Christian church....

At least by March 1957, if not before, attendance at First Baptist had increased to the point that, just as had been the case at Philips Memorial, two services were taking place each Sunday—one at 9 a.m., the other at 11 a.m. The church bulletin for March 17 notes that 271 attended the first service and 375 the second. Sometimes the assistant minister preached at the earlier service, but not always. It's hard to convey the impact his sermons had on his listeners, because so much of their power lay in the resonance and emotion that was so much a part of his delivery. It was obvious that his beliefs and his concerns were coming straight from the heart.

Frank was to stay only three years at Arlington, but one parishioner recalled for the writer two "outreaches" he initiated during that time: Summer union services with two other denominations, Methodist and Congregational; and, the conducting of communion services at the Arlington Rest Homes the first Sunday of each month.

Another occasion while Frank was at First Baptist,

"A Japanese Festival," undated on the announcement, must have reminded him of the visit by the young Japanese-American student, during the war, who'd come to Phillips Memorial to tell us about her own and her family's experience in our concentration camps for the Japanese. On this happier occasion there was to be a portrayal of Japanese traditions by members of First Baptist "with Lani Nakashima, a charming Japanese girl studying at N. E. Conservatory, as member of 'our Japanese family' and our guest speaker—Miss Ayako Yamada of Japan. Japan style refreshments will be served."

†††

The church's home study in 1958 was "Christ, the Church and Race." Appropriately, the February 9th church bulletin, without attributing the source, quoted the following on its front:

> In the midst of racial tensions and world revolution,
> Christians everywhere must be searching their souls for
> an answer to the question: "Do we love our neighbor as
> ourselves?" There are those who insist that they love
> And worship God with their whole heart, and that they
> Love their friends. Yes, they do love God and neighbor,
> but...
> Could it include the thousands of "displaced" Negro people,

many uneducated and unskilled, who are fleeing from the
South into northern cities? We have rushed to show mercy
by sending food, clothing and money to displaced persons
In many lands. What is our response to these "displaced"
citizens in our own country, so near at hand, so far from
our hearts?
—or [what of] the migrant workers right here in our Town?
—or the Indian Americans being moved into industrial
centers everywhere?

WHO IS MY NEIGHBOR?
ANYONE IN NEED WHEREVER HE MAY BE!

† † †

Frank is again emphasizing his belief in inclusiveness when in a Lenten sermon, "Our Confessional," on March 16, 1958, he offers "the working definition" of sin as "anything that separates creatures from the creator and creations from other creations." To emphasize his belief in inclusiveness, the sermon begins:

> There is that in mankind that requires togetherness. We are planned that way: born into a family, protected in a clan, associated in communities, enlarged in nations. Man is a social creature. Anything that separates and divides, defeats

the purpose of Life!

Our togetherness is based upon the unity of life, in the creative plan of living—even divinity is in togetherness: the doctrine of the trinity declares the unity in apparent separateness. Life is in God, with God, thru God, and God is the sum total of all living!...

The day we recognize SIN—our failure to fulfill togetherness with others and with God, that day the heavenly choruses start rejoicing over the repentance of one sinner. That day we start tearing down the barriers that have shut us from reality so much of our lives are spent building self-enclosing prison walls around us—alienating us from God and Man and LIFE!...

This ego crust, these caves of illusion, these isles of isolation, keep us for GROWTH, TRUE DEVELOPMENT, TOGETHERNESS WITH MAN & GOD and they can only be broken thru by confession. "Confess with your lips, that it is Lord, and believe in your heart, and you will be saved."...

On another occasion, Frank, in his exploration of "sin," defines, rather tellingly, the "seven deadly sins":

Anger, Contempt—the will to exclude another from good.

Deceit—erection of barriers to genuine encounter and manipulation of people as things.

Lust—the will to exploit another as a toy to serve one's own nerve ends.

Pride—to set oneself up as judge and God.

Hypocrisy—use of appearances of goodness to excuse from real honest relations.

Anxiety–failure to trust God
Do-Gooder–using charity & organized good works to keep from personal encounters.

Tying it to love, as he had previously, near this sermon's end, Frank quotes C. Hartshorne, "Love is the medicine for the sickness of the world, a prescription often given, too rarely taken."

The Easter Sunday Sermon on April 6, 1958 culminated a week that began with a celebratory service on Palm Sunday, followed by a Maundy Thursday Communion Service, then a shared Good Friday Service with St. John's Episcopal, and, finally, five services on Resurrection Day: the first, city-wide, at 6:30 a.m. at Menotomy Rocks Park; the last, a 5 p.m. service that included a baptism and special musical program by the church's five choirs. For "Doubting Thomas's," Frank had this to say in his Easter Sermon: "If the resurrection were not so, it should be, and with God's help I will live as though it were so–THEN IS LIFE ENNOBLED INDEED!

† † †

The lack of information in Frank's files accessible to this writer leaves us with no warning that he will leave Arlington in August that year. A recently acquired article in the *Arlington Advocate*, August 7, 1958, helps us out. It reads:

> Dr. Francis W. Thompson has resigned as pastor of the First Baptist Church in Arlington to accept a position as vice-president and director of development at the University of Redlands, Redlands, California.
>
> Dr. Thompson, who became pastor here in September of 1955 will preach his last sermon at the

First Baptist Church this Sunday at 9 am. It is titled "Not Farewell, But Fare Forward Voyager."

...In announcing his resignation, Dr. Thompson said, "I greatly appreciated being accepted as a member of this community, an integral part of one of the best known cultural centers in the world, and the chance to share in its New England heritage."

...Since moving to Arlington, Dr. Thompson and his family have been very active in community affairs. Mrs. Thompson was director of the Woman's Club chorus and also directed four youth choirs here.

They have two children, Sara Sue, who will enter Redlands in September and Willard Scott who attended Phillips Andover last year.

The church gave a farewell reception for them on August 13, 1958.

† † †

Frank's decision to leave the pulpit once more, this time after only three years, to return to fundraising, can't help but make one wonder *why. Was there an excessive, bothersome amount of bickering at the church? (something he frequently hinted at, sometimes openly alluded to, in his sermons) Did the thought of returning to Redlands evoke a nostalgia for the earlier, less stressful, perhaps more hopeful years when he was still shedding his view of himself as a "country hick?" Or was it the prestige?* His son, Scott, remembers him once commenting, "Not a bad promotion to go from President of the small Bacone College to become Vice President of the far larger University of Redlands." But, Scott also asserts, "A Vice President is the creature of a President, so it really wasn't a promotion."

Whatever the reason, after only a few short years, Frank was leaving First Baptist at Arlington to become Vice President of Development at his old alma mater, Redlands, the college from which he'd graduated in 1935 and that had awarded him an honorary doctorate in 1954 while he was at Bacone.

Frank would be seeking funds for Redlands at a propitious time: the National Science Foundation, private foundations and industry were all increasing their grants to universities in recognition of the need for improved, more rigorous teaching, especially in the fields of science and mathematics. After the Soviets launched *Sputnik* in October 1957–the world's first satellite that circled the earth for several months–the U.S. found itself in the unaccustomed role of having to play catch up, before it could even consider surpassing the Soviets in space exploration.

14. California & Redlands University Beckon

A group of college students went to that great soul, Helen Keller, to ask her opinion about something. "What," they asked, "do you believe is of the most significance today?" The great lady, deaf and dumb and blind since childhood, read their question by putting her finger tips on their lips and then her sightless eyes, appearing to look off across the centuries, her ears seeming almost open to let in the voices of life, her words came back clear and concise. "The most significant advice to the youth of today is found in the book of Proverbs, "Where there is no vision, the people perish."[1]

†††

If Frank had hoped, in returning to Redlands, to recapture the youth and spirit that had enveloped him while a student there, he soon learned that that was an impossibility, probably in any role, but certainly not as part of the administration. The passion and need to right a wrong that had driven his fund-raising at Bacone was absent in the more formal atmosphere at Redlands: absent was the same sense of community, of "family," he'd felt at Bacone, or even at Phillips Memorial. He would still prove his talent as a fundraiser, but the self-satisfaction, the feeling he was contributing to something larger than himself, was missing. Additionally, according to his son Scott, "The biggest grief of his life was reporting to President Armacost."[2]

†††

In September of 1958, en route to his old alma mater, Frank spent a delightful few days in Muskogee

---

[1] Incident recounted in one of Frank's sermons.

[2] More will be said of this later.

visiting old friends in town and at Bacone College. It would be the most restful time he'd have for some months to come.

The Thompsons' first task at Redlands was finding a place to live. Their first effort, the purchase of a smallish house near campus having proved unsuitable, they felt fortunate to quickly find another that would be impossible for any but the rich to consider today. Located on a mountain overlooking the town, it had a pool and grounds that included eighty-five fruit trees which they loved tending. Their home thus became their retreat and main source of happiness while at Redlands. It was also the site of university events and socializing with staff and others. In addition to her required role as hostess of these events, Loretta also resumed the more fulfilling role of teaching voice as she did everyplace they went.

Oddly, little is said of their affiliation with a local church, but Frank did become chairman of the school board of a small international and avant-garde school a rich European (Swiss) friend of his had set up.

But, for the most part, Frank quickly again became immersed in fundraising. The year *before* he arrived, Redlands' Board of Trustees had adopted the long-range goal of raising $8,000,000 before 1970, of which $5,000,000 would be for endowment. The immediate goal was planning a Jubilee, Fiftieth, Golden Anniversary campaign, that would raise $1,000,000 before June 1959. The goal had hardly been set when Glen Snyder, until then Assistant to the President in charge of fundraising, resigned, leaving management of this ambitious campaign up to Frank. It was a heavy load–and no nationally acclaimed inspiring choir to act as entrée to church and civic groups; the closest equivalent was a theater group that prepared a special anniversary program they presented before church groups, women's clubs, and Baptist conventions. Also the university produced a colorful book depicting campus life that was so well received it was selected as one of the best examples of color photography in the western states in 1959.[3]

Again Frank's position found him frequently "on the road," though more within California than coast to coast as earlier. Eight groups had been identified as "publics to be solicited: (1) alumni, (2) business and industry, (3) church relations, (4) estate planning, (5) parents of University students, (6) Fellows, (7) special friends for capital purposes, and (8) research-grant sponsors and foundations. Appropriate Trustees, administrators, and Development Office staff were allocated to serve within each of the eight divisions."[4]

As described in an article by Jack Cummings, director of alumni relations, that appeared in the summer 1959 edition of *University of Redlands Alumnus magazine*, many of these people, including Frank, went "night after night for several months all over the state holding organization meetings, campaign kick-offs and follow-up meetings." He adds, "Bouquets should be given the wives and families of these men for they saw little of their husbands and fathers during the January to June period."

The same issue of the magazine makes clear their success: by graduation day (June 1959), President Armacost announced that $1,100, 000 had been received in gifts and pledges--more than their goal of $1,000,000. He states,

---

[3] Information from Armacost, Hone, & Mertins, pp. 26-27. Redlands' archivist could not find either a copy of the book nor information about who selected it.

[4] p. 57, Armacost, Hone, & Mertins

"Nearly 1000 alumni and friends participated in the effort." Curiously, however, even though Frank had been in charge of development during that critical year, he is not among the people named by Armacost as active in this fund-raising!

A year later (1960) the university magazine notes that in the ranking of alumni who've contributed to their alma mater, Redlands has moved from near the bottom of the list to sixth place among schools in the "Large Coeducational College" category. An editorial in the summer issue complains that despite this the college received only Honorable Mention in the 1958-1959 American Alumni Council competition (Frank's first year as Vice President of Development). They write:

> We can find no school in the country that has achieved these things during 1958-1959: (1) Tripled the percentage of alumni support and (2) More than quadrupled the amount of alumni giving. The schools who won in our division, large co-educational colleges, went from 41.7% to 43,1%, and 31.7% to 40.0%. Redlands jumped from 14.0% to 44.5%. The amount of money given to the two winning colleges by their alumni increased from $46,225 to $56,403 and $30,055 to $50,066. Redlands' increase was from $27,236 to $155,307.

Redlands claimed that guidelines for the competition stressed percentage increase as the primary consideration, as it had been over the years, but that after the fact this year, the judges had decided to change the rules to stress not just improvement but also achievement. A letter from the executive director of the American Alumni Council, in response to Redlands' complaint, is quoted, in part, as saying:

> On the surface [Redlands truly spectacular climb] does appear more impressive than the record of the two schools judged to be the winners. I am sorry to say that I am unable to say why the decision was made as it was."

The editorial ends with the University and the Alumni Association expressing its "sincere appreciation to all who participated in making [the college's spectacular] record possible." In July, at their General Conference in Washington, D.C., two certificates for "creditable achievement" were presented to Jack Cummings on behalf of the American Alumni Council. They had been especially impressed by the "Khrushchev's Challenge" brochure that played on a quote by Khrushchev: "I challenge you to a fight. Not in a shooting war, but in a war of life and we will beat you. We are winning now and we will continue to win."

On November 4th that year, in recognition of their fifteen years at Redlands, President and Mrs. Armacost were honored with a surprise banquet attended by more than 350 alumni, fellows, faculty, friends and members of the newly formed Development Council, which consisted of representatives of the Board of Trustees Development Committee, the President himself, and members of the Development Office staff.

The Council, with Frank as Director, had held its first meeting earlier that same day. "Over 100 civic leaders, professional and business people, alumni, and faculty representatives" had participated in afternoon workshops prior to attending the evening banquet.[5] This committee was the

---

[5] Information from *U of R Alumnus*, winter 1961 and p. 57, Armacost, Hone, & Mertins

beginning of what would come to be referred to as the college's National Strategy Board, with James Graham Johnston, former Vice-President of IBM World Trade Corporation, as its National Honorary Chairman, and Dwayne Orton, a Redlands' graduate and director of IBM's international education programs, as its Vice General Chairman. Later, after Frank had left, Johnston gave 1.5 million dollars to Redlands for the start-up of a "cluster college" to be named after him—modeled after six such colleges associated with nearby Claremont College.[6]

† † †

A number of events that occurred during this time must have served as gratifying changes of pace for Frank. On April 7, 1959, he greeted Linus Pauling, a man after his own heart, while he was on campus. An article by Ron Smith in the college's *Bulldog Weekly* had this to say of Pauling:

> Originator of the petition calling for a halt to nuclear tests signed by 9,235 scientists, Dr. Linus Pauling will be the speaker in Convocation.
>
> Dr. Pauling, director of the Gates Crellin Laboratories of California Institute of Technology, is today one of the most noted theoretical chemists and also one of the most controversial....
>
> In a letter to *Life* magazine, Dr. Pauling summarized his viewpoints: "It is not only unwise, but also immoral for the people of the world to place their trust in weapons designed to kill hundreds of

---

[6] p. 58, Armacost, Hone, & Mertins and p. 3, Ouellette. Frank (and the reader), in a 1969 letter to him from Armacost, will hear more about Johnston College. The wording of Armacost's letter suggests that the concept of developing cluster colleges at Redlands was something that had been discussed even before Frank left.

millions of people, to devastate the earth.

"The compelling need in the world today is not a need to continue the test of nuclear weapons; it is the need to stop wasting world resources on armaments, to solve international problems by reasonable negotiation, to eliminate war and to bring morality and justice into their proper place of prime importance in the conduct of world affairs."...

† † †

Then, on Sunday, June 7, 1959, Fred A. Seaton, Secretary of the Interior, the main speaker at Redlands' 50th annual commencement held in the Greek Theater was awarded a Doctor of Law degree. As reported in the *Redlands Daily Facts*, despite being surrounded by scary headlines– "Communist talk of a new blockade of Berlin chilled western diplomats," "Nicaragua revolt may be used for sweeping probe," "NATO chief resists rocket-rattling threats from Albania"– Seaton's speech to a packed theater mentioned none of this: his emphasis, rather, was on the need for Redlands' 330 graduates to fight to retain the qualities of liberty and justice promised in our constitution. There is also no indication in the paper's coverage of the event that he met with Frank or that he mentioned Indians and their plight in America, but it is not unreasonable to believe that, during Secretary Seaton's time on campus, Frank would have taken the opportunity to talk to him about his time at Bacone and his continuing interest in the Bureau of Indian Affairs which falls under the Department of the Interior.

† † †

Finally, in 1962 Sara Sue graduated from Redlands and a year later, on June 21, 1963 married.

Frank, Sara Sue & Ken Nies

The fact Sara Sue not only chose to attend Redlands while her dad was a Vice President, but also had lived at home her first two years, suggests that she and her dad had mended fences after the explosion during her high school years that had sent her to live with her Aunt Mary Jo for a time. Only during her junior and senior years did Sara Sue live in a dorm. By then probably dating Ken Neis, a medical student, she would have been particularly anxious to distance herself from her parents. Sue and Ken asked a favorite Professor, Dr. Edwin Gasted, to officiate at their wedding, but unlike Scott when he later married, they asked Frank to assist.

† † †

Prior to this event, late in 1960, Frank heard from Wes and Joan Hall (now married) who had belonged to the youth group at Phillips Memorial when he was pastor there. They had moved to Colorado in 1958 and now were asking Frank to come to their Baptist church in Boulder and preach. Their church's beloved pastor had retired and they'd nominated Frank as a replacement. When the large congregation had invited him to become their pastor, Joan and Wes were thrilled. In recent correspondence, they wrote:

> We felt very honored when Mr. T was invited to visit Boulder and preach; then when he was invited to become our pastor, we were thrilled! JFK had just been elected [inaugurated in January 1961], and Frank informed the church calling committee that he had just been asked if he would be interested in taking on the position of Chief of the Bureau of Indian Affairs. Of course he was interested in doing anything he could to help his beloved American Indians, and he knew that the time involved in decision-making in Washington would be lengthy, so he said that he reluctantly withdrew his candidacy for the position offered by our Boulder Church, as he didn't want to inconvenience us.
>
> Joan and I were so disappointed, but knew that he would be able to do a lot for the Indians. Unfortunately, the job in Washington was not offered to him. Our loss, the Indian's loss, and the nation's loss.

> Regarding the time frame, I think that political factors prevented Mr. T from going to Washington. JFK's assassination did not happen until we were living in Telluride, Colorado, as I had accepted a job as School Superintendent there in 1963.

There are no documents to confirm it, but it is quite possible that Frank's name was brought to the forefront for consideration (as Indian Bureau Chief) by Interior Secretary Seaton who almost certainly would have met him while at Redlands just a few months earlier; perhaps had been impressed by his knowledge of Indian affairs. In any case, Frank had been nominated as U.S. Commissioner for Indian Affairs in the Department of the Interior by several members of Congress. Ed Edmondson, the Congressman from the same district of Oklahoma as Bacone, is quoted as calling Frank "a man of great ability and tremendous effectiveness."[7]

Exhibiting his dislike for what he perceived as "being used" by his father, Scott still seems annoyed as he recalls how Frank woke him up one morning and asked if he'd like him to be Commissioner of Indian Affairs.

> I excitedly said, "Yes," and he said, "Well, can you write President Kennedy?" I was bewildered. I already had a keener political sense than my Dad and knew I couldn't get a letter through to JFK despite the nice things he'd said about me when he came to Stanford as my guest in February 1960 while I was a student there. Eventually I'd had a polite administrative acknowledgement of my letter. Dad was well qualified for the position but over

[7] Neither the name of the newspaper nor the date is on the clipping.

optimistic, and underestimated the degree to which politics drove all that.

In fact Philleo Nash was appointed and remained in the position until 1966, by which time Frank was in Laos. According to the *American National Biography*'s account, Nash had had minimal direct contact with Indians but had studied them extensively as an anthropologist. As commissioner he is said to have promoted the idea of self-sufficiency for Native American communities through, among other things, greater educational opportunities, less emphasis on boarding schools, and attraction of industry to reservations.

Frank would have approved these goals. While still at Bacone, in 1954, he'd written, "Without education, there will be no strengthening of the economic position."

> Uneducated Indians are victims as they have always been to the foul play of conniving traders....The only way Indian people will have equality is to have an education so that they can meet their contemporaries on an equal basis.
>
> The high incidence of tuberculosis from lack of nourishment and poverty, from ignorance and isolation, are factors that must be overcome. Only those of us who have guilty consciences for the treatment our Indian brothers have received in the past will respond. Only those with Christian compassion will help!

Frank must have been bitterly disappointed that he'd lost out on the chance again to serve his beloved Indians, as well as the call to another Church, especially in light of his "constant ego-battle with President Armacost," reflected, perhaps by Armacost's failure to mention him in his reports on fundraising. Their strained relationship may have reached crescendo when the college was unsuccessful in its application, submitted on October 26, 1962, for a grant that had been announced by the Ford Foundation, intended "to strengthen selected independent liberal arts colleges." Though "not included in the first round of recipients in 1963," they were informed that later consideration was a possibility." Frank had left by the time a second application was submitted in 1965.[8]

According to his son, Scott, Frank was constantly venting his frustration, voicing his complaints about Armacost to the family. Scott describes Armacost as a tall arrogant man, Frank's age, who was prone to ordering people around, shouting at them. Frank felt belittled, hurt, and vented his feelings by drinking, many evenings, until he was plastered.

Clearly in search of another job, he talked to Scott about his hope of getting the presidency of one of the colleges in the University of California system. Scott recounts accompanying his father to an impromptu meeting with the chairman of the system–and its aftermath.

> [The meeting] was the day after I had won my Rhodes scholarship [he was a student at Stanford]. It was clear to me, but not to Dad, the interview was going nowhere. They foolishly sold their house on Sunset Avenue after three years because Dad was restless and determined to get out from under Armacost. Then they house-sat for some friends but ended up, eventually, having to buy a house again anyway.

---

[8] pp. 56-57, Armacost, Hone & Mertins.

Still resenting his father's requests of him to use his influence on his behalf, Scott recounts another earlier such occasion (one of many, he says).

> He psychologically made me feel subservient to his needs while I was at Stanford: he used his powerful authority as father, just when a father should be helping the bird to escape from the cage, to get me to live for him, rather than for myself. I was, perhaps, a Stanford junior, when he desired that I go to Stanford President Wallace Sterling and ask him (whom I knew well, but not that kind of 'well') to get him a job at Stanford so that he could escape Armacost. This was an absurd request that he should have known was impossible.

Instead of resenting these requests and believing they showed a growing deterioration of his father, might they not just as well be viewed as a father proud of his son's achievements; proud to be able to call on him at a time of need?

† † †

At the convocation service in Redlands' Memorial Chapel on January 4, 1962, Frank preached the sermon. Titled "Go East, Young Man, Go East," it perhaps reflects his frustration and recent disappointments. Nothing of record is said of this or of his work at Redlands in the years he remained there, but the sermon's title does suggest that he is increasingly bored with a life that consists primarily of asking, year after year, for money. There may well have been a growing, gnawing feeling that he was not achieving anything really worthwhile.

Indeed, it's rather surprising that Frank remained at Redlands for five years: perhaps only because none of the alternatives he'd hoped for came to fruition. But despite these disappointments, there is no question that he was effective during those years; some $3,500,000 was contributed to the university from industry, churches, foundations, alumni and parents; an average of $700,000 a year, more than ever before. President Armacost is quoted as saying: "The amount has been increasing as a result of the effective organization that was built under Dr. Thompson's leadership."[9]

However, this quote seems to have been a rare recognition of Frank's efforts. In the "President's Page: Retrospect and Prophecy" that appears in *Alumnus* in the Winter of 1963, Armacost says not one word about Frank, nor is he mentioned in the "Redlands Report" that same winter. Rather, it states: "Dr. Gilbert L. Brown, Jr., administrative assistant to the president, assumed responsibility for the coordination of the full program [of public relations and development] and is serving as Director of Development." Is this apparently deliberate failure to mention Frank a reflection of the animosity Scott states that existed between his father and President Armacost? Scott insists it was so bad that everyone who knew them was aware of it.

† † †

Whatever precipitated another move by Frank in the Fall of 1963, he did not "Go East," but he did accept the newly created position of West Coast Director of the United World Federalists (now called World Federalist Association), an organization that strongly supported the United Nations, indeed was committed to strengthening it, a concept Frank felt almost as strongly about as he did the American Indians.

Earlier that year Willard Scott graduated from

---

[9] p. 6, United World Federalists, October 1963.

343. California & Redlands University Beckon

California's Stanford University with, as noted earlier, a Rhodes Scholarship in hand for study at Oxford University in England. He would remain there from 1963 until 1967 except for time during 1966 spent in Ghana, the subject of his Ph.D. dissertation.

15. Seeking Peace: United World Federalists[•]

The Widow's Walk atop the International Institute gives one a view of most of what makes San Francisco "everybody's favorite city." Today, however, my heart was saddened–blood was spattered on the window, quivering below was a robin. Why had this redbreasted one aimed too low? Three feet higher and freedom was unlimited–strong pinions, ample buoyancy, yet dying from flying too low.

Had it wanted closer fellowship with groundlings? It was already too high for earthworms or seeds. Had it seen a reflection in the pane of glass? Was it accident, miscalculation, madness?

Well, there's one less harbinger of another spring.

I am wondering if similar fates await others who aim too low. I'm thinking of a group that used to be called "visionary," "far out," or worse, but the ideas once scoffed at have become the common mouthings of many the group has grown, or failed to grow, and now is classed as the conservative wing in its area of flight and fancy. It is so respectable, so proper, and in danger of dashing itself against the panes of image-making substance.

Robins have wings to fly high enough to clear all barriers and find freedom unhampered in the blue beyond.

Thoughts turn to peace on earth this season, but harbingers of peace too often fly too low, fearful of epithets from groundlings, or is it acrophobia?

"The trumpet summons us again/then shall we earn/the eternal thanks of man/and, as peacekeepers,/the eternal blessings of God."

† † †

• Now Citizens for Global Solutions. Quote by Frank is undated.

345. Seeking Peace: United World Federalists

Frank's job with the United World Federalists apparently resulted from a chance conversation between Scott and "Sandy" (Ulma) whom he'd met at a UWF conference in Washington, D.C. when he was there as a Stanford "student leader." Sandy was the director of field operations at national headquarters and the conversation turned to a discussion of Frank as a "believer" who would love to take a job with them.

> Sandy was right when he pointed out that Dad was overqualified. However, there was no dissuading Dad from taking the job at UWF. He couldn't stand Armacost anymore and was considering himself a "sell-out" for not working for his true beliefs, which had become much more focused in an international direction during this period. [You may recall that Frank, while a student at Redlands, had once expressed the intent to use his gift for speaking to enter politics or international affairs.]

It is not, then, surprising that in October 1963, when offered, Frank accepted the newly created job of West Coast Director for United World Federalists. As such, he would still be travelling extensively, organizing for the UWF, and directing the twenty-five UWF chapters located on the West Coast–in Portland, Seattle, Los Angeles, and Santa Barbara, as well as several in the San Francisco area–the city where Frank chose to establish his office. Both he and Loretta were pleased to be in the San Francisco-Oakland area, nearer Sue and Ken who'd just recently married (June 21, 1963). Sue was then teaching French in the Francis Drake High School in San Anselmo, while Ken continued his studies at the University of California medical school, later to become a prominent rheumatologist. As for Frank's opinion of San Francisco, he'd once said:[1]

> [It] is one of the most invigorating places in the world. No matter how sultry, hot, or humid in other places, up Market Street one could always find a veritable cataract-like rush of fresh winds from the Golden Gate. It would bring one up clean out of the world of foggy minds and enervated muscles. There one can't yawn in the face of a gale.

In contrast, Frank called Los Angeles "drowsy and sleepy." The Thompsons bought a nice house in the outskirts of San Francisco near the beach.

† † †

During the transitional months of September-October 1963 when Frank was tying up loose ends at Redlands and opening his office in San Francisco, he gave an interview to the *Fresno Beacon* that goes a long way in explaining his interest in the UWF. A report of the interview (less than two months before President Kennedy's assassination)[2] begins with Frank's statement that the United States has made a "miniscule" turn away from "the dead end street of military spending," by establishing an arms control and disarmament agency. He said of the agency's director that for the first time someone with the ear of the president would be working full time for peace.

> He said studies have shown billions less could be spent by the military without hurting the military's capacity to strike back.
>
> "We have an overkill potential of 1,125" he

---

[1] In his sermon, 5/20/45, "The Rushing Wind of Pentecost."

[2] P. 1-B, *Fresno Beacon*, October 14, 1963

continued, explaining that he means the US has enough weapons and ammunition on hand to kill "each potential enemy" 1,125 times.

The UWF has come under attack periodically since its establishment at the end of World War II, because of its aim of a world government. Some fear the lack of national sovereignty in such a situation.

Frank then talks of hosting in San Francisco an international gathering of delegates from fifty-five nations, planned for 1965, the 20th anniversary of the founding of the United Nations. He continued:

"The main purpose of the United World Federalist is to strengthen the UN, to try in every way possible to get the statesmen of our nation and of other nations to see that there are alternatives to the old war cycle.

"Also, we need to educate people at the local level to show that peacetime will not mean depression."

Indeed, the Declaration of Purpose adopted at the founding of the UWF on November 2, 1947 reads:[3]

WE BELIEVE that peace is not merely the absence of war, but the presence of justice, of law, of order–in short, of government and the institutions of government; that world peace can be created and maintained only under a world federal government, universal and strong enough to prevent armed conflict between nations, and having direct jurisdiction over the individual in those matters within its authority.

---

[3] WFA 1947-1997, 50th Anniversary Historical Survey

THEREFORE, while endorsing the efforts of the United Nations to bring about a world community favorable to peace, we will work to create a world federal government with authority to enact, interpret and enforce world law adequate to maintain peace.

"If You Really Want To Do Something For Me, You Can Take Your Foot Off The Oxygen Tube."

Found on page 35 in "WFA 1947-1997 50th Anniversary Historical Survey" (WFA has no record of source and permission to use.)

Frank would have found the UWF's declaration in keeping with his belief that "we need some unconditional surrender on our own parts if the unconditional surrenderings of WWII are not to be in vain again [as they were after WWI]. However, as Frank continues after this opening of an undated sermon, no doubt given shortly after the end of the war, what he has to say conveys not only what attracted him to the UWF, but also gives a hint as to why he didn't find the UWF as fulfilling as he'd hoped [lacked a religious foundation and any personal responsibility]. Frank's sermon continued:

Millions of young men have had to

unconditionally surrender their time, their loved ones, and their lives to bring this hour into being. They didn't ask to go to war, they were not responsible for this war—they were too young—they were the innocent victims of the world's unconstitutional surrender to self-interest and SIN.

By evasion, self absorption and expediency, we overlooked the inequalities, the starvations, the injustices of our ONE WORLD until they became unbearable. Dictatorial leaders and rabid rulers arose on waves of world rebellion against these inequalities and injustices. Then, instead of correcting the evils, we appeased the dictators and built walls around ourselves until Pearl Harbor, and until its aftermath of tragedy was inevitable! What we sow in evasion and self-interest, we will always reap in destruction and chaos, on an ever greater and greater scale.

UNCONDITIONAL SURRENDER IS WHAT IS NEEDED ALL RIGHT, unconditional surrender to God whose earth this is—not the white man's or the black's. Unconditional surrender to the will to peace, which is and always has been God's will: our only hope.

We must now WAGE PEACE as our beloved youth have waged war—unconditionally. We must wage peace with all we have, with all we are and with all we hope to become. Surely the horror of this war teaches us that never again can we survive another.

Let us resolve that never again will we accept untrue reports of world events, never again will we be too busy to learn the truth, never again will we be too selfish to work out a way WITH our ONE world, not against it. We here resolve before God to surrender unconditionally to Him and His plan for us. For "blessed are the Peacemakers for they shall be called the children of God."

In December, not long after the above-reported interview with the *Fresno Beacon*, Frank spoke to the Unitarian Church in Fresno, California on "Preventative Morality."[4] It was the beginning of what would be his main challenge while with the UWF: implementing plans for an international gathering to be held in San Francisco in 1965—the 20th anniversary of the founding of the United Nations. Delegates were expected from the fifty-five nations that made up the World Association of World Federations (WAWF). This was, in Scott's words, "the plum that made the job professionally worthwhile." Frank needed both his gifts for speaking and for effective writing to inspire the various chapters to become involved.

In the December 1964 *West Coast Digest*, Frank urged each chapter to appoint chairmen to publicize the congress, report names of prospective delegates, and so on. He asked specifically:

> If your chapter will be responsible for transportation for one or more WAWF official? Provide translating equipment for one of the three official languages? Furnish transportation to bring a delegate from Africa or India? Pay registration and banquet fees for members from your chapter? Provide UN flags for banquet tables? Furnish office equipment for the Congress (needed for two weeks)?

---

[4] It appeared in Redlands' Alumnus, March 1964; notes for class of 1935.

> Inform other peace groups in your area of this occasion and the need to coordinate efforts of all citizens in backing the UN now to help prepare for the next step ahead.

As big as this occasion was meant to be, the UWF (now the World Federalist Association) was unable to give this writer any additional information about this event, or on the organization's other work while Frank was there, beyond that found in *WFA's Anniversary Survey for the years 1947-1997* (Frank is not mentioned). The *Survey* includes this information:[5]

> Throughout the 1960s World Federalists renewed their pressure for measures to prevent war instead of continuing to resort to the battlefield. In a telegram to President Lyndon B. Johnson on February 9, 1965, UWF President C. Maxwell Stanley cited the Vietnam War as new evidence of the inevitable consequences of "the absence of an effective world security system and the machinery of enforceable world law."...

[During this time, Frank optimistically, but unfortunately incorrectly, predicted that within two years a revision of the United Nations charter would strengthen the world body and improve its voting system.]

> UWF intensified its defense of the United Nations, which some members of Congress sought to weaken or destroy. On March 7, 1965, the UWF National Executive Council declared that 1965 not only marked the UN's 20th Anniversary, "but also the

---

[5] pp. 13 & 16-19

> beginning of its destruction." A nationwide petition campaign was launched "To Save and Strengthen the United Nations." In San Francisco in June 1965, the World Congress of World Federalists made additional declarations of that need by holding demonstrations in conjunction with the official UN Charter commemoration events. It was also during this world congress that Norman Cousins was elected President of WAWF.

Norman Cousins had been both a leader in founding the UWF and its long-time Honorary President. In 1958, he'd spearheaded the formation of SANE–an organization designed to focus renewed concern on the threat of nuclear weapons and perhaps was influential in seeing that the Senate ratified the Nuclear Test Ban Treaty in 1963.

† † †

The only information available to this writer about the success of the 1965 conference comes from Scott who stated it was a success and resulted in lots of in-house laurels for his dad, but Frank's own feelings were that he'd contributed all he could toward the furtherance of peace through the UWF. As Scott put it:

> He was very thrilled with all the fine things said at the conference about the superb job he'd done organizing the show, but it seemed, at this point, almost too little too late. The job was taking him nowhere and he was losing momentum personally as well.

Scott explains his dad's sentiments this way:

> UWF was a small organization that had

converted its central function from a goal of building a stateless world to one of supporting the UN in a world of states. This made it a kind of contorted bird with one wing flying one way and another another: e.g., UNA had the advantage of no baggage from 'one-worlders,' whereas the true radicals didn't have the baggage of UWF in its attempts to be 'realistic.'

As we shall see in the succeeding section, Frank contemplated leaving the UWF for at least a year prior to actually doing so. He was still searching for a place where he could "make a difference" in ending the inequalities, starvation, and injustices he felt essential to peace and the furtherance of ONE WORLD.

16. Laos: Hoping to Make a Difference

Who is my Neighbor? Anyone in Need, Wherever he may be.... This haunting motif led us to Southeast Asia, there to learn at first hand what our "image" was becoming; there to see if we could offset a bit of the unfortunate press we were getting abroad. No one who hasn't been in that area can begin to grasp the attitudes that people of that far off world have toward "Faranges," the word for "foreigners" which really means intruders....The problem for us and our nation, most dramatic and timely, was the condition of children, for in many ways this unfortunate conflict is a war of genocide and will be for years to come: from six to ten civilians are casualties for every one militarily involved, and because the wars have been going on for three decades in Southeast Asia, the population is more than half juvenile. Children are the innocent victims of the most massive of all offensives in the history of humanity.[1]

† † †

By the time Frank left the World Federalists, Scott had graduated from Stanford and was studying at Oxford in England. Recently he explained to this writer how his "knowing the right people and speaking up for his dad" was responsible for opening the way for Frank's obtaining a job as the "Cultural Coordinator for the Kingdom of Laos representing the United States Information Agency (USIA)." Scott wrote:

I had a friend in the Stanford administration,

[1] From Arlington church bulletin, 2/9/58 & sermon at Alameda church on 11/3/1968.

> Bob Miller, who had been in USIA and still had close friends there (a very tightly knit organization). Bob took a liking to Dad once when he was at Stanford visiting me. After I told Bob that Dad was unsatisfied in his career, things not going well, he said that Dad should work for USIA, heading up one of their educational centers.

Crediting himself with setting the stage for Frank's getting the job with USIA when he introduced him to Bob, Scott writes:

> Bob REALLY liked Dad, and was one of those people came along and opened doors for him. It turned out to be Laos. Recall that our involvement in Vietnam came via Laos, so Laos was considered "front lines" though luckily it was neutralized in due course.

In a letter to his dad from England, dated April 9, 1964, *over a year prior to Frank's actually leaving the World Federalists*, Scott is responding to a suggestion by Frank that he is disappointed with the World Federalists as an organization and is contemplating accepting a job with USIA. Scott confirms that he too is disappointed with them but suggests that taking a job with the USIA may not be a good idea. Of this Scott writes:

> What I'm, of course, saying is that the challenge is there, and poignantly so—so it's a deep personal decision with implications that don't need spelling out. I couldn't be more disappointed that UWF is not catching on as we hoped. All I can say is that you must evaluate in what context USIA would have you over ten years, and if it seems that you could be happy in it, then see it as a higher calling—

very much the synthesis of so much you've been involved in all your life. And if you're quite serious about it, get the hell down to Latin America on your vacation to see what's happening there first! ...Mexico is one of the most exciting countries in the world, increasingly used as an example of underdeveloped world, with a fantastic metropolis that I would far rather see than any in Europe outside of Rome and Paris, from all I hear. One could visit it for more than just the sake of travel– there's so many good scholarly works coming out on it, and one could really get into the village and see what's going on, UN Missions, UNESCO, etc.

The letter gives no indication that Scott had anything to do with Frank's interest in or consideration for the job with USIA; though, of course, this lack of reference to it does not preclude Scott's recent assertion to this writer that it was his introducing Bob Miller to Dad that led ultimately to his being offered the job. Be that as it may, this letter from Scott does make clear that at this time in his life, he shares his dad's liberalism, writing at some length about how Republicans are ruining all hopes of a successful Geneva Conference.[2] He then says:

I'm interested in two things, the two relevant facts of the age: the need for world law, and the dilemma of the developing nations [which no doubt drew him to choose Ghana, Africa as the subject for his Ph.D. dissertation]....

---

[2] In his book, Scott notes that just prior to his leaving for Oxford in 1963, he had participated in the civil rights' March on Washington. P. 41, *Price of Achievement*.

357. Laos: Hoping to Make a Difference

As already noted, Frank remained at UWF for another whole year after he'd first talked of leaving. No doubt sick and tired of fundraising and conference planning, he felt the need to become personally involved in helping the neglected of our ONE WORLD he'd so often preached about.

† † †

In a recent conversation with John O. Sutter, he elaborated for this writer on the connection between Laos and Vietnam. Now President of Northern California's World Federalist Association's office, Sutter had in the 50s and 60s both studied in Southeast Asia, been in the foreign service, and represented the Asia Foundation (headquartered in San Francisco) in a number of countries in that region; hence he was regarded as something of an expert on the area, or, as he prefers, a specialist. Sutter explained:

> At the time Frank was there, the Vietnamese occupied Eastern Laos, while the CIA was working with the Laotian government and hill people, called Hmong, many of whom became refugees in the U.S. In 1965 when I visited the capital, Vientiane, it was nice and quiet, but gradually, as Northern Vietnamese were running their war materials to the Vietcong in South Vietnam, down the Ho Chi Minh trail which was largely inside the border of Laos, the country was far from peaceful for a long time.
>
> However, these cultural centers and libraries like Frank was setting up, financed by the U.S., were quite popular; among other things, they provided English language instruction and everyone wanted to learn English. So, despite the proximity of Vietcong

activities, Frank would not personally have been under any threat at the time; he could have enjoyed his work for a while. The U.S. wasn't forced to close down its embassy until about 1973 or 1975. It's very peaceful now, despite still being Communist; the Buddhists have again become very active.

It may be peaceful now, but Scott suggests why records regarding Frank's time in Laos have been impossible to come by:

> The educational institutions with which Frank was associated tried to preserve an appearance of independence from the embassy and thus kept separate records that no doubt went up in smoke in 1975; whereas, embassy records had backups in Washington.

At one point Frank explains that he does not work directly for the USIA but for the Lao-American Association that is under contract with USIA. A letter from the association's director, Ruth C. Wright, describes the main purpose of the organization this way:

> To promote mutual understanding and sympathetic appreciation between the Lao and American people. The Association accomplishes this purpose by teaching the basic tool of understanding–language–and by sponsoring various cultural, social, and community programs.

† † †

Just one month after the successful UWF conference in June 1965, Frank found himself in Washington, D.C.; Loretta back in California to settle things there. He started what was to have been a three-month orientation/indoctrination before his scheduled departure for Laos in October. Not having yet located an apartment for his stay, Frank's first letter to his "Sweetheart" is written from the Burlington Hotel in DC, postmarked July 2, 1965.

> The big program is a mighty full one. They run us around these mammoth buildings as though we were training for the marathon. So far, not too much that is substantive, but we get down to real business next week, tests on language, intensive study of communism and a lot of American history. There are eight in the group, only two of us as directors, but the overall training is the same for all. They are all younger, in years anyway, and mighty sharp people, so the old man has to put up a brave front, as though in his early thirties again.
>
> ...It will be a long summer. Hope you and Scott [who must be home from Oxford for the summer] can dispose of cars and house soon so we can take as much of this training as possible together....You must be so busy with all that has been thrown at you that you won't be lonely, except perhaps at coffee time, the hardest for me too. I'll be so anxious to know how everything goes and what plans shape up.

Frank closes the letter with "Much love to you and spare some for Bud [Scott]. Then, "Ever and Ever more Love." The letter is addressed to Loretta at 1235 Holman Rd., Oakland, California. [Frank's passport notes 520 Boden Way, Apt. 9, Oakland as his address; in fact, it is his friend's, Beulah Parker's.[3]]

---

[3] You may recall that it was Beulah who gave Frank the money he needed to attend Redlands University. They remained close; Loretta, at times jealous, not quite so happy about their continued friendship.

The five additional letters Frank writes Loretta while in DC are not dated. All are addressed to "Sweetheart," one of them, beginning, "Your letters are so sweet and full and joyously you," reminds us of earlier letters he wrote Loretta when courting. But the letter written after his first week in DC begins: "After a week of this, I am beginning to see what they have in mind for us. It is truly an indoctrination program, but so far it is one that I think we could live with." Frank certainly gives us an insider's look at how the government "prepares" its representatives who are to serve overseas.

> Some of the instructors are old fashioned and dogmatic, but most of them recognize that one sells his country's image best by being his true self—that I hope will be the sum result. Several of us were mighty disturbed when we began to get the pure propaganda line that didn't allow for any questioning, but the others have been more realistic. A Negro named Garnett who had been expelled from the USSR admitted that the U.S. program lacked much of the imagination and subtle impact of the communists because it had been all negative whereas the USSR had been more all-inclusive and informative of events in their larger context. If the implications of his talk are carried out, I think we will find the way to fit in the program.
>
> It will not be an easy assignment—in fact we are getting quite a bit of attention because they recognize that it is a tough post and so will need the most consideration. Soon I will start sending you the info on steps to be taken in preparation. You might start taking your shots as soon as you have finished the hard house work in preparation for sale. You will

need to take shots for about a month since it isn't wise to take more than one at a time. With your good health and rugged constitution, I think you will have minimum trouble—old softie me will be the one to cave in.

Reflecting his nostalgia for the years spent at Phillips Memorial, Frank goes on in this letter to express the wish that they would have time for a real vacation in Rhode Island before embarking. He's also considering the need to be rested: "We are going to have our hands full of entertaining with ample servants and lots of advice—they say we will each need to learn patience, AND LEARN TO GO AT A SLOWER PACE THAN EVER BEFORE."

Telling Loretta he's now moved into an apartment, he writes:

> I leave early in he morn and return pretty late at night. It is a 25 minute walk at top speed, which I have been doing so that the exercise problem is cared for....[but adds] even though it's "cool" for D.C., I am soaked through after a brisk walk, but it's all preparation for what's to come.

Frank closes his letter with a typical comment as to how "full and wonderful" Loretta's letters are. His letter, directed to Scott as well as Loretta, signs off with "love to both."

His next letter reflects the fact that Frank has learned that his orientation period is being cut short so he's hurrying things up, and advises Loretta to get her passport, visa and shots at once. "[The shots] are just about everything they can puncture you with. Your reaction ought to be more mild than mine, being you are a big girl and I'm such a sissy." His immunization record shows that he had three plague shots (in July, August and September), three typhoid shots (two in July, one in August), two typhus shots (July and August), two tetanus shots (August and September), and a gamma globulin in September. [*Too bad there wasn't one for Hepatitis!*]

This letter continues:

> One of our bigger decisions will be the piano. They don't have one in center over there and I think it would be a must for you, but probably not your good piano. Do you feel inclined to buy a small upright; it would be at our own expense, but will be worth it for your use. Next is washer—heat makes much washing necessary, but would washer justify itself with the type of clothes, i.e., all cotton? The house is nearly complete with refrigerator and stove, but you would need your china and silverware for entertaining, unless you think you would rather not risk it. (We might have to pull out on short notice if the commies approach.)

Changing the subject, Frank writes (in long-hand; the rest typed):

> I'm sorry my letters are so uninteresting. I seem to have lost any ability I ever had to write. I love you so much and think of you constantly, but writing has become a chore I never minded before. Hope you and Scott have written much to Sue: she was so plaintive about having no mail and she is such a wonderful correspondent....
>
> Back to business: Plan to bring with you only one or two dresses that aren't tropic weight: those for any possible trips or vacations. They don't wear stockings, hats or gloves—hot weather cocktail dresses

> mainly and cotton washables for work. You will be teaching English (very simple system) and I hope music. I can hire you at $2 per hour—about 3 hours per day—that will pay for servants for house work. ....Much Love, F.

We learn from his next letter that his orientation has been cut in half, and the faster pace of inoculations is causing him to suffer. Not able to study, he took off for a quick trip to Rhode Island, visiting with the Kenneys, and, for the first time, dropping in unannounced at Phillips Memorial on Sunday morning, and, he writes, "It was fun, though but few there. Rev. Snell is in holy land getting his reward for his long tenure." [*Do we detect a bit of jealousy/maybe envy in realizing his replacement's longevity, and, perhaps, satisfaction in observing few attending church, so unlike when he was there?*]

It becomes clear in this letter that Loretta not only is not going to share in any part of the orientation in DC, as they'd originally planned, but is not even going to have things sufficiently settled in California to be able to accompany him to Laos. Frank strikes a positive note regarding this, telling her that it's a miserable time of year there:

> If I get there first I can size things up a lot better than from here. Another reason for having you come later is that I will have to go to Bangkok [Thailand] for a week of modern English-teaching techniques which I am missing out on here because of the change of plans...that would leave you alone in a new area for a whole week, whereas if you come after the monsoons, you will find it much easier to acclimate, etc....

364. Justice, Peace & God

In his next letter from DC, Frank tells Loretta that he will have a short time, August 13th to 17th, with her in California before leaving for Laos. He alludes to the great letters that both Scott and Sara Sue write and states "they will be chief among the morale builders we will have through the long stay abroad." He then writes: "The news from Laos grows more ominous each day—power-struggle-wise I mean, but the Laos-American Association seems to be on a good footing, and there are many reasons to think that it will be one of the most interesting posts of all the USIA." Frank ends the letter with some advice:

> Don't be too worried about the house. Even though your son said I have proved not too successful a business man, I still feel it would be better to rent than to take any real loss in this dull market. Our equity would continue to build up, and California property can't go anywhere but up unless we have a major shift, and in that case the whole economy will change anyway.

The final letter from DC begins with a greeting in the Laotian language. He then writes:

> As you undoubtedly know, that is my greeting in Laotian. It's quite a language and very much beyond my present ability, but one we will need at least to recognize....I am so full of vaccines I can hardly sit up, but so it goes.

Frank again laments not having a "month in the wilds with you" instead of having to depart on PanAm at 2:45, Tuesday, 17th after only a short 4-day visit. He concludes:

> You'd never guess my Saturday activity. This one anyway! Cleaning apartment and washing clothes!

365. Laos: Hoping to Make a Difference

It's my turn to have the gang in for drinks. All trainees let down on Saturday and have a bout and so I must fit in the scheme and the apartment has had its first attention today.

† † †

Frank's next letter to "Darlings all" is from Tokyo, Japan, a stop-over en route to Laos. It ends with a very clear statement of what drives his life:

> Here in the land of the rising sun—it was setting for so many hours of the flight that one fails to comprehend it would ever need a new beginning. The sun was a many-colored blur against the plane. Anchorage, Alaska was as bright and fresh as San Francisco. Tokyo is hot, but no more so than Kansas City or Muskogee. How Vientiane Laos will be, can only be hinted at. Not having slept, I was not up to much nite life in this land of Geishas, but I took a turn around the nite spots where "soliciting" is much more in evidence than in Western cities....
>
> The long sunset ride was good for loafing, loving and anticipating—loafing in present, loving in memory and anticipation, and realizing what a lucky guy I am to have such a help-mate who has helped to bring such a precious pair of "plusses" [a word he often uses in referring to his children] to this point. Not least of my gratitude goes to **that nature within that will not let me rest until some semblance of fulfillment of the call to service has been answered and those who shared that urge are such a large part of the substance.** So now off to the next leg of the long nite's journey to write the next chapter. Love, love, love to each, multiplied for all.

366. Justice, Peace & God

† † †

Frank's first letter from Laos is full of optimism and wonderfully conveys his first impressions: [*Remember how he recently proclaimed to Loretta that he'd lost his ability to write!*]

> At last I know what the space age is! It's an age in which time can lose its entire meaning. The plane which took me from the arms of two loved ones [Loretta and Scott] and several devoted friends flew straight into the afternoon sun with not a move by the latter for 22 hours except the one spent refueling in Anchorage.... Somewhere along the route a day of life was left behind—to be regained two years from now [the length of time he expected to serve in Laos].
>
> After a day of rest and sightseeing in teeming Tokyo, we gained back two hours as night came on faster than seemed possible after the other experience of never ending sun. Hong Kong and Bangkok were incidental stops that bear revisiting as soon as priority allows. Of course, the adrenaline pump was out of kilt with time, but there was enough zip left to make the flight into Laos thrilling. Lush green, lofty mountains afar and the mighty Mekong lazy and brown under the false sheen of silver.
>
> Then there it was—Vientiane—where a new adventure was to start for the "moveable Ts." Washington DC had hinted there might be a committee to meet the plane, but returning personnel had warned me not to expect much on a late Friday P.M., but there they were, everybody but the Ambassador [William Sullivan], and even he had sent a personal envoy.... I was moved more than for many a day....

> Perhaps most unbelievable of all was the weather—you know the long months of agonizing dread that had built up regarding that ever present topic of chit chat. But here it was delightful after the monsoon had passed—far less humid than Muskogee had been on that former hi-day, July 14, 1948. Ceremonies over, the U.S. officials escorted me to Wat-Chan, our home.

Frank found it "more than adequate," but the Public Affairs Officer (a position just above Frank's as Cultural Affairs Officer), looking around, told his assistant, "Get some more furniture and fixings for this place at once!" After everyone left, Frank lay down for a "wink or two," and slept right through the banquet scheduled that evening in his honor. The letter then continues:

> I awoke at 4:30 a.m. to the most amazing bass chorus I have ever heard. The rains had turned Wat Chan #1 (Buddhist temple across the street) into a small lake and a bullfrog chorus showed years of harmonic training. I already envision Loretta writing the Lao-Frog anthem. Soon the night chorus was aided by the rhythm of many drums—later explained as the monks' morning meditation to the rising sun. No words will ever describe the above chorus and accompaniment. It must be heard to grasp, and then only dimly. The morning was graced with a steaming thermos of coffee and goodies brought over by the Assistant Cultural Affairs Officer...
>
> At dusk I walked 100 meters to the banks of one of the world's largest rivers and there watched two worlds mingle, Lao fishermen and families

> feasting along the banks—some truly picnicking, some squatting in place contemplating the twilight glow. On the river the modern world of water skiers and skin-divers made me wonder all over again where I was.

He ends this first letter from Laos with an assurance to Loretta and others that the "cultural shock, so forebodingly warned about, is no more than that experienced at Bacone, and again the future looks as bright as the stationary sun that wavered not nor diminished on that long flight between time."

A letter on September 5th suggests that Loretta plan to arrive in Bangkok on October 7th by which time he'll have a car and can meet her, thus sparing her some "cultural shocks" and also giving them a "few days together in that fascinating city [before] the nice drive up to Vientiane. The letter also indicates that Frank was about to leave on his "first field trip into the river villages."

About a week later Frank is writing about the theft of a borrowed tape recorder and the camera that Scott gave him, the primitive nature of the police, and the interrogation of their maid Toye.

> The police apparently worked her over good—she came back crying and ready to leave for Thailand if "Massy think iss thiff."[4] Massy no think so, but one can never be sure: it was such an "inside job."

After a long discussion about what to bring and what not, Frank closes:

> You're right, this can be an exciting adventure. We have many uses for you and your talents, and with

---

[4] Frank's attempt to duplicate the maid's fractured English.

the freedom you will have from your age-long slavery to housework [because they'll have servants], you ought to soar as so often you have. But most of all, you can again be sweetheart to one who misses you keenly. So come along, but not so fast as to upset plans there for careful shipping, selling and forwarding.

Frank with a Laotian student in his office

In a letter written September 12th, Frank writes that "the buildings are being readied for the crush of the largest enrollment in history and a whole new set of courses and classes." So many have enrolled that our home is going to have to be used for some of the classes. He also talks of the country's love for holidays that disrupt the year.

This was rice planting day–a time to give thanks for the past and hope for the future. Long lines of candle carriers were serpentining and singing up and down the river. Practically every house was lighted a la Christmas in New England, except these were all white lights—each San Law (the rickshaws of Laos) had its strings of candles and happy crowds were dancing in the streets. They are such simple and happy people and yet so bedeviled by their animistic fears. I haven't been able to get the psychology at all.

You will be shocked at the carelessness in so many parts of the city—in spite of the millions the U.S. has poured into the country. They tell me that the royal city of Luang Prabang is much cleaner and more charming, but why the capital city would be thus is beyond my comprehension as yet.

During a quiet spell this week I went across the river in a fascinating long boat to Nung Kai, which is in Thailand. There it was as different as any contrast could be: neat shops, clean streets, attractive little park, and a fairy-land of shoppers....The contrast makes one wonder why the difference in so short a space, and they each came from the same original tribes. Our Ambassador (Sullivan) said to me that when he was in Thailand 18 years ago, it was exactly like Laos today, so maybe we are again in a pioneering setting.

Thoreau has been my pleasure reading the past week. He is the ONE to say what needs to be said to ME these days—never have meditative words had significance and been freighted with more meaning than his quiet assertions from that charming little pond whose ripples have been felt around the world. "If all around you seem to march to different tunes, perhaps it is because you hear some distant drums unheeded in their rush," and, of course, our old favorite, "Only that day dawns to which we are awake."

The letter continues at some length, ending, not for the first time, with a recognition of Loretta as the person who has made his life possible:

> This has been anything but a love letter and yet you know it covers much of what the larger meaning of love includes, and along with the practice goes, as always, my tenderest love and deepest appreciation of the thrilling life you have made possible by your constant faith and abiding love. And, of course, "There are more days to dawn, the sun is a morning star."

By Frank's mid-September letter, he's experiencing the monsoon season, at first no worse than Oakland, but then on the 15th the water was so high around the post office, he couldn't get there to mail a letter. Frank tells of awaking one morning after it poured all night to find the yard under two feet of water. The electricity in the whole area went off during their first night classes.

> The gathering monsoon was making the air very heavy, and then without fans, and with many candles, you can imagine what the heat was like. It's only at such times as that that the weather is terribly uncomfortable....Anyway, the power went back on after I had gotten home ready to sweat out a nite sans air-conditioner or fans, so all was well.

† † †

While Frank awaits the arrival of Loretta, at last, on October 3rd, he writes a sort of overall view of what's been going on, directed at friends back in the U.S. He begins by talking of the "moveable Ts," the five of them having spent a part of the year on five different continents.

> Sue and Ken have returned from a study program for 18 of her French students, spent in LaRochele and Paris. Scott has studied and traveled in Europe, Africa and the near east, and after a summer of research at Stanford and Washington, DC, will take a third year on the largesse of Cecil Rhodes (Rhodes scholarship) in London, Paris, Africa and hopefully, Laos. I say hopefully Laos, because Loretta and I will be in Vientiane, Laos for at least the next two years. I am director of the Lao-American Association here under contract with USIA. Could you think of any farther spot for us to rove, unless it were outer space?

To Loretta Frank expresses his belief that she

Loretta, after her arrival, busy with her Laotian students as predicted by Frank

"will have her hands full with a burgeoning program of music–which we hope to make a large part of the acculturation program."

Loretta serving punch to her students

Frank then says of Laos:

Laos is what most lectures call a UN country. It really has no excuse for existing as a separate entity. There is, as you know, a fragile eggshell-thin neutrality accord in effect here. As a pawn in the power struggle between East and West, it will signal a new dimension of diplomacy if this "accord" can be held. Never has there been more intimate and dramatic evidence of the need for a strengthened UN and a world governed by law than this section of the world demonstrates now.

> The United World Federalists, for whom we have worked the past two years, has the only viable answer to this kind of political situation. I am so glad that we took the plunge to come out here, because one can't possibly see the forces of incipient nationalism, and outmoded paternalism clashing more dramatically than here–and all the reading or TVing does not suffice to put the issues across. I cannot write openly of many of the involvements.
>
> Vientiane, the political capital of Laos, is the royal capital where the figurehead king sits. It is a replica of a "Gunsmoke" setting, with an oriental cast....
>
> Laos is a notion and not a nation, it is the "land of a million elephants." The Laotians are charming people in many ways. They have a happy-go-lucky way of taking whatever comes, shrugging off the serious atavistic demands of foreigners with an ease that is almost enviable. "We know you rushing Americans! We know the French and all they got out of their 'schemes' was ulcers, and you too!" Although there are signs of changing. More and more Lao are going to America for higher educational programs–and all such must go through the program I am mainly responsible for.

Frank then describes the building, where his 1400 students are jammed in, as "an ancient brothel." Then he tells of his plans to erect a new cultural center for his program, adding, "Those of you from Phillips Memorial and Bacone and Redlands will remember that the Leopard never changes, or one who is supposed to be a builder never escapes even in far off Laos."

†††

Loretta now with him, we have fewer of Frank's writings to share, but there is another long piece that was written to his "in-laws and out-laws" in May 1966. Titled "The *Immobile* Ts," the account gives no indication that they plan to cut short their anticipated two-year stay in Laos despite Frank's recent incapacitating siege of hepatitis.

Of the illness, John Sutter, mentioned earlier, told this writer how easy it was to get hepatitis in Laos—caused by eating food contaminated by food-handlers who don't wash their hands after toilet use. It's very debilitating, takes a long time, many months, for recovery. Sutter saw his wife suffer when she got hepatitis while working in one of the Red Cross centers set up for refugees in 1969, but they had weathered it without the need to return to the U.S.[5]

As for Frank, in this piece to folks back home, he had this to say of his hepatitis: "I have been immobilized for nearly three months with hepatitis. Part of the time in a Bangkok hospital with no fan or air-conditioner in one of the hottest cities in the world. Part of the time in the unusually cool spring of Vientiane." Frank gives the impression he is fully recovered and gives no indication that he is not up to the job or has any thoughts of leaving.

Early-on in March, Sara Sue had written that the Nieses [her in-laws] had called, "very concerned about Dad." She continues, "Yes, hepatitis is much worse with older people although Ken's brother missed over a month of work

---

[5] An article in the *Providence Journal*, 12/31/2002, concerns "blood tainted with hepatitis B was one of more than 2000 violations the Food and Drug Administration found during its latest inspection of Red Cross headquarters" (in the U.S.). The Red Cross had reports of 134 people, including one who died, who got hepatitis after blood transfusions....

and still had to take it easy." In a later letter she writes that Ken [her soon-to-be-doctor husband] "had planned to write you to lend some knowledge on hepatitis but had to leave in a rush."

Sara Sue wrote her dad regularly but mostly about dinners they give or go to and such. Regarding Ken's doctor studies while in the surgery phase, she wrote: "He hates surgery and calls all surgeons the Prima Donna's of the medical profession."

In June, 1966, Sue writes of Ken's graduation– "Believe me, he's often been discouraged by the profession and its future. Well, now he's a doctor and his learning is just beginning." She had written of their hope he'd get an internship in a San Francisco hospital, and of their disappointment when it didn't happen. Neither is very happy that they're going to Los Angeles. Ken writes: "We are currently in a mess after moving from our beautiful city by the bay to this land of smog, sun and bumper stickers." He continues: "I would like to thank you for the Laotian 'gong' which blends in quite well with our examples of African and American Indian art which currently adorn our living room. In fact, besides a couch and stereo system, these are the only objects which occupy the living room at present."

Meanwhile, Frank has sent a copy of his May 1966 back-home-report to Jack Cummings at the University of Redlands with a cover letter indicating: "The war clouds [are] growing darker all the time. We can't write much about it but this could be a very hot area ere long, especially if the red hordes decide to start moving south into the great rice bread basket of the Thailand, Cambodia deltas." The enclosure, he says, "gives a little picture of the life here. At least that which we can write about." And so, even though censored, what Frank has to say in his report gives us an insight as to why so much of our aid to other countries is so ineffective, at least in winning hearts:

> This country is incredibly primitive despite uncounted millions poured in by large nations, especially the U.S. The flood of funds has resulted in tragically little progress that can be observed. Probably the answer is the funds have been given for utilitarian purposes hoping that they alone would provide a bulwark against the on-sweep of communism. The tragedy is compounded by a lack of consistency in the use of the funds. The U.S., for instance, at one time lavished military funds on one general who was, at the time, waging intensive war against another general who was, at the same time, receiving economic aid from the U.S. The Lao people see these inconsistencies and shrug off any accusation of expediency in their own use of funds.
>
> A one word description of Laos would be "contrast." Baroque and lavish houses built by the French in their imperialistic hay-day along side crude native huts reeking in local squalor. Majestic gold embossed temples on lots surrounded by primitive twelfth century poverty.
>
> The sweet and gentle natured natives smiling as they meet you and yet giving one the sense that under the smile there is a smirk of deep misunderstanding. Understanding that they too must use every means of getting material advantages from those who wish to use them. The smiling natives on one side, the little soldiers trying to look ferocious, assuming the grimace they think a warrior should have, standing at military gates. I have seen Boy Scouts more formidable.

> Up in the hills a short drive from the city, the Pathet Lao, disciplined and dedicated, waiting to wrest the opulence from faranges [foreigners]. During a picnic at the very edge of a Pathet Lao domain, we talked with no holds barred, among Lao friends. Their most persistent question was, "How can we call out the same dedication by 'our people' that the Pathet Lao calls for theirs?" They are waiting for the opportunity to take over that which looks so luxurious to them from the distance. They go through great agony to exist against all odds and yet they persist for they think history is on their side. It's the age-old haunting question, the haves and the have nots. Was it General Eisenhower who said, "Hungry people always have to go to war, well-fed nations, never"?
>
> Some call these natives pagan but we find a deep sense of reverence that indicates an innate awareness of the higher meaning of life. Our yard boy, for instance, kneeling at the foot of my bed the first morning home from the hospital. I wasn't sure what was happening but the maid interpreted that he was praying to Buddha and trying to tell me that unless I exorcised the evil spirits within me, I would die.

Frank then refers to the regular, weekly power failures; the "little island of Americans separated and guarded at the gates from contact with the world around;" "an un-country struggling to gain national pride, but still torn by tribal loyalties." After some elaboration on these faults, Frank continues:

> Perhaps the contrasts in my own recent illness illustrate something of what we're facing. Gamma-globulin is considered 90% effective in treating

> hepatitis but the little technician who gave me my shot gave only half a dose so I contracted the dread disease and have spent nearly three months on the shelf. All of the magic and technique of modern medicine dependent on the know-how and wisdom of the one administering it.
>
> Great issues are at stake here as the war clouds thicken and the monsoon returns. Talks toward a solution in UN were "rumored" underway when religious controversy flared up. So now there will be another round of escalation with our area more critically drawn in. All in all, it's an adrenaline producing-time, one we wouldn't have missed for all the rice in the paddies. Whether our tour is concluded next month or next year, we will have been enriched, and hopefully trained, for more productive service in the next stage of the T saga.

This same report gives an overview of the doings of the Thompson children, including the fact we've already mentioned that Sue and Ken, in Frank's words, "will soon be leaving their favorite city by the Golden Gate to continue in Southern California. Ken will do his residency in Los Angeles hospitals." Frank continues:

> Sue is taking another group of students to France this summer for continued practice in her favorite foreign language. Scott is continuing to do research and work on his doctorate under the guidance of Oxford University in Legon.[6] He has had grandstand seats at two of the coups in Africa.

---

[6] Legon is the site of the University of Ghana, founded in 1948 as an affiliate of the University of London. It achieved university status in 1961.

His story about Ghana appears in the May *Atlantic Monthly*. It's an unsigned article in the section "Atlantic Report." Loretta will be finishing her first year of teaching and choral directing at the American School in time for us to take our R & R in Malaya [in Malaysia]. We plan to visit Singapore to have our dental work done, then to the Cameron Highlands hopefully high enough to escape the heat.

† † †

Frank obviously has started a correspondence with Jack Cummings, his successor (though with a different title) at Redlands, who is keeping him up to date regarding fundraising there. They certainly don't sound like he left his job at Redlands with any hard feelings. Frank, for his part, is keeping Jack up to date regarding his time in Laos. Again, he shows no indication that he is still or again ill, or that he has any plans to leave Laos. On June 28th Frank writes Jack:

> As you have no doubt noted from the skimpy bits of news which filter through, the pressure doesn't seem to let up over here. Loretta and I have just returned from an R & R trip to Singapore and Malaysia. We couldn't believe what a different world it is down there where the British have been in control for so long. The papers scarcely mentioned Vietnam and other than that item we didn't see the U.S. mentioned, but once or twice during a fortnight stay.
>
> People we talked with, both officials and semi-officials, shrugged their shoulders and said, "Well, the U.S. has made its bed, let it lie in it. You people from the States think you have all the answers so you have to go on killing off your boys and innocent natives rather than trust the people of little countries to work out

their own destiny more or less the way we British did. Now look at what our former possessions are doing and compare their records with those in which you are involved."

I suppose it's a bit of a jealous review and yet there's an element of truth in it. Certainly the recent solutions in Singapore, Indonesia and Malaysia indicate that the confidence Britain showed in her former subservients indicates that faith does reward the one who has that faith, quite often. British officials scoff at our domino theory and point to the independence and independent thinking of their own former colonies as evidence that these people are not about to adopt communism even though the hawks in Washington have made that theory almost indisputable.

†††

The Thompsons' children were probably the first to learn that the Thompsons planned to leave Laos. In a letter from Sue to her "folks" dated July 7th Sue begins: "Stunned is the only word which describes my reaction to the news of your leaving. I have mixed emotions–am elated that you're returning to the U.S., and particularly to California, but am not sure if I understand why you're leaving, other than your health, but I think I'm safe in saying that that's not the primary reason. So, I'll comment more when I've heard more from you."

Frank's letter to Jack Cummings dated August 3, 1966, just before he left, probably offers the best explanation we'll get for his leaving Laos after only a year. Though he discusses, in it, his past health problems, Frank sounds less like he's leaving for health reasons than that he is being "eased out" for "fighting the reins" of American propaganda regarding what is happening in Laos and neighboring countries. After all, he'd closed his prior letter to Jack by referring to it as "a report from the heretic." In this letter, Frank writes:

> Just when you get the latest plates made for our current address, the moveable Ts are on the move again. The medics of the area feel that my bout with hepatitis makes me vulnerable to Southeast Asian bugs. If I were ten years younger, they say, there would be no problem but at my advanced age [57], I had better look out for number one. This alone would not have discouraged us but the stepping up of the paramilitary operations and the de-emphasizing of cultural activities seems to be a handwriting on the wall. I am no hawk and I'm not about to give all my efforts to an illegal war activity in a supposedly neutral country.
>
> It's been a wonderful year for us despite the three months incarceration with the bug. As I said in my mimeo newsletter, we wouldn't have missed it for all the rice in the paddies, but we're going to be mighty pleased to be back in the home land. We have no definite appointment. There are two or three items in the fire, one that could be quite exciting. However, it will take some near miracles to bring about the marriage of two old institutions in order to provide an opportunity to be the nominal leader of a merged effort.

[Frank's experience after his return gives us only the slimmest of clues as to what he is referring to here! However, the next paragraph, the very person to whom the letter is addressed, and the later letter to him from Redlands President Armacost [to be

included later] does lead one to speculate that he might have been envisioning Bacone College as a "cluster college" associated with Redlands University, each still having a President, but with him as CEO, *in a manner of speaking. Two clues support this interpretation: while President of Bacone, Frank had regularly referred Bacone's better students to Redlands, and while VP of Development at Redlands the idea of adding a "cluster college" to that University had been talked of. Further, Frank was probably aware of the fact that funds to open a cluster college had been included in the grant proposal Redlands submitted to Ford in 1965.]*

Frank's letter continued:

> Am writing to Prexy [President Armitage at Redlands] to offer what part-time help we can give to the Ford Challenge in the Bay Area. I know you have big plans for a major effort up there. With all of the affluent grads and the very top level parents of students, I would think your goal would be three quarters of a million dollars from the Bay Area. *Perhaps you and other members of the development team will have a full time director in that area which would certainly seem justifiable with the objective as great as it is. [Writer's italics]*
>
> We're finishing up our work here with the usual round of farewell parties and "baci." The baci is a very sacred institution and original with Laos. Loretta and I feel quite honored to have several of the prominent Lao families throwing bacis for us, which seems to be a little unusual for one who is such a newcomer as we are.
>
> We expect to visit the Holy Land and Athens and then hopefully the airline strike will be over so that we can proceed from there to Rome and Paris

where we will meet Sue who is there with a group of her students studying French. The big disappointment of our trip is that Scott can't get away from Ghana at this time to escort us around Oxford and England. Since you have always been so kindly disposed with our heir apparent, you might be interested in looking in the September or October *Atlantic Monthly*....We don't know which one yet [will have his long article], but it's quite a tribute to his mother's influence that he is crashing the number one literary publication of America.

Whatever differences he had with his children, infuriating both Scott and Sara Sue on occasion, Frank clearly was very proud of them both. Calling Frank a "distant father," Scott partially blames this on the fact he belonged to "a generation that didn't know how to 'take in' or relate to their children." But he also quotes his mom as having "pointed out that [Frank] had never really been loved growing up and thus didn't know how to love back."

† † †

Since Frank suggested several times that he was limited in what he was allowed to say in his reports home, the writer thinks it appropriate to give some background as to just what was going on in Laos–not just while Frank was there. William Blum in the chapter "Laos 1957-1973" of his book, *Killing Hope*,[7] proved an excellent source for laying out the U.S.'s

---

[7] Unless otherwise noted, the following quotes and information are from **Blum, pp. 140-145**. The account heavily footnoted; refer to the book to ascertain the government documents, newspapers and other sources he used. You might also want to find on the internet, William M. Leary, **Supporting the "Secret War": CIA Air Operations in Laos, 1955-1974**, and an article from *Asian Survey*, Vol. VII, #1, "Laos: The Troubled

initial interest in this "impoverished and primitive land of peasants," and revealing the nature of U.S. involvement.

Blum tells us that the U.S. interest in Laos began in 1957 [almost ten years prior to Frank's sojourn] when John Foster Dulles was Secretary of State, when the fear of all things Communist and the "domino theory" dominated our foreign policy.

That year, Pathet Lao, then part of the Laotian government, called for diplomatic relations with the countries of the Soviet bloc and acceptance of aid from them. Following a variety of pseudo-legal maneuvers, by January 1959, they had been excluded from the government; a series of coups and counter-coups followed.

> There were, as well, government-rigged elections, with the CIA stuffing ballot boxes [American wheeling and dealing centered around giving power to CIA's handpicked], different regimes-cum warlords governing simultaneously from different 'capitals', their armies fighting each other, switching allies and enemies when it suited them; hundreds of millions of US dollars pouring into a tiny kingdom which was 99 percent agricultural, with an economy based more on barter than money, the result being 'unimaginable bribery, graft, currency manipulation and waste.'...
>
> No study of Laos of this period appears to have had notable success in untangling the muddle of who exactly replaced whom, and when, and how, and why. After returning from Laos, writer Norman Cousins

---

Neutral," by Arthur J. Dommen. (1964). It might also be time to read again Graham Greene's political novel, *The Quiet American*, written in 1955, that predicts the US's disastrous involvement in Vietnam.

stated in 1961 that 'if you want to get a sense of the universe unraveling, come to Laos. Complexity such as this has to be respected.'

To this mix, the CIA paid for a Royal Laotian Army; inserted its own American military into the country under various guises; built airfields throughout the country; forced whole villages to move; Americans killed in Laos were listed as Vietnam war dead; and on and on. Blum calls Laos "an American plantation," a "CIA playground." To counter US involvement, the Soviet Union began to send military supplies to the Pathet Lao, and, beginning in the early 1960s, the North Vietnamese also sent aid.

> Hanoi [and the Soviet Union] was concerned not only by the American political and military operations in Laos, but by the actions of US Special Forces teams which were entering North Vietnam to engage in espionage, sabotage, and assassination, and by the bombings of the country being carried out by the US Air Force at a time when the war in South Vietnam was still but a shadow of what was to come. Later, as the wars in Vietnam and Laos became intertwined, Laos formed part of the Ho Chi Minh Trail, the principal route to protect it as well as attacking American radar installations in Laos used to aid US bombing on North Vietnam....
>
> Eventually, in 1962, a multi-nation conference in Geneva signed an agreement for a coalition government in Laos. But in the mountains and the plains of the country, this was no longer a viable option. The CIA had too much time, effort, material and emotion invested in its Secret Army...And the Pathet Lao were much stronger now

> than a few years earlier...Both sides regularly accused each other of violating the agreement, and not without justification....Thus it was that the fighting dragged on, though only sporadically.

After the Pathet Lao were once again excluded from the government in 1964 elections, they took the offensive and "scored significant advances. Then the American bombing began."

Between 1965 [the year Frank went to Laos] and 1973, more than two million tons of bombs rained down upon the people of Laos, considerably more than the US had dropped on both Germany and Japan during the Second World War....There was no happy way out for the Laotian people....By 1975, Laos had become a land of nomads, without villages, without farms;...[and] the worst of Washington's fears had come to pass: All of Indochina had fallen to the Communists.

After his year in Laos, Frank would surely have concurred with Blum's rationale for heading his chapter on Laos by juxtaposing the following two quotes. Unfortunately, they reflect a way of thinking as relevant today as then [and explain why so much of the world hates us]—and a way of thinking that Frank clearly was unable to affect as he'd hoped he might.

The first from the *Far Eastern Economic Review*, Hong Kong, 1970:

> For the past two years the US has carried out one of the most sustained bombing campaigns in history against essentially civilian targets in northeastern Laos...American jets have destroyed the great majority of villages and towns in the northeast...Refugees from the

Plain of Jars report they were bombed almost daily by American jets last year. They say they spent most of the past two years living in caves or holes.

The second by Alexis Johnson, US Under Secretary of State, 1971:

> [The Laos operation] is something of which we can be proud as Americans. It has involved virtually no American casualties. What we are getting for our money there...is, I think, to use the old phrase, very cost effective.

17. "Suffering"

Brimstone and ashes inevitably cling to one's clothing after a sojourn in hell. Brush as I may I can't seem to dislodge the effects of this past year in Southeast Asia. Though we were stationed in the so-called neutral Kingdom of Laos we saw the whole ghastly rehearsal of forces girding for Armageddon.... Out there on the hinterlands of Armageddon, Napalm and Phosphorus bombs and even clean civilized weapons rip and sear, and gangrene pervades the very air you breath–until one either turns to drink, to opium or suddenly begins to relate in a small way to the agony of the Cross.

Of course, it wasn't the physical pain that made Jesus cry out...His was the anguish of LOST CAUSES– "O, Jerusalem, Jerusalem, if only you had known the things that belong to PEACE. I came to bring LIFE and you chose death." ...The brimstone and ashes wont leave as memory recalls our great nation making a parking lot of a small country which was "backward" enough to engage in civil war–and know that it is being USED as a utilitarian tool of expedient self-interest.[1]

†††

Frank had left Laos earlier than planned but nonetheless full of enthusiasm for what he called "an incredible experience." And he left convinced that now he had the experience and training that would enable him to serve mankind in a greater way than ever before. That he would soon find this anything but the truth must have been crucifying to the soul. As the months went by, unable to find a place where he was wanted, where he could fulfill his

---

[1] From a Good Friday sermon in 1967

desire to serve, he increasingly felt lost, at loose ends, a failure.

Since they'd sold their home before leaving for Laos, Beulah Parker, Frank's wealthy friend whose financial support had enabled him to attend college, provided Frank and Loretta with a small apartment in her building. He commented on this in a letter to "Bud" [Scott] written September 12, 1966, barely a month after his return from Laos: "Mother is being paid for choirs, and I am getting assorted expense money for speaking around and Beulah has refused rent since I am painting 80 to 100 hours per month for her."

Frank & Loretta back in Oakland, California (undated)

In this letter Frank sounded hopeful about two churches that were "in process," but meanwhile, while awaiting word from the churches, he writes: "Some medical men want me to take on a program of crash relief for Vietnamese children, napalm victims, but with no organization and no tax deductibility it would be another grind. Strange how I get sucked into causes every time I aim for a more settled existence." [Maybe because that's where his heart lies!] As for his "speaking around," he says his speeches have been "real shock treatment for apathetic Americans."

Later in this letter Frank sounds less positive as he waits to hear about a Church calling him. He writes:

> The only sanity restoring rationale I can make for this blank period in our existence is that the good Lord intends that I shall know all of experience, for unemployment was the one major shock of society that I hadn't known, though having tried so often to help others who were going through it. I now can empathize first-hand with same. Of course, there is a more sanguine way to view this period--we actually made as much money in 1966 as we had any other year, and that with only four months of work, counting my three months of hepatitis, and doctors have assured me that a year of "inactivity" is expected after such a bout as I had. The one snag that hurts our planned timing is the loss of the Morris [an English car] but who could have counted on "an act of God" to wash it away. Perhaps if we had been in Vientiane we would have lost even more, or some other Pollyanna.

In a letter soon after this, Frank said he was "not very hopeful" about getting a call from any church in the San Francisco bay area:

> They have many prominent men under consideration, and so many eastern big-wigs wanting to get out here. The establishment of the church is such that Mother and I are beginning to wonder if we belong in the church after all. The exec of United

> Church of Christ, Norberg, said he just couldn't understand why they have not grabbed us up, but it's probably age and too liberal in views, as your criticisms have implied.

Clearly the hoped-for miracle Frank had written Jack Cummings about while in Laos hadn't happened [*surmised to have been a hoped-for reconstituting of Bacone College as a "cluster college" of Redlands University; himself as* CEO]. However, at least at first, his involvement with the Committee of Responsibility (COR), a project he called "a hot one," seemed to fill his ever-burning need to "make a difference." COR was an effort by doctors to form a nation-wide organization to bring burned Vietnamese children to the States for treatment unavailable to them in Vietnam.

In his letter to Scott about this time Frank wrote, "If we can pull this off and bring 100 or so of these dramatically burned Vietnamese children here, it will make people realize, as nothing else will, the genocidal nature of this mess. I shot for the top echelon of San Francisco to head the thing but was not able to pull that off."

But only a month later, Frank called COR "a nebulous thing," despite its having held an international conference attended by 2000 doctors. He wrote Scott:

> I thought it would be great from the humanitarian angle but none of the liberal leaders in the bay area will touch it openly. They all think it would be good if the State Department approved, and it were determined that the children could be best served over here. After the negative response I have gotten on so many approaches, I have determined it is just not for me. I don't have the stature to command followers, nor the long time

> involvement in liberal causes to make the effort and the risk worthwhile [*of doing this full-time, I believe he means*]. So I will now tell the local men that my original offer of a month's help will have to stand–it has actually been two months– and very small pay, but it's been an effort anyway.

Later in this letter Frank indicates that nothing had come through from the churches as he'd hoped. He writes:

> Since I think my presentation before the two different ones was as strong as I can make, we have determined that it's age and liberality against us and have started the wheels in New England. It seems a bit cruel to run out on Beulah at this time of her trials with Jane (her older sister) but she has said she must not hold us back, and with the diminishing returns on the estate apparent, and her own longevity fairly well assured, we just must move to get a position where I can have a pension and hospitalization coverage. Regarding the estate, her equity in Boden Way is not as large as I had thought, and she has been drawing on the income from the other property to pay for Jane's nurse, etc. So you see why we have never felt that the feet of the rainbow had too big a pot and is now turning out to be an almost negligible consideration. (They had been counting on an inheritance from her for their retirement.)

Frank had been making guest appearances at churches in the San Francisco/Oakland area, hoping to be called to a permanent position, but without success. A letter from Walt Mueller, written July 31, 1966 while he was still in Laos, indicates that Frank had tried to line up a church position even before he left Laos, but Mueller had written:

"There is not too much that can be done until you are here on the ground where you can be interviewed by some pastoral committee in person. The letter had continued:

> This democratic procedure in our Congregational churches sometimes seems slow and cumbersome, but we all have to put up with it....No one knows just what situations may be available by the time you return. Dr. Dick Norberg [whom, the letter indicated, Frank also had written about his desire to get located in a good church on his return], assures me that he felt there would be no difficulty in your finding a church when you get there. Sometimes these things take a little time, and my recommendation would be to wait until something you really like opens up. I shall do everything I can to help...

Mueller's letter also indicated how sorry he was to hear about Frank's hepatitis but pleased to learn he had recovered. Mueller also writes:

> It has been good to get your letters, although somewhat disturbing as one hears and thinks about a few more of the world's "unsolved problems." And Laos certainly has its share, along with the rest of Southeast Asia. ...I write to welcome you back to the land of affluence, power and good plumbing. Perhaps your most useful place is here to help man the barracks, while some of the younger men man the trenches on the firing line.

As the months passed and no church "called" him, Frank must increasingly have felt a failure, and increasingly have sought solace in drink. What previously had been only "social drinking" became more than that. As Scott described it: "He was having to use mints and gum all the time to hide the booze on his breath." In an e-mail to this writer, Scott went on to say:

> The first time I saw him drink was around 1954 [Scott would have been 12] at a rich person's house in Muskogee, crème de mènthe. I knew he had a small bottle in his bureau at all times, but quantities were small until after Laos.
>
> Booze represented the big bad devil, the Jungian bad side to him. [On one occasion he told me] how when working with lumberjacks as a young man, they'd swish down whiskey after work. That represented "MEN" and he loved the image. Later, booze represented escape from the superego problems of being a role model as a pastor. It wasn't just a genetic defect (though that too) but a psychological problem coming from his circumstances.

Apparently, as Frank began to drink more heavily, he forgot, or chose to ignore, his own past references in sermons to drink as "immoral," an "escapism that offered a false 'train' to the good life, a train that needed to be rerouted toward Christ."

† † †

After almost eight frustrating months back in the U.S., finally, in March 1967 Frank received a call to the position of Associate Minister at the First Congregational Church in San Francisco. One might surmise that the gratitude and relief he felt to again be in the pulpit was tempered somewhat by a feeling of humiliation that he would be only an "Associate." However, Loretta, in a letter to

Scott states, "We like the feeling of not having total responsibility of church." She indicates that there will be double services on Sundays and that Frank will preach at both every other Sunday. In the same letter, Loretta states that their savings "haven't been touched, luckily, since we both brought in bits and our rent has been low." She describes the Church as a "beautiful Greek structure with Ionic columns!"

After the "calling" but before he assumed his duties at the church, Frank writes Scott how he's trying to wind up his role with the COR project and will be "walking out in three days." He states that the minister (Rev. Brown) has been wonderful but "swamping both mother and me, throwing so many things my way." But, Frank adds, "So far we seem to have carte blanch to go-go." He refers to the Good Friday service when he'd first preached there: attended by 2300 people [*could he have meant 230?*], including Sue and Ken who had brought a Jewish friend with them. Sue said that afterwards her friend said "I converted her and she wants to read up on the Protestant Church now."

In a long article by James Clark Brown, the minister, in "The Columns," the church newsletter of March 27, 1967, he urges the congregation to welcome "Dr. and Mrs. Francis W. Thompson on the occasion of Dr. Thompson assuming his full-time relationship to us as Associate Minister. Be on hand to express your personal word of welcome to both of them."

The annual report indicates that they had an "all church fun party to welcome them" and the Browns too "on their first year with us." The Church newsletter included a lengthy review of Frank's past accomplishments, ending by quoting a letter the minister had received that week from Ed

Edmondson, the member of Congress from Oklahoma in whose district Bacone College is located. It reads:

> Dear Jim: I was delighted to learn that Dr. Francis Thompson is to be Associate Pastor in your church, beginning in April. Dr. Thompson won the hearts of all Oklahomans during the period that he served as President of Bacone College, which is one of Oklahoma's leading institutions of higher learning for Indians. He is a man of great ability and tremendous effectiveness, and I know his ministry will enrich your church. Please give our very best to him and to your family.

† † †

Frank had always incorporated his own experiences into his sermons, part of what made them meaningful to his listeners, and now was no exception. One early one, called "The Altar Test," is based on Micah 6: 6-8 and Matthew 5: 21-24, the latter two verses, perhaps of the greatest significance:

> 23. If thou bring thy gift to the altar, and there rememberest that thy brother hath ought against thee;
> 24. Leave there thy gift, and go thy way; first be reconciled to thy brother, and then come and offer thy gift.

He opened the sermon with the question: "Have you ever wondered what would happen if we actually carried out the teaching of Jesus? Let some of his strong sayings come alive!" Frank's talking about making peace with our brothers and coming back to the altar "purified by the purging power of reconciling love in action." As he has often in the past, he's talking about a growing circle of concern that encompasses brothers everywhere; he emphasizes how deeply his experience in Southeast Asia has affected him, how the conflict there is decimating the children.

> After our tour of duty abroad we returned with hopes that we could awaken our churches and our nation to the true issues. When one has been through hell one inevitably collects brimstone and ashes on one's clothes and soul. In an effort to expiate our souls of the guilt we felt, and hopefully to clear away some of the brimstone and ashes, we threw ourselves into a program to rescue burned and war-injured Vietnamese children—a program set up by prominent physicians and humanitarians to bring children who were inoperable and untreatable in Vietnam's overcrowded and inadequate hospitals to our great hospitals where skilled physicians were volunteering....

Frank went on to say:

> It matters not how one feels about the war in Vietnam, these little brothers of ours are being burned by napalm, and phosphorous, which we are dropping, and dropping mainly in south Vietnam on friend and foe alike. In treating them, hopefully, we prepare ourselves for soul clearing services at the Altar of the God of all!

Frank may have given up any paid, or full-time, position with COR, but had not lost his interest in it. About the only memory Janet Farmer, one of the church's members, has of his time there is the June evening the young married group (her family was fairly new at the church; they had two small children) met at her house. She told this writer how passionate Frank had been when he talked about Vietnam's innocent children, made victims by our own bombs, and this program, the Committee of Responsibility (COR), designed to help them. At his urging, an office was opened at their church, as at others "all across the land," that helped cut through much of the red tape involved in bringing these needy children here. A report from the Fortnighters (a group for those who were single and over the age of 50) noted that Rev. Thompson also met with them.[2]

† † †

In another sermon, "The Call for a New Reformation," Frank has come to terms with his earlier dislike of Catholicism. He has this to say:

> It is now a day to think together with our Roman Catholic brothers about our common tasks, our likenesses, and our complementary assists in the cause of a Christian imperative for a godless world....We are interested in a united front against common opponents, unity of concern without uniformity of structure.
>
> Surely the patience of Almighty God must have been strained beyond any human understanding during these centuries of blood-letting divisions "in the body of His son our Lord Christ." It is not by accident that some of the leading secular thinkers of the ages have called Christian disunity the Scandal of History....The Irish wit says it so well: "Would that we all were heathen so we could live together like Christians."

---

[2] The writer could locate no information about the history, impact or endurance of this organization.

Frank then returns to his experience in Southeast Asia:

> This whole scandalous division was one of the most embarrassing questions we had to answer. The Buddhist leaders would ask in their quiet subservient but gracious manner: "Why do you Christians expect us to leave our Buddha, who teaches that all men are brothers, to join your churches which fight and argue with each other all the time?"
>
> I could dialogue with these Buddhists because I was not known as a churchman, but as a minor official of the U.S. government. ...Interestingly enough, that discussion nearly always led to a second embarrassing question, which is dramatically linked to the first. The second question: "Why does your government talk to us about bringing us democracy and coming to help us and then run our country by military machine–control our economy for your benefit and then tell us that we must fight against your enemies, when all we want is peace and a chance to solve our problems in our own way? You Americans have a word HYPOCRISY. Isn't that what you do to us?"

Having brought up issues that were asked again even today as the U.S. embarked on a war against Iraq [April 2003], Frank, still very much the pacifist, goes on to ask his congregation– "Well, do you get the frightening implications of these two questions?" As a believer in the power of the Christian church, if only it would unite and make its presence felt, Frank continues:

> A divided and ineffective church, that ought to be making every effort to save the world, is

completely helpless to guide and guard the destiny of this our beloved country which seems to so many of us to be following the pattern of history where power became god and expediency the only measure of diplomacy....Look what the combined church forces were able to accomplish in Civil Rights once they became involved and once they found common ground to launch creative action. This reformation Sunday prompts us to ask if it isn't time for a second reformation!

Frank quotes "the brilliant Roman Catholic, Prof. Mickael Novak," who in his call for a second reformation touches on issues that have always been in the forefront of Frank's concerns. He quotes Novak as saying:

> What is at stake in the new reformation is not only the purity of the Christian church. At stake also is the fate of the black peoples, the yellow, the brown and the white peoples of the earth. Unless we open our eyes to the misery and horror of life on this planet–to starvation, desperate illness and poverty, napalm and military technology, stupidity and blindness–this strongest nation of all history will share the fate of all great nations of the past–and lead itself and the world into destruction....

Frank then concludes:

> We all stand under the judgement of God for what we have done–all of us, our leaders and ourselves. When we look upon the destruction we are reeking upon human beings, and the suffering we are allowing, despite our wealth, and when we recognize the thick layers of self-satisfaction in our

> rhetoric and secret love of ourselves, we know with Martin Luther that we have need of an immense and overwhelming mercy. Only a massive effort to have ourselves purged by the awful righteousness of God, and in true humility come together seeking the purifying love of a divine redemption will there be hope for Christianity and for the world that is so in need of creative therapy.
>
> He closes with a brief prayer:
>
> PURIFY THY CHURCH, O GOD, STARTING WITH ME–SO THAT WITH THEE I MAY START OVER AGAIN HELPING THEE TO BRING PEACE ON EARTH, GOOD WILL AMONG ALL MEN & NATIONS!

Clearly Frank continued to harp on Vietnam and the U.S. as a bully-nation, for he concludes a sermon in July by stating: "You undoubtedly are sick at heart and almighty tired of hearing about Vietnam." He continues:

> Some of you have written on "I wish" cards that you wish the minister would not always speak about Vietnam. And yet is there any more overriding fact in today's world? And is there any more stark and startling reality than the fact that this great and beloved nation of ours is in danger of losing its soul because it is using a little nation to prepare a staging ground for larger conflict? More than one half of the civilians of that little country are burned and damaged by napalm, and more than half of the remaining civilians are children under 16 years of age, because that nation has been used not only by us, but by others for three decades as staging ground

> for the false philosophy of means to an end. If this travesty had not such widespread opposition, it would not be a matter to be constantly discussed especially from the pulpit. But when one has been around the world and has talked with leaders in most of the major nations and is convinced that we have not one single friend or willing partner in this sad military venture, then one would be false not to speak out at every occasion and at every opportunity.

That fall, Frank was the headline speaker at the Valley Plaza Town Hall[3] on United Nations Day; the program arranged to celebrate the organization's founding on October 24, 1945. This certainly would have been one of those opportunities Frank looked forward to that enabled him to talk about Vietnam and the need to strengthen the UN in order for it to counter the forces of war and become a more effective, much needed, vehicle for solving the world's problems peacefully.

The story Frank told in one sermon emphasizes his belief that we might be seeing a dying world if we do not change. He said:

> In Pittsburgh, before that city had cleansed the soot from its airways, a lady was seen grabbing every child that came by, wiping his face with a moist towel. Someone said, "How good of you lady. But why are you cleaning all these children's faces?" Her reply, "I am looking for Willie."
>
> In clearing the smog from the air, the muck from our feet, the smut from our souls, we just might

---

[3] Neither the city where this was located nor the paper that reported it could not be located by this writer.

> find Willie, and God, and ourselves. "For God is not dead; God is not dying; God is love; God is hiding."
>
> [And then his challenge to his congregants] Will you join in an heroic search for the hidden God, so needed in this dying world?

Asking his congregation, in another sermon, to "wrestle with me over the very personal problem of Evil and Suffering in our otherwise glorious world," Frank makes the connection with the contemporary popularity of the "Death of God" theologians. In his powerful voice, he exclaims:

> These shocking young thinkers have tired of people's immature reliance on a grey-bearded pie-in-the-sky God, rescuing them from the just consequences of personal or social "SOWING TO THE WIND AND EXPECTING TO REAP OTHER THAN THE WHIRLWIND." These theologians have resorted, like the medical profession often does, to shock treatment to jar patients loose from debilitating patterns of apathetic acting and reacting. Look around us: In this best of all worlds so filled with the worst of all actions, is there anything less than shock that will awaken us?

Frank goes on to suggest that rather than trying to rationalize trouble or to explain good and evil, we "admit that God and all the metaphysical ideas related are in the realms of mystery." But then he asks if we are not better off to act as though there were a God– "to stake everything on the divine postulate"–than to "eat, drink and be merry for tomorrow we die." He continues:

> Given this divine assumption–we can then move into erecting the ladder of hope St. Paul

constructs [in Romans 5: 1-5]—We all know trouble, but out of trouble comes patience, out of patience endurance, and out of endurance character, and from character springs hope. HOPE THAT NEVER FAILS...

This formula calls for us to admit trouble (so much of our effort is the attempt to ESCAPE).

[*If his own drinking had by now become excessive, as has been reported by his son, this advice takes on a certain irony. One might feel he was trying to convince himself.*]

[Escapes through] drugs, excessive drinking, pell-mell rushing, retreat to suburbia—today's social amnesia—pseudo philosophies and theologies that deny the existence of evil—neo-Buddhistic attempts at negation of reality....IN THE MIDST OF THE STARK, STARING TRAGEDIES OF EXISTENCE, DO SOMETHING BETTER. TRANSFORM IT. LET IT BE THE BEDROCK AGAINST WHICH WE ERECT OUR LADDER TO LIFE ABUNDANT!

You see, the act of recognizing we have troubles; that we can't "go it alone" clears the deck of pride and arrogance, puts us in the aura of humility and LO THE VERY COSMIC FORCES START TO PULL UPWARD.

† † †

On the last Sunday in December 1967, just nine months after his welcome as Associate Minister at the First Congregational Church, San Francisco, Frank resigned[4] to

[4] Records from the San Francisco church give not even a hint as to why he left there. Could it have been that he felt so completely confident he

accept an interim pastorate at Redwood City First Congregational Church. It's not surprising that even as he served as an Associate at the San Francisco church, Frank continued to search for a church that wanted him as *the* minister. And in serving at the Redwood City church in an interim capacity, he almost certainly hoped this would lead to his being called as their permanent minister. His son, Scott, suggests that he was quite optimistic that this would happen.

> He aimed ever so intently on the Redwood City Congregational Church, and thought it his destiny because of "Redlands," "Redman," Redwood," but it didn't work. He had built so many hopes on that one and was crushed by the fact that it didn't work. Again, he saw destiny in the names and didn't sufficiently concentrate on the politics, I suspect. [Not understanding politics, which Scott feels himself adept at, is a failure of Frank's that Scott has alluded to many times.]

Referring to his "brief ministry among you," Frank apparently preached his last sermon at the Redwood City Church only three days after the assassination of Martin Luther King on April 4, 1968. He reminds the congregation of King's triumphant cry, "I have been to the mountain top, and I have seen the promised land." And of his widow's statement that his death had come as no surprise: "We knew it was inevitable"–the price he'd pay for what he knew was right– "I have a dream, We shall Overcome."

Frank correctly predicts–"These phrases will outlive

---

would be called by the Redwood City Church as their permanent minster that he'd resigned? If so, not getting the call must have been doubly hard to take.

the days of our years," but not so correctly, that they "will stir to greatness a nation too long in arrears to its black brothers." He continued:

> These words may yet prompt us to understand our master when he said on that last night, "In the world we shall have tribulations, but be of good cheer, I have overcome the world!" He hadn't done away with its sorrow and its heartache, but he had done something better: He had transformed his losses into ladders for others to climb to their own Mountain Tops....
>
> King was naïve enough to think he could serve his country best by calling on the church of Jesus Christ to lead his country back to its lost dreams–and when he felt the church falter, he turned to a wider following....
>
> To millions, the assassin's bullet Thursday night was but a repetition of those crude nails and bitter spears [Christ encountered]....
>
> MLK modeled his whole life on Christ, and he knew he must share his Master's fate. Each knew what awaited him at his Jerusalem, whether it was Beal Street where the blues were born and turned sour, or the ancient city that killed the prophets and knew not the time of its salvation....
>
> Christ knew the palm branches on the road [that cheered him earlier] would soon crumble to dust to be used to throw in his face. It was a cross, not a crown, he saw above the escarpment of the city. But it was worth even that to prove to them and to us that evil need not win, that death was not the end, and never would be. And what a tragedy it is, that this shot in the dark should strike down the one

that best exemplified the Christ for uncountable hosts.

Frank concludes his sermon by declaring that Christ's message would be for each of us not to despair, but to ascend our own mountain top to gain our own vision—and make royal preparations for our own death. He ends with a quote by Bishop Meyers made that Friday: "We must never talk of the Negro problem again—it's the white man's problem, and above all it's the Christian's call for a new crusade." Regrettably, Frank's hope that "such a crusade is taking shape even as the bells of mourning toll" was not to be.

† † †

When the Redwood church did not work out, Frank must have been depressed as he found himself once more at loose ends; not chosen; all the hopes he'd nourished when he left Laos of making a real contribution seemed crushed. And, as if this was not enough, his physical body began to betray him as well. In late July, his appendix ruptured, resulting in peritonitis that "damn near killed him," according to Scott. Scott was then back in this country from England, a newly appointed Assistant Professor at Tufts University's Fletcher School of Law and Diplomacy. Still poorly paid and fearing his father was dying, he asked a friend for financial help in case he needed it in making the trip to California. For the next several dreadful months, while Frank underwent five operations trying to get the skin to set, his recovery remained touch and go.

† † †

It's not clear just when Frank resumed preaching, or if he was fully recovered when he did. We do know that he preached the sermon at the First Congregational Church in

Alameda on November 3, 1968, and that the church bulletin that day refers to him as their "new minister." Of this appointment Scott writes:

> He was overqualified for the First Congregational in Alameda, but the options had narrowed dramatically. It was a smallish church but a pleasant one with some very nice middle-class folks, and Mom and Dad made some nice friendships. The place was filled with people affiliated with the military base in Alameda, bank vice-presidents, retired folks, all nice white folks.

More recently, the Church Office Coordinator (noting that Alameda was on an island off the California coast near the San Francisco/Oakland area), described the city to this writer as replete with lovely old homes, and as "a playground for San Franciscans," but, he also said, the church had a legacy of providing social services for the homeless, addicts and other poor who lived in an impoverished Oakland. However else Frank may have felt about being called to this Church, its commitment to serving those in need would have appealed to him.

18. Frank's Last "Call"

The proper functioning of the physical heart is essential to human life. Yet we know that unless the physical heart functions in surroundings of loving care, a person remains largely a biological animal. The heart of that loving care finds its focus in him who "emptied himself, taking the form of a servant." What seeks to work in us is the Spirit that forms our lives into the shape of a servant who brings light to the world and enhances the quality of human life. How much do we let the heart of that Spirit throb and grow within us?[1]

† † †

We cannot know whether or not Frank felt "overqualified," as his son suggested, when he accepted the call to the Alameda First Congregational Church; whether,

---

[1] This was chosen by Frank for the back cover of the bulletin for the January 11, 1970 church service.

possibly, he felt demeaned by the offer. It would seem to this writer more likely that by the fall of 1968, having faced near-death from the complications that followed a ruptured appendix, he'd not only have given up his earlier hopes, on leaving Laos, of finding some grandiose opportunity to serve, but would simply have been grateful to again be full-time in a pulpit. All we know is that whatever his initial feelings may have been, and whatever he felt as the years passed, Frank remained at the Alameda church for the next 6½ years; until he retired in 1975.

† † †

Frank's first annual report—for the year 1968—indicates that the church's recent years had been trying and, in his words, only the congregation's "passionate intensity," its "intense devotion to the just causes of church and society," had accomplished the "veritable miracle" that kept it going. He gives no clue as to what its problems were. In closing this report, Frank asks:

> Will you spend a little uninterrupted time researching or brainstorming ways you feel Loretta and I could be more effective servants of our church's need? We have not one scintilla of personal ambition, but we are passionately dedicated to finding the abundant life for you and yours.
>
> There is absolutely no limit to the progress here with a dedicated group of laymen working together for the greatest cause on earth. With the immortal Livingston, we repeat, "We will go anywhere so long as it is forward."

These words certainly don't sound like a man who has "given up" and turned to drink as solace. But Frank may well have begun to look for a way to escape from the burdens of ill health and disappointments that seemed to be piling up. Although the letter he received from Redlands University's President, George Armacost, dated January 20, 1969, was exceedingly friendly, it may nonetheless have elicited painful reminders of what was and what might have been. Armacost wrote:

> I am sorry to hear of the ruptured appendix and complications which followed thereafter. Such affairs are not only painful and unpleasant, but also expensive even though one has hospital insurance. I sincerely hope the complications have all been cleared up and you are now first rate again.
>
> We were pleased to see that Scott has married such a fine young person. I know he will do unusually well and has a great future ahead for him.....
>
> I am glad to hear you are the pastor of the First Congregational Church of Alameda and certainly wish you great success in your leadership. Our very best wishes to you and Loretta for 1969.

The wording of this next statement by Armacost lends credence to our earlier speculation that Frank knew of Redlands' plans for adding "cluster colleges" to Redlands and his hope on leaving Laos that Bacone would be one such with him as CEO over all. If we were correct, Armacost's information about Johnston College, six years after he left Redlands and almost three years after leaving Laos, must have been especially difficult for him to contemplate.

> Johnston College is finally taking shape with Pressley C. McCoy as Chancellor and three or four members of the staff are now busily working on

> curriculum for opening in September. As you will recall, the international and intercultural aspects of education will be the principal points of emphasis in the curriculum at Johnston College.[2]

†††

On December 12, 1968, Scott married Nina Nitze of a wealthy, politically prominent family.[3] Frank attended, but was excluded from any official role. Scott explained that he wanted Frank for once to be "JUST father." He goes on to say, "Of course Dad wanted to be high priest." He continued:

> The Nitzes had arranged for Bishop Angus Dun, the retired dean of the Cathedral and ex-bishop of DC, to preside; an awesome figure who'd presided alone in the East Room funeral of FDR.

---

[2] Johnston College had a ten-year contentious history as an independent cluster college that made use of Redlands' Administration services and library. However, it never solved the problem of who had final say on curriculum and financial matters and over who should decide how much freedom its students should have (Redlands objecting to the freedom granted students at Johnston). Eventually Johnston was dissolved as an independent college and in 1979 reborn as the Johnston Center for Integrated Studies. In addition to the piece by Ouellette (see Resources), this writer had various e-mail exchanges and phone conversations about the history of Johnston College with Redlands' archivist Jim Hoffer, and Bill McDonald who was a member of Johnston College's original faculty and is still at Redlands as a professor of English.

[3] After becoming wealthy as an investment banker, in 1940 Nina's father began his government service to a number of presidents–as director of the U.S. Dept. of State policy planning staff, Secretary of the Navy, deputy Secretary of Defense, member of the US delegation to the Strategic Arms Limitation Talks –and on and on. In 1989 the Johns Hopkins University's School of Advanced International Studies that he helped found was named in his honor.

> [Their wedding was to take place in the Cathedral of St. Peter and St. Paul in DC; better known as the National Cathedral.] Well, Frank, during the little pre-ceremony chat Dun was having with Nina and me, managed to barge in saying he was just looking for a place to put his coat. He hoped for a last chance to have a role in the ceremony, which I had long since ruled out. Maybe wrong on my part, but necessary psychologically.

Scott, clearly finding his father's behavior an embarrassment, goes on to say that Frank, while surrounded by a lot of powerful folks, had made "a terrible faux pas" at the wedding dinner the night before—held at the F Street Club, located in "an old mansion that Nina's grandmother had coincidentally rented while she was a member of Congress from the East Side."

> The event was rather grand—Dean Acheson and people like that were there--and there was just no way for me to satisfy Dad's constant need for assurance. I had never known how thin-skinned he was and short on self-assurance once he got out of cocoons like Phillips Memorial where he'd built an admiring world.

And so Scott explains what he'd thought to be "the terrible faux pas":

> Unnecessarily offering "proof" that he really was my father (and thus entitled to status at the grand party), Dad gave a toast saying he'd had measles after I was born, leaving him impotent, and so presumptively those before were indeed his--perhaps meant to be funny, it wasn't. It was quickly glossed over, but didn't help me. It was another sign of

Dad's feeling sorry for himself.

In a later discussion of this incident, Scott had this to say:

> Looking back, I'm sympathetic. The circumstances were more or less overwhelming to Dad; he was out of his depth. I'd had a year of 'getting used to it' [*presumably meaning the ways of the rich and powerful*], but he hadn't.

† † †

Was it accidental that Frank began his sermon of January 4, 1970, titled, "A Rumor of Angels in 1970," with an anecdote relating to marriage?

> You have heard of the maiden lady of uncertain age to whom her pastor asked, "What's this rumor I hear about you getting married?" She replied, "There's nothing to it, but thank God for the rumor."

This opening was a lead-in to a discussion of the supernatural forces that were being expressed in recent theology. "Thank God," Frank says, "for the rumor if not the reality. For it just might indicate that man is recognizing he can't go it alone. He may at long last be looking for assistance from above." Adding to this common theme of Frank's, in another sermon he said:

> As well command the east wind cease, the tide from rising, as to attempt to stop sin by our own efforts. We can cry, preach, rant, scream or tear our hair ever more, but we can't conquer it in our own power—only God can, with the help of others.

Returning to this sermon: after describing a few

unexplainable instances that he's observed, Frank asserts, "an iconoclast would have difficulty convincing me there isn't a higher world, a mystical order beyond our ordinary phenomena."

It's interesting that late in the sermon, Frank once more alludes to the wrongness of drugs and alcohol. *Is he challenging himself?*

> I can't love God if I don't love my own self enough to treat my body and soul as though they belonged to God–and therefore are not to be destroyed by hate, or fear, or lust, or drugs, or tobacco, or alcohol.

Frank makes clear that he is not suggesting that the existence of "angels" implies remoteness, but rather that their existence requires careful attention to each human need and gesture that we encounter–because, just as the Bible says, it is in the midst of mankind's affairs that "some have entertained angels unawares." As so often in the past, Frank urges us to start where we are in paying attention to what is around us; gradually "moving out to where we ought to be; always aware of the rustle of angel wings, remembering that "the gods bring threads to a web begun." Perhaps, he suggests, this church will start this New Year by "Letting God's love, His angels of love, turn us on."

In a later sermon, Frank tells of an experience that so shocked him that he felt he was back in Southeast Asia "where fatalism is the way of life, where the wheel of fortune and fate determined every day's acts and attitudes." *[Though not posed as such in this sermon, maybe this example, and perhaps others discussed in this sermon, should serve as a warning to us to be careful what we attribute to angels!]*

417. Frank's Last "Call"

> I [Frank] visited a home where an outstanding young athlete was seriously ill. "Tom's case is terminal," the Doctors say, unless he is operated on at once. "Which hospital is he in?" I asked. "Oh, we're not letting him go," they said, "come in here and we'll show you why, and they led me into the kitchen. Seated around the table they took out a ouija board and shushed us into a momentary trance. Then, in an unbelievable performance, they had the 12 year old sister of the dying brother trace the answers to questions put to the ouija board. "Shall we submit Tom to surgery?" "No," the answer came. "Will Tom get well?" "Yes," the answer came. "Are we right with God?" "Yes." "Will this minister agree with us?" "Yes!"
>
> Frankly I was so shocked, I found but few words to answer them. How could a rational response convince this family whose conclusion had been reached far outside the realm of reason! So I prayed.
>
> The sequel to the story is that after Tom's funeral the parents wrote me a letter asking me to pray for God's forgiveness for their aberration. "If only we had listened to your prayers. If only we had believed that Doctor." Of course, there is no proof that medicine would have been successful, but oh the anguish and guilt that would have been spared those parents.

Frank goes on to talk about the burgeoning of the occult in "this age of Aquarius. Gurus started using private planes to leap from one campus to another, stockbrokers installed cubicles for astrologists to study their Zodiac signs before investing; the late Bishop Pike's records of his communication with his suicidal son zoomed to the best seller list...." After added examples, Frank ends the sermon:

> Many may be the explanations for the age of Aquarius, but to me it's most negative aspect lies at the door of our neglect of true religious principle. When the Great God is neglected, the Half-gods are spawned....If nothing commands my utmost devotion, then I'll create gods in my own image–a comfortable fatalism in time of war to assuage my guilt and calm my fears....My thesis is that a serious study, a constant rededication, a fresh mastery of the language of faith would reap far more lasting insights, and produce effective living in the now and evermore!

It was in another February sermon that Frank dealt with the difficulties of love in a society that sees men in masses, "generalized by race, creed, color, or manner of dress," rather than as individuals–in *not* seeing "every ragged, tattered, wayward waif as a child of God."

As the war rages in Vietnam, Frank quotes the series of questions posed by George Wald, the Nobel Prize Scientist of Harvard, that Wald says must be considered "before every action, every political plan, economic program, or social venture":

> 'Is it good for children? Are hydrogen bombs, whether American, Russian or Chinese, good for children? Are polluted skies and streams good for children? Is hunger good for children?'... A little child shall lead them to save a society and a World.

On February 8, 1970, Frank's sermon is concerned with "World Law or No World." Stating that it is "Brotherhood Month," "Race Relations Sunday," he contends that overriding these is "the crucial need for world law, if there is to be a world remaining in which to practice brotherhood, racial justice and any form of social order." He expresses his concern that the UN has not lived up to its original design, primarily from lack of sustained commitment and support.

> *However, we know that he has never entirely abandoned his hopes for the UN, for once again, at the East Bay's 26th anniversary celebration of its founding, Frank is the keynote speaker, his speech titled "The UN–Good for Children and Other Living Things."*

Continuing this sermon, he accuses the World Federalists, which he also clearly still admires, as too often "talking only to itself" when enunciating its goals of strengthening the UN and bringing world peace. Frank states that, in his opinion, it is "the most effective group of opinion makers," adding, "its message should be blazoned from every TV screen and supported by all thinkers." Once more, Frank reiterates his belief that the church "could become the agency most effective in pleading the cause of mankind, since the church has the largest group of nominal members–and has the highest commission from God himself! He declares they will be ineffective, however, unless there are strong stirrings that don't seem to exist today.

[*You can* hear *Frank's doubts now as compared to his certainty of earlier years that the church would be in the forefront of solving all our problems.*]

Frank now has this to say:

> After the excruciating horrors in Vietnam grind to a stalemate, we must find what William James

> called, "A moral equivalent to war," no less than an all-out crusade to end war itself....[Then he quotes Kennedy], "In a nuclear war it will be the dead who are the fortunate ones."

Acknowledging that the number now committed are few, Frank closes this sermon with these thoughts:

> Some of the finest minds on this planet are devoted to the cause of World Peace through World Law—all they lack is grassroots support from opinion-makers and voters with concern. It's not an easy task we call you to take on. It's not as popular as ranting about pollution, learning about ecology, fuming about Revolutionaries, petitioning against a South Bay crossing, or castigating the effete snobs, but those of us who have been in war, and those of you who unfortunately are still in it, know that time is of the essence. And all these other evils can and will be solved if we could transfer our major efforts and the majority of our money from negative non-producing war, to the pursuit of happiness and the establishment of justice.

Having heard once again the drum-beat of war in March/April 2003, maybe we should agree with Frank when he said, in his later years, that he felt he was a failure. Perhaps he was not so much expressing a feeling of personal failure, as of his obvious failure to rouse Christians to unite and forcefully act together on behalf of peace and the elimination of all sorts of the world's evils—inequalities, hunger, poverty, et al.—a theme that pervaded so many of his sermons. And then, as suggested in his annual report for 1970, he must still, or again, have been having health problems; surely as hard on his psyche as his body, especially for one who'd always been so active.

421. Frank's Last "Call"

Frank begins the report with a reference to the congregation's "constant prayerful words of encouragement during my disabling times," also explaining, perhaps, why this writer found none of his sermons for 1970 after April.

But the report's emphasis is on the coming year, asking for assistance in three areas–strengthening the teaching program for both youth and adults; defining our place in the local and larger religious community; and, the need to "share our facilities with other groups, both sacred and secular, in order to relieve our financial strain." The first two of these have always been a concern of Frank's; the third he seemed to be confronted with, in one way or another, at every church he served.

†††

If, as has been suggested, Frank is drinking heavily at this period of his life, one may read into many of his sermons preached during this time, a lesson to himself–*or*, in contrast, conclude from them that he was *not* then drinking. An example is the one he preached on March 7, 1971, titled "The Magic of the Mirror" (James 1: 19-27). He says, "A mirror is honest, it reflects what it faces, but it takes honesty and imagination to interpret what is seen!"

> To many of us we see what we want to see, not what is....Our worship experience each week is an opportunity to hold a spiritual mirror before us. To see ourselves in the eyes of God, to see ourselves as we appear to others, to see what we are–and with God's help what we may yet become....
>
> Perhaps some here are discouraged because they fear they have done so much wrong God can never forgive them...If we believe in God we must believe Him when He says He will forgive all honest repentance. If we

will not forgive ourselves, we should hardly expect God to forgive us. The mirror will reveal our own need of forgiveness....The time to be discouraged is when we look in the mirror and are satisfied....

On September 19, 1971 it is the "Call to Meditation" that is of more significance to us than the sermon, "The Unquenchable Holy Spirit." It reads:

Leader: O God, I am filled with questions. I want to believe you are there to help me know the answers.

People: Why do we long to be loved by others, yet don't know how or are afraid to give love?

Leader: Why do we make rules that insult the humanity in others, yet wonder why there is no respect for authority?

People: Why do we say, "You can learn from your mistakes," yet we reject those who stumble and fall?

Leader: Why do we want to be free, yet don't know how to be responsible with that freedom?

People: Why do we say all men are equal in your sight, yet ignore those in need at home and away from home?

Leader: Why do we call the quiet peacemaker a weakling, yet fear any force that threatens us?

People: Why do we demand the truth from others, but when the truth hurts us we don't hear it?

Leader: O God, is this why they crucified your son?

People: Is this why we still crucify your peacemakers, reformers, truth-speakers, prophets, and dreamers?

Unison: Eternal God, we bring these questions and our questing spirits in confidence that you will give the answers if we have the will to hear and heed.

Incorporating this same message in an undated sermon, Frank states that "the church is in the world for one purpose and one purpose only: to reconcile men with each other and with their God." He concludes that "if the church, this blessed fellowship of lost souls, is not helping individuals to be reconciled to themselves, with others, and for all groups and nations [there's his expanding circles again], then it should close its doors and stop the agony of trying to balance budgets and teach children and save souls." His "Call to Meditation" on November 14, 1971, is in this same vein.

Minister: That commerce within our nations and between the nations of the earth, may become imbued with a spirit of cooperation and service, that all may have their fair share of freedom, health, and abundant living, we pray, O God.

People: That the spirit of love and sacrificial service may prevail in our hearts and in the hearts of men everywhere, and that human brotherhood may dominate the minds and wills of men of all nations and races, we implore thee, O God.

Frank begins the prayer that follows with "Thy love unites men in brotherhood and common purposes," and concludes it with "May Thy Spirit so prevail in our churches and in our societies that we may hasten the coming of Thy Kingdom on earth."

† † †

In his annual report for 1971, Frank notes that although the Church hasn't grown in numbers, it has shown signs of "a deepening spirit of concern on the part of many."

For 1972, his emphasis is on "innovation," especially in the area of Christian Education. The report concludes: "The successful churches today are those that are innovating... [and in our church] whether they be feeble or fulfilling will depend on each of us being willing to "expect great things of God and attempt great things for God."

Frank's annual report for 1972 is unusually brief as he praises their small church's survival despite the resignation of its "outstanding music leaders who have done so much to build the reputation of First Church as tops in music for a quarter century." As for the coming year he advises they remember that "where there is HOPE, there is life." He concludes:

> This report contains the deep conviction that Alameda needs our type of free and liberal thinkers and God needs our continued dedication to get his message of social justice and personal involvement across to a society where "the best lack all conviction and the worst are filled with passionate intensity," to repeat the words of Yeats. Perhaps our hope and theme for 1973 could be summarized in the words of [President Kennedy] who said [*one of Frank's favorite quotes*]: "Some men see things as they are and ask, why? I dream of things that never were and ask, why not?"

Personally, on July 12, 1972, Frank had been honored with a Distinguished Service Award from Bacone College in Muskogee, Oklahoma. He received the plaque from Dr. Stanley McNair, President of the college's board of trustees, who paid a visit to the Alameda minister. According to the newspaper report, "The citation and plaque from Bacone College underscore that the Rev. Thompson's 'greatest ministry is to disadvantaged people who need and receive his best effort toward their self-discovery and preparation for reliable citizenry.'"[4]

† † †

Clearly Frank was still in touch with Bacone, and the Christmas card (undated) he received from its President, Charles Hollyman, suggests a friendship. Addressed to "*President and Mrs. Thompson,*" it read: "*We want you to come so much. Let's get together over the telephone during the holidays for finals. I'll call. Charley.*" Hollyman had been in the same position as Frank, Vice President of Development, from 1967-1973 while Gerold Holstein was President. Hollyman then succeeded him as President. His very successful administration was "interrupted in February of 1976 when he suffered a stroke. After a lengthy convalescence he resumed his work, but soon announced his resignation."[5] Frank, who had suffered a heart attack himself by then, and had resigned his position at the Alameda Church in 1975, may nonetheless have cherished the hope that he, not Dr. Wesley Haines, would be chosen as the interim president; and then, still optimistic, hoped he would be selected as president. But it was Dr. Dean Chavers, a Lumbee Indian, who became President of Bacone in 1978.

It's quite likely that Frank was considered for a position at Bacone, but his health problems could hardly have been overlooked and may have been the deciding factor against him. On July 9, 1973, just a few days before the news of the taping system in Nixon's desk hit the news, Frank had had a massive heart attack. Scott writes:

---

[4] Clipping sent by Alameda Free Library.

[5] Williams and Meredith, pp. 121-122

He was in intensive care at the Alameda Hospital for a least ten days, not expected to pull out of it. He couldn't speak until after a week, he was so weak. The doctors told him he'd have no more that five years at most to live unless he gave up tobacco (he was fond of cigars) and liquor. We discussed this with him, though at that point we were more focused (alas) on the smoking [than the drinking which was the greater problem].

Describing Frank as a "craggy faced minister," on July 31, 1973, the *Alameda Times Star* ran a long article based on an interview the day before with the reporter at Frank's home "where he's recovering from a nearly fatal heart attack he suffered July 9." His near-death experience obviously didn't dim his strong interest in the Indians and the oppressed generally in this country. He told the reporter that "he still feels as 'weak as the dickens,' but hopes to return to his church in another month."

The reporter goes on to say:

Rev. Thompson's concern for the Indians and the peoples of Southeast Asia is more than a minister's natural concern for humanity. It's the result of working with both peoples and discovering that, in their relationship with the United States they share many parallels. No racial group has been more mistreated in this country than the Indians.

The article opened with this opinion of Frank's:

> The American debacle in Southeast Asia began more than 100 years ago when this country started its great rush westward across lands that Indians had roamed for centuries.

Referring to his time in Laos, the article states:

> What he learned in Southeast Asia sadly convinced him the United States has never learned the tragic lesson of its mistreatment of the American Indian.... "The history book picture of the warlike Indians is one of the greatest travesties ever. There is a double suffrage of having owned the land and having all the promises made to him which were never kept."
>
> Years later, in Laos, he found the U.S. repeating the "same old stunt over again." American advisors were treating the people like Indians—demanding that Laotians "do it our way or not at all."...
>
> "The American people are a good people," he firmly believes. "But we have never learned to accept the fact that others may have good ideas too." [*An accusation again put forward in the Spring 2003, especially by opponents of President Bush's stated policy justifying "preemptive war" as he prepared to attack Iraq.*]

After a brief overview of his life, the article returns to discussing Frank's views regarding the United .States' Indian policies.

The federal government has never developed a consistent Indian policy, he says. "Every administration has taken a new tack."

He's especially critical of the government's relocation program for Indians that began about 10 years ago. Twenty-five thousand Indians were brought to the Bay Area, a terrible mistake, Rev. Thompson believes. "It's practically an impossibility for a people to come from a barren, God-forsaken land, and fit into a complex, mechanized urban society." The answer, he believes, is his Marshall Plan for American Indians. The idea is to give Indians the help they need,...[but] instead of the white man telling the Indian to do it my way or not at all, we should let the Indian do it his way.

Asked what he thinks of the American Indian's new militant image, Frank has this to say:

"I think it's as justifiable as any of the efforts by any of the racial groups. The country is in an age in which the only thing that pays off is violence and in which people are only awarded for excesses."

Indian protests like those at Alcatraz Island and Wounded Knee, South Dakota, are "terribly necessary because we're living in such an apathetic age that only the dramatic will cause a stir."

Clearly Frank is not considering being side-tracked as a voice for the Indians, and the voiceless generally. He may even hope that having so much to say about the Indians, at this time, will strengthen his chances of being chosen for a position at Bacone even as he recovers from his second near-death experience in recent years.

429. Frank's Last "Call"

† † †

Frank has this to say of his illness in his "Minister's Report for 1973:"

> No matter what our personal belief regarding a devil or devils, we have all seen the power and goodness of God at work in our midst. Loretta and I are more confident than ever that the Grace of God does manifest itself; certainly His Grace has been with the physicians and you good people who have seen me through my time of troubles. I say "through" advisedly for such positive good health has returned that I no longer feel as though living on borrowed time, but spared for more and richer service to you and His causes here and anywhere His Spirit leads.
>
> The outpouring of concern, and the willingness of so many to assume larger shares of responsibilities in our beloved church have been tonics beyond professional prescription. We repeat with the great Apostle "I thank my God daily for each of you." Now let us "press on toward the Mark of the Prize." Let us look beyond the negatives of our age to the fulfillment of His plan for our church and society.

Frank closes the Report with these words:

> Above all we will, in the words of a song popular during WWII, "Accentuate the Positive, Eliminate the Negative." Our heartfelt prayer is that we may continue and strengthen the bonds that were forged in times of trouble that such bonds may hold us all closer together and nearer to Him who is our

Hope and our Salvation.

By the Fall of 1973, Frank had resumed his ministry and weekly sermons as he'd anticipated, yet for reasons that are far from clear, he says goodbye to the congregation in his Annual Report for 1974—giving the impression that age and health have forced him to retire, *yet that does not seem his intent exactly.*

> Loretta and I are faring into an unknown area and experience—like many others we never believed the time would come for us to retire or step out of the frenetic rat race. We know not where we'll go but we'll be searching for the horizon; someplace someway we can serve our Lord and His people. We go with only Medicare and Social Security to sustain our physical needs, but with assurance that God can use even those who belong to the geriatrics class.
>
> We go with heartfelt gratitude for the compassion you have had during our many illnesses. We go regretful that so little has been accomplished on the numerical scale, but confident that many have been led to see that they are instruments of His will and way and love.
>
> Our departure leaves you to carry forward whatever impetus may have been generated by our six years of togetherness. First Church is a volunteer organization with all the plus and minus meanings of that label. But it is more: it is an integral part of the "body of Christ." Each of you is a member of a larger—all encompassing—host of living witnesses. Each of you is a significant portion of whatever lies ahead. Each of you can build bridges to the real and needy world across the estuary [remember Alameda

> is on an island across from Oakland]. You each represent the God of all mankind. Life abundant which Jesus promised all who took up their cross and followed him can be yours.
>
> We trust and pray you and your next minister will find a new day dawning for Alameda and the world.

Exactly when they're leaving can be found in the annual report for 1975 written by the church Moderator. The reason given for their departure is curious indeed, perhaps reflecting a hope that has been discussed previously, one we know that was not realized.

> Dr. Francis W. Thompson indicated his desire to terminate his Ministry after the Easter service so that he might proceed to Bacone College. A reception was held on March 22nd and friends from throughout the community were present to wish him well in his new post.

No mention was made in either of the announcements of Frank's departure that on February 25, 1975 he had been seen at the Alameda Medical Group where Dr. White had diagnosed him with "Anginal syndrome." The chest pains that had frightened him apparently were temporary and not indicative of another heart attack. Nonetheless, they would be an additional reason why Bacone's Trustees, looking for a new President, would not have wanted to appoint someone in such fragile health to fill such a high-stress position.

19. Worn Out "Racing the Wind"

"Why should we fear death? It is life's finest form of adventure," said a man once. That man wasn't a preacher standing in a flower-surrounded pulpit, not sitting comfortably in a chair before a fire where such philosophy is easy–It was spoken by Charles Frohman on the decks of the Lusitania as she settled to her watery grave. "Why fear death, it is life's greatest adventure." It is if we live each moment with the attitude of a discoverer, and if we see the eternal best in every man, woman and child, and give our lives to bringing eternal values to them, and lastly if we have faith that the God who put us here has not yet exhausted all his resourcefulness and can find another world for us after death.[1]

† † †

On his retirement in April 1975, Frank was not quite as badly off financially as he'd suggested in his report to the Alameda congregation–as having only Medicare and Social Security: he also had a small pastor's pension and income from modest investments. It's true, however, that the Thompsons didn't have much. Frank had never worried about retirement because he believed his "godmother," Beulah Parker, ten or fifteen years older than him, who'd helped him out so often since his days as a student at Redlands University, would have demised and left him her considerable estate by the time he retired.

The fact Beulah was still alive explains why Scott was surprised that Frank had retired when he did with such minimal income. However, immediately following Frank's

---

[1] From sermon, "Preparing for Eternity," preached 3/24/40. He notes at the top of his copy that 300 were present at both church services.

retirement, Beulah did again help them out by providing an apartment on Boden Way (#8) and paying Frank to manage the apartments (which she owned). That is the address he gives on May 1, 1975 when he assumes the job of "West Coast representative for Bacone College."

What exactly precipitated this appointment we don't know (or even what it entailed), but Scott recalls one visit Frank made to Bacone about this time, after which he felt "devastated;" was not even invited to see the new President's house which he had raised the money for. This quite likely refers to a visit he made either shortly before or just after he left the Alameda church—still holding on to the idea that he might be selected as president.[2] Perhaps his appointment as Bacone's West Coast Representative shortly afterwards was meant as a modest consolation for not having selected him, as a token of their appreciation of his past service to the college, and as a recognition of his fundraising abilities.

There's no doubt Frank would have liked more, but he nonetheless had a generous supply of attractive business cards printed that note him as "West Coast Representative."[3] They give both Bacone's address and that on Boden Way in Oakland, as well as both phone numbers. There is no record of what success Frank had in this position, either in recruiting students or in fundraising. What is clear from the flyer announcing his appointment is the fact that his love of the

---

[2] As noted previously, Dr. Wesley Haines was chosen as their interim president in 1976, Dean Chaves, as president in 1978. If the visit was earlier than 1976, his friend Charles Hollyman was still president, but ill

[3] Quoted previously, this was probably the position, part-time, that he tells Jack Cummings in a letter 8/3/66, he's written President Armitage about. It's very unlikely that it is the full-time, more responsible job, he suggests to Cummings as needed to raise money in the Bay area to fulfill the Ford Challenge.

Indians had not waned. The two quotes confirm his continuing views:

> The Indian has been constantly misunderstood and his acts of violence during the last few years demonstrated leadership and a breakthrough long needed, although it is unfortunate that the leadership has been in negative areas. Bacone is geared to train leaders for creative and positive areas.
>
> I feel Bacone justifies its existence for many reasons but if for no other reason than that it helps the young Indian boy and girl shed a lifelong resentment and to know that they have a right to make mistakes, and to learn by making them, in order to be better leaders of the Indian people.

Soon after that, Beulah gave the Thompsons the money for the down payment on a house in the mountains—at 19986 Echo Blue Drive, Lake Wildwood, a new development in Northern California, not far from Grass Valley and Nevada City, but far inland from the coast. How Frank expected this to fit with his new appointment as a Bacone representative is unclear, but, according to Scott, Frank *was* under the impression that up in the mountains there would be a big need for him. If so, Frank was quickly disillusioned of that when his offer to be a stand-in, summertime, was rejected by several churches.

† † †

By the time Frank left the Alameda Church and had made a trip back East hoping to find an assistant pastorate in one of its small churches, he was, according to Scott, already drinking too much. A small clipping found in Frank's files suggest his first stop in New England had been at Phillips Memorial. [*It indicates that he was the guest minister there twenty-six years after he left, which would have been* 1974.] It's hard to imagine how he must have felt giving his first sermon in the now completed church that he had initiated.

As for the small churches, there were three, one in East Greenwich, where he was being considered. None panned out. Scott recalls that Frank came from one meeting with a church committee clearly smelling of alcohol, a sufficient if not necessarily the only explanation of his failure. Clearly Frank was devastated when he came up to Hadley Hill Farm, Scott's home in New Hampshire. Not wanting to admit his failure, he played down the whole thing and drank himself to sleep. But first, Scott recalls, he had joined his dad in getting roaring drunk, and in having what Scott described as "a terrible psychological fight." Thinking he was throwing at his dad the worst possible thing, Scott shouted that he was gay—at which, to his surprise, "Dad turned pastoral, understanding, and sympathetic in the best Christian sense. I always treasure that memory," proclaims Scott.[4]

† † †

It's not unusual for a person to feel "lost" after retirement, have no idea what to do with their time, and for family relationships to deteriorate as a result. If Frank tried to bury *his* feelings of emptiness with drink, his behavior and relationships could only have gotten worse as he faced rejection after rejection. And those friends who visited him at this time all report they could smell alcohol on his breath. Ford, the half-brother he was closest to, was one of those.

---

[4] This incident occurred before Scott actually came out—in 1985, he told this writer.

They had a good visit early in October, barely a month before Frank died, but Ford came away concerned that Frank was depressed and drinking too much. Loretta clearly was concerned.

Photo taken by Ford during his visit October 1980
He died a month later

On occasion Frank did seem to stop drinking, but it never lasted. One such time was during a visit of their friends Dickson and Ginny Kenney; Loretta happily told them he had stopped drinking, and that seemed to be the case. They ate together at a Chinese restaurant in Oakland, near where he was then minister. Frank ordered wine, tasted it and disapproved, sent it back. But other than that taste, Frank didn't drink during the meal or during their visit. They thought he had stopped, but regrettably that was not the case.

437. Worn Out "Racing the Wind"

For some time the family did not understand about alcoholism, didn't recognize it as a disease; they just knew he drank way too much; they didn't understand that he needed help to stop.

The effect his drinking had on the family in Frank's final years, at least as it was perceived by Scott, is best told in Scott's own words:

> Frank would complain that Mom didn't "get it," that she was "being negative," meaning that she was objecting to the booze. At one point, Mom came back to Boston to visit Nina [Scott's wife] and me and she left Dad a casserole per night so that he had absolutely nothing to do but heat it up. However, he complained to my sister [Sara Sue] and me that she had abandoned him, there was nothing to eat, and the reason he was raving mad—literally crazed on the phone—was that there wasn't any food and all he had was booze. We lost sympathy at this point because he simply wasn't being reasonable; he was behaving like a child when his full-time maid [his wife Loretta] wasn't there to cope with his needs, etc, etc.
>
> This was before I discovered, perhaps a year later, an article in *Newsweek* about alcoholism, how it was a disease, not weakness of will. It had Dad written all over it. For the first time we realized what the real problem was, that he needed serious and sustained medical help if he was to recover, but it was too late. By the mid-80s he was drinking huge amounts.
>
> The last time I saw him in mid-1980, I brought the children to their place and I had to leave earlier than the kids. The problem was how to ensure that Mom drove them to the airport—down

> the mountain road– and NOT FRANK. Loretta was so subservient to Frank that we were scared he'd commandeer the car and risk the kids' lives to prove his manhood. Well, Frank loved Scotch, which was at least twice as expensive as the Vodka he usually drank–consumed liters of it a day. Well, I bought a $25 tank of Scotch and told him I'd give it to him if he ABSOLUTELY promised not to touch the car when the kids went back to the Sacramento Airport.

But there was also another side of Frank that is told by one of Sara Sue's children, Cory:

> Grandpa T, as we grandchildren called him, seemed to enjoy teaching me. Most notably, I remember him teaching me how to box. Grandpa T claimed to have been an able boxer and he wanted to share his skills with me. He took me out to our garage once while he was visiting on a holiday. There he showed me how to hold my fist and take a proper fighting stance. Then he demonstrated a jab and other punches, accentuating the "cork screw" action my fist needed to take upon delivery of every punch. He was adamant about this "cork screw" delivery as he argued it was the source from which a punch drew its power.
>
> Grandpa T seemed to enjoy telling me about his boxing prowess and teaching me proper stance and punches. This is certainly the most vivid memory I have of Grandpa T. But I do remember that in Wildwood Grandpa T enjoyed taking me fishing. We never caught anything big but had a good time just sitting and talking. Whenever we did catch a fish, he insisted on teaching me how to clean

it. To his dismay, I always chickened out and coaxed Grandma T into cleaning the fish.

I also remember Grandpa T often reading in his leather chair, smelling of sweet pipe smoke, the smell I always associated with him. He seemed to enjoy reading to us, and sharing history, politics and Indian culture.

But Cory was not entirely sheltered from his drinking:

I know Frank used to keep vodka in the freezer in Wildwood. I recall seeing him pour drinks from a bottle in the freezer and I curiously questioned him about it. Unfortunately I do not recall the conversations that ensued.

Having previously made use of it, we also know that during his last months, Frank began writing his autobiography for his grandchildren. All these positive acts, realized despite his heavy drinking, plus the fact he was able, if he wanted, to hide his problem reasonably well when there were visitors, all suggest just how conflicted he was within himself. Even so, there were other times when his inhibitions were so loosened by his drinking that he let fly all his resentments, and his ravings became so outlandish that it seemed he knew he needed committal. He seemed to regard booze as "the big bad devil, the Jungian bad side of him."

Scott said:

His behavior got so bad at one point that Loretta was thinking of leaving him, something she discussed at length with me. This threat so scared Dad that he committed himself at a hospital for help. Unfortunately, however, after a few days, he checked himself out, telling us it was they who needed his help, rather than the other way around.

Ken, Sara Sue's husband, in retrospect, reflected: "How sad it was to see such a charismatic and successful man deteriorate from alcohol abuse." Ken spoke of Frank as though he were one of the most passionate and interesting men in his life.

† † †

Frank clearly had lost sight of the message in some of his most powerful sermons. One he preached in 1947, "Custodians of the Temple," is a good example. After acknowledging and praising the custodians of his and other churches, he turns to the greater concern of our own temple. He quotes Paul: *"Know ye not that ye are the temple of the Lord, and that the spirit of God dwells in You!"* Frank then continues: "He who tampers with the human body, is tampering with the very citadel of God–and God will destroy such a tamperer!

Later in the sermon Frank discusses the need for laws to deal with drink.

> [The fact that this body is the temple of the Lord] is why this whole battle with bottles must be fought. Of course we can't legislate righteousness. Can't make people take care of their bodies if they don't want to. Impossible to prohibit man from destroying their higher sensibilities if they insist on it. So the one attempt at legal prohibition failed.
>
> [Frank points out that] more people are injured as a result of drunkenness than were injured by the most ghastly war of history!...I am no staunch advocate of legal prohibition. I think there is a better way, but if that better way is not taken, then prohibition may be necessary again...

> You see we may so dissipate this God-given freedom of ours as custodians of the temple that we may have to turn our bodies over to total control! ...Moments of devotion would reveal the holiness of this body, as a host to God's spirit and as a sacred meeting place for man and mate.

This was not the only sermon Frank preached that attacked drink as an evil. We may conclude that Frank has lost the vision he proclaimed as necessary in another sermon, undated, "Those Fearful Flying Saucers":

> When human beings have no clear-cut, positive goal in sight, they turn inward and cause confusion and chaos....When he loses his outward vision he discovers inward illusion....It is a time of disillusionment—no forward-reaching program, no soul-expanding challenge.

There is no doubt that Frank was without a goal at this point; had no soul-expanding challenge left. And just as happened in his case, in this sermon Frank talks of those who try to escape "the confusion and disillusion of the day by the method of drink. The whole sordid industry recognizing the instability of man within himself, it plays upon the finer instincts of man...and at the same time brings out his lowest animal natures." And so, regrettably, we see Frank.

† † †

We turn again to Scott for the only account available of Frank's last days.

> All I remember is that during the night of November 19, 1980, (prior to his 70th birthday), Dad had complained of chest pains, and toward the

> morning clearly was having another heart attack, so Mom called an ambulance. Plainly he made it to the hospital because when I got the first news, just prior to lunch eastern time, he was still alive. I set out for California as soon as I got the news from Reagan's ambassador to Korea and a friend of mine, during a lunch break of the conference I was attending. So Frank must have died around 8 to 9 a.m. [West Coast time]. According to the doctors, it was a "massive myocardial infarction with complications of alcoholism," and I doubt he ever had a chance of recovery. Following the attack in 1973, he had not stopped smoking, he drank more and more, and he didn't reform his eating habits (bacon, fatty junk, etc.)
>
> Mom and I went to the funeral home and told them he wanted to give his body to medical research, which, of course, saved us a bunch of money and a lot of nuisance. This was on the next day, and was the usual therapeutic bureaucratic stuff that was necessary.

The obituary in *The Union*, a Grass Valley newspaper, highlights the fact that Frank, who had died Friday in Grass Valley, had wanted no funeral services. It states, "arrangements for donating his remains to science have been made under the direction of Hooper & Weaver Mortuary."

Scott's account continues:

> The question was then whether we should have a service; I guess posed cuz we were scared no one would show up, given how long since he'd been in Alameda and the fact that he hadn't any meaningful friends up at the lake. But we decided we

should have a service; it would be a good thing even if it was just for us.

But the folks in Alameda took over and arranged a service in their church–several days later–which was very very nice. I was pleasantly and happily surprised by the reaction to Dad's death. The sanctuary was about half full and over and over people got up and "shared" and told of intervention in their lives which Frank had made which they could never forget, etc. It was very good for both Sue and me to know that our father hadn't entirely thrown away the last phase of his life; to know that he had a real ministry there even if a shell of that at Phillips Memorial.

Perhaps not then, but at a later time, Scott, too, shared his feelings about his dad.

Dad plainly made a meaningful contribution to many lives, and too few of us are given to make such a mark. Lots of people may make lots of noise and be talked about, or hold high office and get press notice daily, but that's different from making a difference as Frank did. Not too many people at any level whom I've known have made a difference in their lives, at least a positive one. Obviously Frank did. When I think how people from his early days still kept in touch through all the years, and note the absence of that in most peoples lives, and hear the stories about him in his various incarnations, I know that he set a very high standard. I rose way above him in worldly, even professional, terms, and yet have a very modest view of what I've done in comparison to him. But that holds true for most of the folks I've viewed up close. Frank made a lot of mistakes, including some major ones with his family, but the balance sheet still comes out ahead. The urge to keep doing for others never left him.

An interesting footnote to Dad's death is that Sue was unable to show any emotion at all during the three or four days we were in California together. We went out to restaurants every night and talked and talked but she couldn't let go. Interestingly, a week or so later, she went ballistic at the death of John Lennon (shot on 12/8/80 in front of his upper west side apartment in Manhattan). She was so overwrought that she had to be sedated by her husband, Ken. Characteristic of "psychological displacement," a death she really didn't care about allowed her, finally, to grieve over Dad's death.

† † †

Frank summed up the philosophy that had carried him through life when, in a sermon in 1942, he started with a quote from the early Christians:

> "If I live in luxury while my brother lives in want, I am a partner to him." It seems to me there is only one spirit to help us thru the ages, one attitude that will send us out, not giving a rap what the world thinks of us but to make the world take a place of leadership, and that is the spirit we should have.

Frank had helped so many in his life, yet it was not enough in the end to sustain him. Nor could the friends and relatives who cared deeply for this charismatic man stop his downward spiral. Perhaps he'd just given too much; had worn himself out seeking to make a difference–racing the wind. This writer was only in high school when she knew him at Phillips Memorial, but can still hear his powerful voice, see his arm raised to bless us, giving the benediction from the rear of the church before we left the Sunday service. It's time now to say it, altered, for him:

> Over your life may the sunlight of heaven
> Shine with a light that never grows dim.
> Filling your heart with the grace of God's presence
> Until you are safely enfolded in Him.

20. Afterword

"For the love of God is broader
Than the measures of man's mind,
And the heart of the Eternal
Is most wonderfully kind."[1]

† † †

Beulah Parker, who had helped Frank out so many times financially, died several years after Frank and left her estate to the young girl who had stayed by her and taken care of her. Scott comments:

> Even though Mom had never lifted a finger for Beulah after Dad died, she was bitter, thinking she deserved the estate. She threatened to sue on the grounds of verbal contract and expectation (we had courted Beulah for years with the expectation of inheritance), but her lawyer pointed out the obvious: Loretta had 'moved away,' and Beulah had done what would have been expected.
>
> After Dad died, Loretta had done nothing but make fun of Beulah. She hated her, seeing her as her 'competition.'" Scott advised his mother that she couldn't expect to inherit unless she was the caregiver, and "as best as I can determine, why should she have accepted that role? She had enough money and 'taking care of Beulah' might have been fatal for them both."

† † †

Soon after Frank's death, Loretta came to stay with Scott and his wife Nina,[2] occupying the four-room maid's

---

[1] A poem, author not stated, included in one of Frank's 1940s sermons.

quarters of the big house at Chestnut Hill in Brookline, Massachusetts. At Christmas Loretta went with them to Aspen for their annual Christmas holiday of skiing, then returned to California. But Loretta was not doing well alone, and Scott invited her to return to Chestnut Hill, explaining that she could help with the kids (they had three young children) – even though in fact there was little for her to do since they had a full-time nanny.

It's usually difficult for a mother and married son to live peaceably together, and Loretta and Scott were no exception. In this case, Loretta seemed to have thrown off the subservient behavior she'd always shown around Frank, and to have become a "control freak," as Scott perceived it, to a degree that made up for lost time. What one really sees is the clashing of two people desiring to be in control.

In Scott's own words:

> Nina wrote her a strict letter of admonitions of where she was and was not to interfere in the running of the household. Mom couldn't bear not to be in control, but she was sufficiently freaked out by Nina's wealth to be respectful once told what she could and couldn't do. Well, it nonetheless was a tense time and we were all relieved when it somehow transpired that she was needed at Bacone. They needed her enough to provide a small half-house [one of campus apartments].

† † †

Linea Harman, who'd been friends with Loretta since when Frank had been President of Bacone, talked to

---

[2] Scott and Nina did not divorce until May 1984; Scott did not "come out" as gay until 1985.

this writer about Loretta's return to the college as a volunteer. She remembered how they resumed their very pleasant friendship; how Loretta had returned the same year, 1982, that her niece came to live with her and go to school. Linea recalled what a beautiful voice Loretta had; how her niece was one of the many who took voice lessons with her; how the lessons really helped her niece's voice. Loretta also helped with the choir, then under the direction of a George Stevenson; she acted as chaperone on trips away from campus.

In 1985, ending a four-year stay at Bacone, Loretta embarked on a trip with the long-time friends of the Thompsons, Dickson and Ginny Kenny. Recently, Dickson talked to this writer about the trip which they planned to last from three weeks to a month:

> It was very meaningful and enjoyable, really beautiful country. We were able to get into parts of Indian reservations not usually accessible to "ordinary people," because some of Loretta's students lived there and she knew their parents. Loretta had talked of the Indians and had suggested they go on this trip together. We flew out and she met us in Tulsa; showed us around Bacone first; then we went through Oklahoma, Albuquerque, New Mexico, Arizona, and Nevada; ended up at Sue's in California.

It was about this same time that Scott noticed something odd going on with Loretta's house in California:

> I checked on her finances monthly and noted that the buyer of her house, which she'd sold in 1981 before she went to Bacone, for about $60k,

wasn't making his payments. She told me it was ok, he had called her and would soon catch up. After several more months of this, I called a lawyer and we began planning to sue to get the house back. We'd learned that the buyer was a "slick guy" who had a practice of buying from widows, then not paying the mortgage and sweet-talking them until they died. In the case of Loretta, fate intervened and it was he who died; killed when his car blew up. Loretta got the house back for her sale price, and was so delighted to get it back that she moved in and immediately set out to enlarge it. She felt that the house was a fulfillment; that a way of life was re-legitimized.

Loretta, Tanya, Sara Sue, Xmas 1988

†††

Perhaps it was because she was so absorbed by the house at the time, and was not really a Willard anyway, that in 1985 Loretta did not go to the Willard Family Association Reunion held that year in Cottonwood,

Arizona, where Frank's branch of that family had pioneered. Lucille, wife of Frank's half-brother, Ford (then deceased), recently wrote this writer about it.

> We were both there as well as his half sister, Mary Jo, with her husband, Dave Partington, also Frank's half-brother, Lynn Gano, and Frank's daughter, Sara Sue Nies. It was a two-day affair and a great chance for me to get acquainted with my husband's relatives. We visited the spot where the Wallace Willard house had stood, on the banks of the Verde River. I really liked Sara Sue. She told us about her teaching experiences in a California college. I particularly remember her telling us that she did not count off for misspelled words in her students' compositions as that was not the point of the course.
>
> I thought things had changed since I was in school. Sara Sue and Lynn just seemed to click during this gathering. They enjoyed each other's quick wit and Sue invited Lynn to come to her home for

Ken, Cory, Tanya, Sara Sue (seated) 1989

Thanksgiving that year, which he did.

Loretta remained in her California home fairly contentedly until near the end of 1993 when she sold it. The deciding factor was Sara Sue's death on March 13, 1992. Sue had died of pancreatic and liver cancer (an irony since she didn't either drink or smoke) after a long and painful illness that had included surgery and chemotherapy. When Sue went, she was at home on their couch, surrounded by friends and family. Loretta was there and would have been there earlier, but, according to Scott, Sara Sue, during her months battling the cancer, had been in denial that it was fatal, and had refused to allow her mother to visit, as she had, until then, been in the habit of doing.

Regarding Loretta's decision to sell her house soon after Sara Sue's death, Scott says:

> Loretta had drifted apart from her California family and there was nothing else Ken (Sue's husband) could do for her, even though he had been extremely helpful, dutiful, as an arthritis specialist [actually, a rheumatologist] at UCLA, even making Mom a supportive cast for her legs to help her get around as her arthritis worsened. By 1992, Ken had told there was nothing more medicine could do beyond giving her more aspirin. So the logic of moving back to my home in Virginia increased.

† † †

Scott must have been reluctant to have her back, so was pleased she had chosen to build a house for herself on the spacious grounds near the main house, rather than actually move in with him [by then both divorced and come out as gay]. Loretta was at war with his new lifestyle. Scott describes it this way:

> It was a control issue. She kept saying how much more I could "serve" if I hadn't come out, etc.–if I'd continued to throttle my life and live in the closet. I suggested whenever she said I should go back to the straight world that she try coming into the gay world, which would be about equally easy. She deeply resented my then companion, a Latino. She fought me every inch of the way for control of my farm house, which I owned 100% (there had been a long fight during the divorce over the properties they'd owned together, and over custody of their three children). Loretta simply didn't get it. And she simply wasn't prepared to accept my lifestyle because she preferred to be unreasonable.

Before moving back, Loretta came back several times–for her 80th birthday on February 27th, and to oversee the house being built for her near the main house at the farm–only its beautiful shell finished by the time she died. She was still living in the main house when, in October, Scott describes an "extremely strange, never before fit, she had, throwing pans against the wall, screaming, etc. I finally calmed her down," he says, "and she got quiet and passive and apologetic. She couldn't believe her behavior."

> The next week she complained of an ache in her left shoulder, a symptom that is clear to a physician but of which I had never heard. I called Kenny [Nies, his son-in-law] to ask if I should take her to the hospital, even though she wasn't, she said, in real pain.

453. Afterword

Scott hadn't heard back from Ken who was traveling, and had concluded Loretta's condition wasn't serious, so he'd asked her to help out with one of his drunken friends who'd stayed over with him that weekend. He wrote:

> Curiously, I had had a guest, Tim Dickinson, that weekend before she died, and he got so drunk he went into a stupor and couldn't be awakened to go back to Washington when planned. I took the plane, as usual, to Boston in the early morning [Monday, October 24, 1994]. I'd left exact instructions for Loretta telling her how to take him to the bus for Washington. In the nine months she'd been here, Loretta had never ventured into Washington on her own. However, Tim connived to get her to drive him all the way in, which I deduce she agreed to because she wanted to use him as an influence on me to get me back to the straight and narrow.
>
> She had a smile on her dead body, according to my caretakers who found her, having collapsed on her return from Washington, reaching for a tea-cup. Tim told me she'd been in fine form during the drive to DC.

Dickson and Ginny Kenney had visited Loretta once after she'd moved into her not-yet-finished house on the grounds of Scott's farm in Virginia and had been looking forward to another visit. They told this writer:

> We were shook up to learn she'd unexpectedly died the same day we'd planned our reunion. She had a heart problem but had not really been ill prior to her sudden death. We learned she had died of a stroke that Monday, mid-day, soon after her return from a trip to DC.

Loretta's funeral was more a celebration, held at her new house which had a cathedral ceiling and was very apt for the service; only family, the Kenneys and a few local friends were there. Scott's son, Nick, composed a guitar piece, especially appropriate since his primary memory of Loretta is the time they spent together while he played his guitar and she sang, both loving music. At the service they also played the largo from Handel's comic opera, Xerxes, which Loretta had often sung as contralto. "Loretta's local pastor, a gal, presided, Scott says, continuing:

> Mom had only started going to that church shortly before her death. Rather than connecting with the local community, she had wanted only to hang out with my friends, obviously not to my liking and something she had committed not to do before I invited her to live at my house. I scared her a little by mentioning that when she died, it would be embarrassing if she had no friends: so suddenly she was all over the place making friends, as if in anticipation [of death?]. About 50 locals showed up after she died, bringing cakes, pies, all the usual.
>
> After everybody had left—my three kids, the Kenneys, Aunt Mary Jo and Uncle Dave were left, spending the night. We had Martinis, oh did we have martinis. I said something the effect that, "Well, yes, Loretta was a wonderful woman, but it wasn't all roses having her live with me these past eight months." I came to realize Loretta was a little bit nuts while she was living with me at the end. Although older people are entitled to be a little more idiosyncratic, or, let's say, their defects become larger and larger, Mom carried it to something of an extreme.

Maybe the relationship between Mother and Son was especially volatile near the end of Loretta's life, more so than that with others Loretta came into contact with, but surely it can be understood in the context of what she'd been through during those years—first she had lost a beloved husband to drink, then to death; then she lost her daughter to cancer. It would not be surprising if the sweet, smiling person so many had delighted in for so many years had disappeared.

† † †

Frank and Loretta left one son, Willard Scott, (Sara Sue already deceased) and five grandchildren:

Scott and Nina Nitze Thompson's children:

Phyllis Elizabeth Pratt Thompson Reid (born February 9, 1974)
Nicholas (Nicky) Edwin Scott Thompson (born July 23, 1975)
Heidi Alexandra Nitze Thompson (born June 4, 1979)

Ken and Sara Sue Thompson Nies's children:

Tanya Nies (born July 30, 1967)
Corin (Cory) Nies (born February 7, 1969)

Appendix 1: Family Tree: Ancestors of Francis Willard Thompson

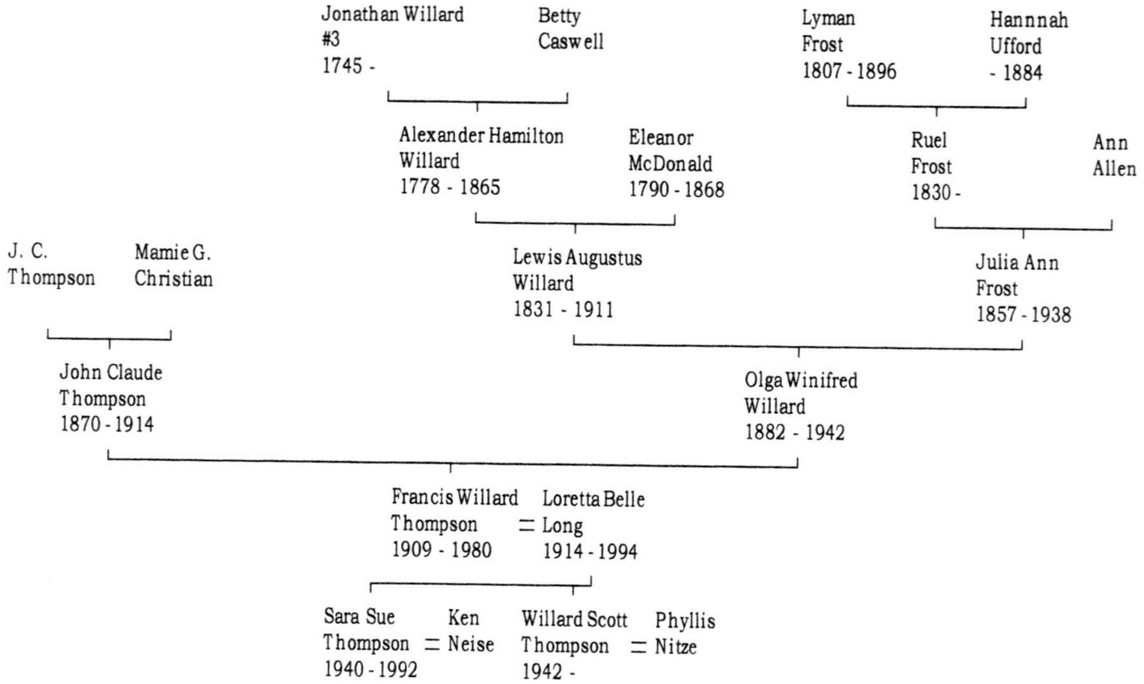

Appendix 2: Family Tree of Frank's Father

James
b: 1814
Muhlenberg County, Kentucky

Mary J.
b: 1819
Logan County, Kentucky

J. C. Thompson
b: 1842
Logan County Kentucky
m: November 02, 1869

Nannie G. Christian
b: 1849
Todd County Kentucky

John Claude Thompson
b: November 21, 1870
Muhlenberg County, Kentucky
d: July 04, 1914
Greenfield, Monterey, Callifornia

=

Olga Winifred Willard
b: June 26, 1882
Elko, Nevada
m: September 06, 1900
d: March 03, 1942
Mesa, Maricopa, Arizona
2nd Marriage: October 24, 1912
to Paul Gano
Divorced: December 05, 1912

Francis Willard Thompson
b: November 20, 1909
Phoenix, Maricopa, Arizona
d: November 19, 1980
Lake Wildwood, CA

=

Loretta Belle Long
b: February 27, 1914
m: July 02, 1939
d: October 24, 1994

Doris

=

John Lewis Thompson
b: October 22, 1901
Lompoc, California
d: January 20, 1975

=

Marie Drake
b: 1912
m: June 01, 1938

Appendix 3: Family of Olga Thompson Gano

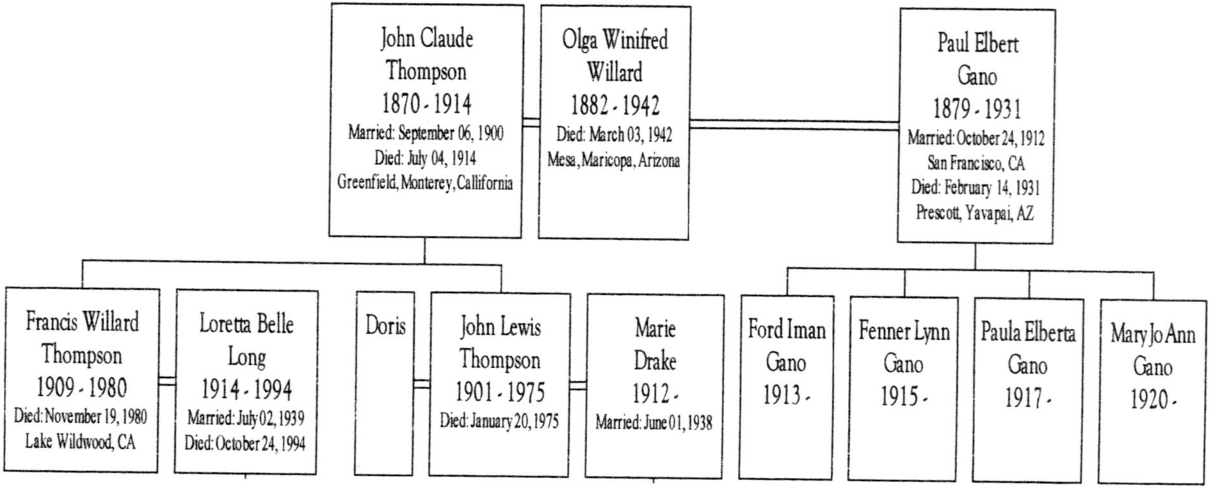

Resources

Most of the quotes in Frank's biography are from the originals of letters, sermons (some on disintegrating paper, some handwritten and barely legible, most hand typed), and church bulletins found in Frank's files, as were most of the photos, news clippings, and other of his writings. The majority of other memorabilia were sent to this writer for use in this biography. Permission was sought and graciously given for quotes from William Blum, Gary Moulton, ed., and the World Federalist Association (resources listed below). A few other quotes fall under "fair use" or © holder could not be located.

Memoirs, etc.

Gano, Ford Iman. "The Autobiography of Ford Gano," dictated 1994-1997. Transcribed by Elizabeth Osborn, Longmont, CO, privately published, 1999. (See also "Liz"<liz@csd.net> & www.csd.net/~liz/gano/la.htm)

Nichols, Frances Edna, "Memoirs"

Thompson, Francis Willard, Memoirs, "Frank's Odyssey for Our Grandchildren," 1980.

———Account of his experience during RI's 1938 hurricane.

Willard, Julia Ann Frost, *Pioneer Stories of Arizona's Verde Valley*, 1954

Willard, Frances E., *Glimpses of Fifty Years*, a brief autobiography published by the Women's Temperance Publication Association, 1889

Willard, Lewis Augustus Obituary, Obituary Book, p. 476, Sharlot Hall Museum Archives, 415 Gurley Street, Prescott Arizona 86301 (Laurie Carlson, 1-928-445-3122).

Willard, Don, "An Old-Timer's Scrapbook." No publisher or date noted. (Also, titled, "Those Early Years: Old-Time Memoirs" 1968).

Books & Other Publications

Anasi, Robert, *The Gloves: A Boxing Chronicle*, North Point Press, Farrar, Straus & Giroux, ©2002.

Archaelogia Americana Dictionary of American Biography.

Armacost, George H., Ralph E. Hone & Esther N. Mertins, "Whose Emblem Shines Afar" A Commemorative Account of the Universty of Redlands, 1945-1982, Redlands, Calif 1983.

Blum, William, "*Killing Hope*: Laos 1957-1971" pp. 140-145, Common Courage Press, P.O. Box 702, Monroe, ME 04951, 207-525-0900, Revised & expanded, ©1986/1995

Buford, Kate, *Burt Lancaster: An American Life*, Alfred A. Knopf, NY, ©2000.

Dommen, Arthur J., "Laos: The Troubled Neutral," *Asian Survey*, Vol. VII, #1, (1964).

Fishgall, Gary, *Against Type: The Biography of Burt Lancaster*, Scribner, ©1995.

Gromyko, Andrei, *Memories: From Stalin to Gorbachev*, translated by Harold Shukman, Arrow Books, London, ©1989

International Boxing Hall of Fame Official Record Book, McBooks, NY, ©1999

Leary, William M., "Supporting the "Secret War": CIA Air Operations in Laos, 1955-1974"

Moulton, Gary, ed., *The Journals of the Lewis & Clark Expedition*, (especially Vols. 2 and 7 of 13 volumes), Univ. of Nebraska Press, ©1986. See also www.aartsci.wusl.edu˜landc/html/clarke.html

Ouellete, Eugene G., "Johnston College-A Rebirth," a paper presented at the Fortnightly Club of Redlands on October 3, 2002. Found on the internet at http//www.redlandsfortnightly.org/ouellete02.htm

Panganiban, Rex & Walker, Barbara, *A Vision of the World*, World Federalist Association publication, 47pp.(no other information on booklet)

Rothbert, Otto, *History of Muhlenberg*, John P. Morton & Co. Louisville, ©1913.

Sugar, B.R. (Chief Editor), *The Ring*, Ring Publishing Corp. NY, ©1981.

Thompson, W. Scott, *The Price of Achievement: Coming Out in Reagan Days*, Cassell, Wellington House, London, 1995.

Williams, John & Howard L. Meredith, *Bacone Indian University: A History*, Oklahoma Heritage Assoc., ©1980.

World Federalist Association, 50th Anniversary Historical Survey, 1947-1997, 46 pp .(no other information on booklet).

Barbara Mills was born in Daytona Beach, Florida; spent her childhood in Jackson, Kentucky. She graduated from Brown University in 1950 and has Masters Degrees from the University of Birmingham, England (in Social Studies) and from Rutgers University (in Library Services). She was an activist and officer with Baltimore, Maryland's CORE (Congress of Racial Equality) chapter in the 1960s. Since her divorce in 1974, she has worked as an inner city school librarian and headed agencies working with delinquents, mentally ill, the homeless, prisoners and abused women. The author has two children, both attorneys (Susan primarily services immigrants; Alan, primarily tenants and prisoners) and two grand-children. Now 77 and diagnosed with Parkinson's Disease, she lives in Cranston, Rhode Island near her daughter.

Previous books: *"...And Justice For All," The Double Life of Fred Weisgal, Attorney & Musician; Providence: 1630-1800, Women are Part of Its History;* and *"Got My Mind Set on Freedom," Maryland's Story of Black & White Activism, 1663-2000. The latter* a finalist in 2003 Organization of American Historians' Liberty Legacy Foundation Award.

463. Index

ABOUT THE AUTHOR

Barbara Mills was born in Daytona Beach, Florida. She spent her childhood in "Bloody Breathitt," (Jackson) Kentucky. Graduate of Brown University, Providence, Rhode Island; Masters (in Social Studies) from University of Birmingham, England, and Master of Library Services from Rutgers University, New Brunswick, New Jersey. Activist and Officer with Baltimore, Maryland's CORE (Congress of Racial Equality) chapter in the 1960s. After divorce, worked as inner city school librarian, then headed agencies working with delinquents, mentally ill, homeless, prisoners and abused women. Retired in 1991 and began writing non-fiction. Two children, both attorneys: Susan, servicing primarily immigrants; Alan, primarily tenants and prisoners. Two grand-children. Now 77 and diagnosed with Parkinson's Disease, lives in Cranston, Rhode Island, near her daughter.

Previous books: *"...And Justice For All," The Double Life of Fred Weisgal, Attorney & Musician; Providence: 1630-1800, Women are Part of Its History;* and *"Got My Mind Set on Freedom," Maryland's Story of Black & White Activism, 1663-2000.* The latter, a finalist in 2003 Organization of American Historians' Liberty Legacy Foundation Award.